SEX, GENDER, AND THE BODY

Sex, Gender and the Body

The Student Edition of
What Is a Woman?

TORIL MOI

OXFORD
UNIVERSITY PRESS

OXFORD
UNIVERSITY PRESS

Great Clarendon Street, Oxford OX2 6DP

Oxford University Press is a department of the University of Oxford.
It furthers the University's objective of excellence in research, scholarship,
and education by publishing worldwide in

Oxford New York

Auckland Cape Town Dar es Salaam Hong Kong Karachi
Kuala Lumpur Madrid Melbourne Mexico City Nairobi
New Delhi Shanghai Taipei Toronto

With offices in

Argentina Austria Brazil Chile Czech Republic France Greece
Guatemala Hungary Italy Japan South Korea Poland Portugal
Singapore Switzerland Thailand Turkey Ukraine Vietnam

Published in the United States
by Oxford University Press Inc., New York

First published as part of *What is a Woman? And Other Essays* 1999

British Library Cataloguing in Publication Data

Data available

Library of Congress Cataloging in Publication Data

Data available

ISBN 0–19–927622–6 (pbk)

1 3 5 7 9 10 8 6 4 2

Typeset by
Cambrian Typesetters, Frimley, Surrey
Printed in Great Britain
on acid-free paper by
Biddles Ltd, Kings Lynn, Norfolk

For
DAVID

Preface

This book is published in response to teachers who told me that they wanted their students to read the first two essays in my *What Is a Woman? And Other Essays* (1999). They had been using the essays in courses concerned with sex and/or gender in literature, philosophy, English, French, history, anthropology, political theory, sociology, and women's studies, and in all kinds of inter-disciplinary contexts. Because the existing book is too big and expensive for students to buy, they asked for a smaller, cheaper book, pointing out that given the length of the two essays, a reasonably priced paperback would cost no more than a full set of photocopies, and would be far handier to use. This, then, is the student edition requested. It makes the first two essays from *What Is a Woman?* available in full.

In these essays I set out to find a third way for feminist theory, one that steers a course between the Scylla of traditional essentialism and biologism, and the Charybdis of the idealist obsession with 'discourse' and 'construction'. They are the beginning of a larger project, namely to rethink feminism without having recourse to the exhausted categories of identity and difference. For such a project, Simone de Beauvoir's feminism of freedom is an obvious cornerstone. These essays also arise from a wish to make feminist theory responsive to historical specificity. To be more precise: my project is to analyse key concepts in feminist theory in a way that makes it possible to reconnect them with history, society, and women's everyday experiences.

I started working on these essays in the late 1990s. At the time I was deeply dissatisfied with the state of feminist theory, and felt that a new way of thinking about old questions, particularly questions concerning the body and language, was desperately needed. It seemed to me that feminist theory had managed to paint itself into a corner, in which all it could ever do was to denounce 'essentialism', embrace 'constructionism', and generally proclaim the unwisdom of ever using the word woman (these are all subjects discussed in Chapter 1). There had also developed, I felt, an unhappy divide between feminists committed to the personal (autobiography, narrative, confessions) and feminists dedicated to theory. The divide between the personal and the theoretical or the philosophical is often aligned with a series of oppositions that have long been contentious in poststructuralist theory: first person/third person, speaking as/speaking for, subjective/objective, personal/impersonal, and particular/universal (these are discussed in Chapter 2).

These essays try to undo the kind of thinking that makes such oppositions look compulsory for theorists. I found the intellectual resources required to do this in the existentialist feminism of Simone de Beauvoir and the ordinary language philosophy of Stanley Cavell, J. L. Austin, and Ludwig Wittgenstein. These essays show that at least some of the oppositions that concern contemporary theorists are 'pictures that hold us captive', as Wittgenstein puts it (PI §115).

Poststructuralist feminist theory is based on the idea that language is a system, and that reference is particularly emblematic of the way language works. This book is based on a very different idea, namely that in most cases, the meaning of a word is its use in the language (see Wittgenstein, PI §43). In order to find out what meanings a word has, we need to consider who says what to whom under what specific circumstances. Only in that way can we hope to get clear on the criteria we are actually relying on, for example when we count a person as a woman.

A key idea underpinning these essays is that poststructuralist theory tends to 'absolutize' its central terms. This means that it tends to take them out of every conceivable context of significant use, to proceed without regard to the many different situations in which one might actually use the word in question. This procedure turns concepts into metaphysical entities that no longer respond to any specific criteria of meaning. In Chapter 1 I show that this is precisely what has happened to the word 'woman' in much feminist theory.

These essays also represent a return to Simone de Beauvoir's *The Second Sex* (1949), not as a historical document illustrating a long past moment in feminist thought, but as a source of vital new insights for contemporary feminist theory. *The Second Sex* is a gold mine for feminist theorists, and I certainly have not exhausted its riches. One Beauvoirean theme I pursue in these essays is her thought-provoking understanding of the body. In Chapter 1 I elaborate on her claim that the body is a *situation*, and show that this is a concept which undercuts the sex/gender division and gets us out of the usual stalemate between 'sex' and 'gender', 'essence' and 'construction'. In Chapter 2, I show that *The Second Sex* also contains another way of conceptualizing the body, namely as a *background*. These concepts are flexible, open to social and historical change, and allow us to grasp the body in its everyday incarnations, without ever assigning it one (or a set of) given meanings, and without finding ourselves obliged to deny the obvious, namely that there are men and women in the world.

Unfortunately, there is still no acceptable English translation of *The Second Sex*. To get a sense of what the difficulties with the English text are, I urge readers of this book to read Margaret Simons's pioneering essay on the translation, as well as my own recent article on the subject, which also contains information on the reasons why a new translation is unlikely to appear any time soon (see Simons, and Moi, 'While We Wait'). If anyone who reads this knows how to persuade Random House, the owner of the Knopf and Vintage imprints, to agree to the publication of a new English translation and edition of *The Second Sex*, I hope he or she will take immediate action.

The first essay in this book is entitled 'What Is a Woman? Sex, Gender and the Body in Feminist Theory'. It arose from my sense of astonishment at the trouble the word 'woman' was causing feminist theory. How did we land ourselves in a position where feminists genuinely felt that they had to surround woman by quotation marks to avoid essentialism and other theoretical sins? The aim of the essay is to liberate the word 'woman' from the binary straitjacket in which contemporary sex and gender theory imprisons it, so as to recuperate it for feminist use.

The essay starts by sketching the history of the rise of the sex/gender distinction in English, before engaging critically with the powerful poststructuralist revision of the sex/gender paradigm. This is followed by an account of a positive alternative, namely Beauvoir's suggestion that the body is a *situation*. Finally, the resulting understanding of what a woman is, is tested, as it were, on some legal cases concerning femininity and sex changes. The last part of the essay (section V) is crucial to its overall goals, for it shows what it means to try to think concretely as opposed to metaphysically about what a woman is.

My answer to the question 'What Is a Woman?', then, is that there is not one answer to that question. If pressed, I would simply answer: 'It depends.' The criteria that make us count a person as a woman depend on who is speaking, to whom they are speaking, what they are talking about, in what situation they find themselves. This is, I think, a far better way of thinking about the question than to lay down theoretical requirements for what the word 'woman' *must* mean, which is simply another way of removing it from its contexts of significant use.

Chapter 2, entitled ' "I Am a Woman": The Personal and the Philosophical', goes further than Chapter 1 in engineering an encounter between Beauvoir and Cavell, Wittgenstein and Austin. It does so by focusing on the question of voice and style in theory and philosophy. How can I write theory without losing myself? How can I speak for others without silencing them? Do women always speak as women? What else can we speak as? How would you react if someone said to you in a theoretical discussion: 'You think that because you are a woman'? Can a woman intellectual insist on being called an intellectual, not a woman intellectual, without betraying her sex (or gender)? In short: What is at stake in the innocuous little sentence 'I am a woman?' and its equally innocuous companion: 'You are a woman'?

This chapter uncovers Beauvoir's radical analysis of a dilemma that women in a sexist society regularly have to confront. This is the situation in which women are invited to 'choose' between being imprisoned in their gendered subjectivity (their 'femininity') and having to eliminate that subjectivity altogether in the name of some ungendered general humanity. A woman, in short, is often invited to choose between calling herself a woman, and calling herself a human being. (Through a brief discussion of Frantz Fanon's *White Skin, Black Masks*, I show that raced subjects in a racist society often find themselves in a structurally similar dilemma.)

The genius of Beauvoir's analysis is that she shows that both options are equally disastrous for a woman's aspirations to social justice and equality. In the first case she is locked up in her particularity, and so loses the right to represent humanity, to speak for all. In the second case she is forced to abandon her particularity in favour of an impossibly ungendered generality. Then she can aspire to speak for all (or to speak the truth, as Beauvoir puts it) only if she pretends that her gendered experiences in the world are of no relevance to her words. ('I am a writer, not a woman writer' is a phrase exemplifying this attitude.) Men do not have to choose between their masculinity and their humanity. I have never heard a male writer say, 'I am a writer, not a male writer'. He does not need to, for it goes without saying that there is no contradiction between his gendered particularity and his access to the universal category, in this case that of writer. This analysis explains, in part, why Beauvoir insists that the goal of feminism must be for women to gain access to the universal as women, not as some curiously ungendered person.

This crucially important theory in *The Second Sex* has often been overlooked. As a result, feminist theorists have found themselves caught on the horns of the dilemma described by Beauvoir. Instead of refusing its terms, they have ended up generating theories in which 'sameness', 'equality', and 'identity' are pitted against 'difference' with tedious predictability. But Beauvoir is precisely not recommending that we choose 'difference' against 'identity'. She is not recommending that we choose a (poorly defined) sense of 'sameness' or 'equality' against 'difference' either. Were we to choose either one, we would not escape, but rather be caught in the sexist trap she analyses.

Chapter 2 is concerned above all with women's ambition to write theory and philosophy, that is to say, to write with the aspiration to the universal. The question is how to find a personal voice for such a project. Through a detailed reading of the beginning of *The Second Sex* I show that Beauvoir managed to find a voice, a way to write personally and philosophically at the same time, without abandoning the outrageous ambition of speaking for all, and without silencing others. This is what makes Beauvoir's use of herself in *The Second Sex* exemplary.

2004

Acknowledgements

In 1994–5 I was the fortunate recipient of a Rockefeller Fellowship at the National Humanities Center (NHC) in North Carolina, and of a Senior Fellowship from the American Council of Learned Societies (ACLS). Duke University granted me sabbatical leave for the same year. In the autumn of 1998, Duke University granted me another semester's leave, without which Chapter 2 of this book would never have been finished.

The philosophical groundwork for the essays in this volume—the intense study of Wittgenstein, Austin, and Cavell, and the rereading of Beauvoir and Sartre—was done at the National Humanities Center. At the NHC I profited immensely from conversations with my philosophical colleagues Richard Moran and George Wilson, and with my literary colleagues Sarah Beckwith and Jonathan Freedman. Above all, however, I owe great thanks to Martin Stone who first showed me what I could learn from turning to ordinary language philosophy. I have learned a lot from his philosophical example. Further acknowledgements will be found in the notes to each essay.

The cartoon by Tom Cheney in Chapter 2 appears by permission from:

© *The New Yorker Collection* 1996 Tom Cheney from cartoonbank.com. All Rights Reserved.

This student edition was prepared with the help of my wonderful research assistant Fiona Barnett. Without the steady support of my editor at OUP, Sophie Goldsworthy, this edition would simply not exist.

T.M.

Contents

A Note on the Text

The text that follows is the text of the two first chapters in the 1999 hardback and the 2001 paperback editions of *What Is a Woman? And Other Essays*. No changes have been made, except that some quotations, notes and references have been updated to reflect the publication of texts referred to as 'forthcoming' in 1999.

In this book I use the MLA reference system, as outlined in the MLA Style Manual. As far as possible references are given in the text. Cumbersome and very long references are nevertheless exiled to footnotes. The context is supposed to make it clear what author and what work is being cited. Full references can be located by consulting the list of Works Cited at the end of the book. Multiple entries under one author's name (Beauvoir, Cavell, Freud) are organized alphabetically. I list quoted translations under their English title, but add the original reference whenever I feel it should be there.

Throughout this book the abbreviation 'TA' indicates that the published translation has been amended by me. This happens particularly often when I am quoting *The Second Sex*. In this volume I always refer both to the English translation and the French original of *The Second Sex*. Page references to some frequently used texts are preceded by the following abbreviations. The editions used are those listed in the 'Works Cited' section at the end of the book.

By Simone de Beauvoir:

DSa	*Le deuxième sexe*, vol. i
DSb	*Le deuxième sexe*, vol. ii
FA	*La force de l'âge*
FC	*Force of Circumstance*
FCa	*La force des choses*, vol. i

FCb	*La force des choses,* vol. ii
MDD	*Memories of a Dutiful Daughter*
MJF	*Mémoires d'une jeune fille rangée*
PC	*Pyrrhus et Cinéas*
PL	*The Prime of Life*

By Freud:

SE	*Standard Edition*

By Wittgenstein:

PI	*Philosophical Investigations*

In truth there is no divorce between philosophy and life.
(*Simone de Beauvoir*)

What Is a Woman? Sex, Gender, and the Body in Feminist Theory

INTRODUCTION

Since the 1960s English-speaking feminists have routinely distinguished between *sex* as a biological and *gender* as a social or cultural category. The sex/gender distinction provides the basic framework for a great deal of feminist theory, and it has become widely accepted in society at large.[1] Over the past ten years or so, the distinction has nevertheless become highly contentious among feminist theorists. Feminists inspired by psychoanalysis, French feminist theory, and queer theory have questioned its value.[2] Poststructuralist theorists of sex and gender such as Donna Haraway and Judith Butler have subjected it to merciless critique.[3]

I want to thank Kate Bartlett, Sarah Beckwith, Sara Danius, Terry Eagleton, Maria Farland, Sibylle Fischer, Sally Haslanger, Julia Hell, Alice Kaplan, Eva Lundgren-Gothlin, Diana Knight, Walter Benn Michaels, Mats Rosengren, Vigdis Songe-Møller, Martin Stone, Lisa Van Alstyne, and Jennifer Wicke for much needed critical feedback on earlier versions of this essay. The fabulous participants in my seminar on 'Sex, Gender and the Body' at the School of Criticism and Theory at Cornell University in the summer of 1997 helped me to put the finishing touches to this paper.

[1] Handbooks in non-sexist usage routinely recommend that we use 'sex to mean the biological categories of male and female and gender to designate the cultural and other kinds of identities and attributions associated with each sex' (Frank and Treichler 14).

[2] Moira Gatens's eloquent 1983 defence of the concept of sexuality is the best and earliest example of a psychoanalytic critique of the sex/gender distinction. Eve Sedgwick's discussion of the distinction in *Epistemology of the Closet* exemplifies the queer critique. Tina Chanter argues that the sex/gender distinction makes it impossible to understand French psychoanalytically inspired feminism, and particularly the work of Luce Irigaray.

[3] Here and throughout this essay, I use the term 'poststructuralist' to indicate English-language critics working on the sex/gender distinction from a poststructuralist perspective. (For obvious reasons, theorists who do not write in

For them, the original 1960s understanding of the concepts has the
merit of stressing that gender is a social construction and the
demerit of turning sex into an essence. Considered as an essence,
sex becomes immobile, stable, coherent, fixed, prediscursive,
natural, and ahistorical: the mere surface on which the script of
gender is written. Poststructuralist theorists of sex and gender
reject this picture of sex. Their aim is to understand 'sex or the
body' as a concrete, historical and social phenomenon, not as an
essence.[4] Although they want radically to change our understanding of sex and gender, they retain these concepts as starting
points for their theories of subjectivity, identity, and bodily sexual
difference. With respect to sex and gender poststructuralists are
reformist rather than revolutionary.[5]

   In this paper I too am trying to work out a theory of the sexually different body. Unlike the poststructuralist theorists of sex and
gender, however, I have come to the conclusion that no amount of
rethinking of the concepts of sex and gender will produce a good
theory of the body or subjectivity. The distinction between sex and
gender is simply irrelevant to the task of producing a concrete,
historical understanding of what it means to be a woman (or a

---

English usually do not discuss this particular distinction. Foucault, for example,
uses the word *sexe* in much the same way as Beauvoir.) I take the most influential of these theorists to be Judith Butler and Donna Haraway. Their analyses of
sex and gender have been accepted by a great number of contemporary feminist critics and theorists. I also draw on Elizabeth Grosz's work on the body, since
it provides a particularly clear example of the way Butler and Haraway's critiques
of the sex/gender distinction have been taken up by other theorists.

   4 The formulation 'sex or the body' is widely used in poststructuralist
theory. It is theoretically confusing in that it makes us believe that it makes sense
to ask questions such as 'Is sex the same thing as the body?', 'Will a theory of
"sex" be the same thing as a theory of the "body"'? As this paper will show, such
questions are based on a confused picture of sex, gender, and the body, and can
have no clear answer.

   5 Donna Haraway dreams of a deconstructed and reconfigured understanding of sex and gender (see 148). Judith Butler's two books *Gender Trouble* and
Bodies That Matter come across as massive attempts to hammer the sex/gender
distinction into poststructuralist shape. After showing that *gender* is performative,
Butler aims to prove that *sex* is as constructed as gender. In her pursuit of a historical and political understanding of the body, Butler never asks whether the
sex/gender distinction actually is the best framework for her own project.

man) in a given society. No feminist has produced a better theory of the embodied, sexually different human being than Simone de Beauvoir in *The Second Sex*. Because contemporary English-language critics have read Beauvoir's 1949 essay through the lens of the 1960s sex/gender distinction, they have failed to see that her essay provides exactly the kind of non-essentialist, concrete, historical and social understanding of the body that so many contemporary feminists are looking for. In short, Beauvoir's claim that 'one is not born, but rather becomes a woman' has been sorely misunderstood by contemporary feminists.[6] Lacan returned to Freud; it is time for feminist theorists to return to Beauvoir.

I do not mean to say that the distinction between sex and gender does no useful work at all. That we sometimes need to distinguish between natural and cultural sex differences is obvious. The feminists who first appropriated the sex/gender distinction for their own political purposes were looking for a strong defence against biological determinism, and in many cases the sex/gender distinction delivered precisely that. I agree that feminists have to reject the claims of biological determinism in order to produce a forceful defence of women's freedom. But feminists managed to make a convincing case against biological determinism long before they had two different words for sex to choose from. Even in a language without the sex/gender distinction it is not difficult to convey one's opposition to the idea that people in possession of ovaries are naturally unsuited to sports, intellectual work, or public careers. From the fact that Norwegian or French have only one word for sex (*kjønn*; *sexe*), it hardly follows that Norwegian or French feminists are unable to distinguish between sex and gender.[7] Working in German, another language with only

---

[6] Sara Heinämaa is an exception to this rule. See her excellent critique of the tendency to project the sex/gender distinction on to Beauvoir, particularly in 'What Is a Woman?'.

[7] In much feminist work in Norway expressions such as 'social sex' and 'biological sex' have been used. Swedish feminist theorists on the other hand introduced a distinction between *kön* and *genus* modelled on the English distinction in the 1980s. For a Swedish discussion of sex and gender, see Danius. In French neither Simone de Beauvoir nor Monique Wittig have had any trouble criticizing the belief that sex alone can explain social behaviour. Recently, however, Christine Delphy and other feminists have been struggling to introduce

one word for sex, in 1920 Freud had already developed a theory
of subjectivity that explicitly distinguished between 'physical
sexual characters', 'mental sexual characters', and 'kind of
[sexual] object choice' ('The Psychogenesis of a Case of
Homosexuality in a Woman', *SE* 18: 170).

I do not claim, then, that a distinction between sex and gender
is irrelevant to every feminist project. Rather I start my investigation of sex and gender in feminist theory by asking: In what
circumstances do we need to draw on distinctions of this kind? In
this essay, my main project is to show that there is at least one case
in which the distinction does no useful work at all, and that is
when it comes to producing a good theory of subjectivity. In other
contexts the sex/gender distinction nevertheless remains of
crucial importance to feminism. In the first part of this essay I
discuss biological determinism such as it emerged towards the
end of the nineteenth century. At this time biological determinism is characterized by two features: (1) a sexual ideology which I
shall label the 'pervasive picture of sex'; and (2) the belief that
science in general and biology in particular both could and
should settle questions about women's role in society. In my view,
the combination of these two features created a historical and
conceptual situation which made it necessary and urgent to
respond by distinguishing between nature and social norms. I
return to some significant texts from the late nineteenth century
because Simone de Beauvoir still finds it necessary to argue
against them, and because I think that the sex/gender distinction
in contemporary feminist theory is designed to counter this kind
of biological determinism. It follows that the distinction may not
work as well for other purposes as it does for this one.

My account of biological determinism is followed by a discussion
of the 1960s and 1970s formulation of the sex/gender distinction,
particularly in the influential work of Gayle Rubin. In Section III
the poststructuralist attempt to revise the 1960s formulation

----

the word *genre* as an equivalent to the English gender (see Delphy, 'Rapports').
Whatever one thinks of this as a feminist strategy, the attempt shows that in the
1990s the sex/gender distinction is still not operative in ordinary French
language.

becomes the subject of critical analysis. In Section IV I show that Simone de Beauvoir's understanding of the body as a situation offers a powerful alternative to sex/gender theories, and in Section V I bring the Beauvoirean approach to bear on some legal cases. The point of this section is to show through concrete examples that Simone de Beauvoir's understanding of what a woman is makes a political and practical difference in the conflicts of everyday life. In contemporary feminist theory so much energy is spent keeping the spectre of biologically based essentialism at bay that it is easy to forget that generalizations about gender may be just as oppressive as generalizations about sex. In many situations today biological determinism is not the most pressing obstacle to an emancipatory understanding of what a woman is. *The Second Sex* shows that every general theory of gender or 'femininity' will produce a reified and clichéd view of women. The final afterword is subtitled 'The Point of Theory'. Here I summarize some of my findings, and ask what concrete investigations the theoretical work in this essay might lead to. I end by asking what kind of work feminist theory might usefully carry out, and what we need it for.

Finally, I want to say a few words about the wider feminist and theoretical issues I seek to engage with. Taking Wittgenstein's deceptively simple phrase 'the meaning of a word is its use in the language' (*PI* §43) as my source of inspiration,[8] I have tried to show that what Susan Gubar has wittily labelled feminist theory's 'bad case of critical anorexia', namely the tendency to make the word woman slim down to nothing (901), is a problem of our own (I mean 'us feminist theorists' own') making. Through a careful investigation of the concepts of sex and gender, this essay tries to show (rather than just claim) that the belief that any use of the word 'woman' (and any answer to the question 'What is a woman?') must entail a philosophical commitment to metaphysics and essentialism, is mistaken. It follows that efforts to rescue the word 'woman' from its so-called inherent essentialism, for instance

---

[8] To be exact, what Wittgenstein actually writes is this: 'For a *large* class of cases—though not for all—in which we employ the word "meaning" it can be defined thus: the meaning of a word is its use in the language.' In my view, all the cases in which feminists discuss the meaning of the words *woman, sex,* and *gender* belong to the '*large* class of cases' Wittgenstein has in mind.

by claiming that one only uses it 'strategically', or that one really thinks of it as an 'umbrella term', or that one really ought only to speak of various *kinds* of women, or that one always mentally must add quotation marks to the word in order to place it under deconstructive erasure, are misguided because they are unnecessary.

Whether it is to reaffirm or to deconstruct the concept, most feminist theories today rely on a universalized and reified concept of 'femininity'. In this essay I first show that a feminist theory that starts from an ordinary understanding of what a woman is, namely a person with a female body, will not necessarily be either metaphysical or essentialist. I also show that such a theory does not have to be committed to the belief that sex and/or gender differences always manifest themselves in all cultural and personal activities, or that whenever they do, then they are always the most important features of a person or a practice. Women's bodies are human as well as female.[9] Women have interests, capacities, and ambitions that reach far beyond the realm of sexual differences, however one defines these. Investigations of the meaning of femininity in specific historical and theoretical contexts are indispensable to the feminist project of understanding and transforming sexist cultural practices and traditions. Yet any given woman will transcend the category of femininity, however it is defined. A feminism that reduces women to their sexual difference can only ever be the negative mirror image of sexism. It is because Simone de Beauvoir never forgot that one of the many possible answers to the question 'What is a woman?' is 'a human being', that I have been able to make such extensive use of *The Second Sex* in this essay. Yet it is as oppressive and theoretically unsatisfactory to reduce women to their 'general humanity' as it is to reduce them to their femininity. Beauvoir herself writes: 'Surely woman is, like man, a human being, but such a declaration is abstract. The fact is that every concrete human being is always in a specific situation' (*SS* xx; *DSa* 13; TA).[10]

---

[9] None of this is meant to block serious inquiry into the question of sexually ambiguous or intersexed bodies. For a beginning of such discussions, see the analysis of various questions raised by the existence of transsexuals in this essay.

[10] In French: 'le fait est que tout être humain concret est toujours *singulièrement situé* (my emphasis). Parshley translates this as 'The fact is that every concrete human being is always a singular, separate individual'.

As Beauvoir shows, the question of what a woman is instantly raises the question of the relationship between the particular and the general.[11]

The answer to the question of what a woman is, is not one. To say this, moreover, is specifically to deny that the answer is that woman is not one.[12] It may be that, in some situations, it makes sense to understand a given woman or a given group of women as, say, plural and decentred. Yet to generalize this or any other view is to fabricate yet another reified concept of femininity. Too many forms of contemporary feminism appear unable to understand women who do not conform to their own more or less narrow vision of what a woman is or ought to be. The predictable result is the proliferation of accusations of 'exclusionism' against this or that theory. What we need today more than ever is a feminism committed to seeking justice and equality for women, in the most ordinary sense of the word. Only such a feminism will be able adequately to grasp the complexity of women's concrete, everyday concerns. That feminism, I am happy to say, exists. Moreover, usually even the most anti-metaphysical feminist theorists support it in practice. No feminist I know is incapable of understanding what it means to say that the Taliban are depriving Afghan women of their most elementary human rights just because they are women. The problem is not the meaning of these words, but the fact that too many academic feminists, whether students or professors, fear that if they were to use such sentences in their intellectual work, they would sound dreadfully naive and unsophisticated. Such fear, incidentally, is not only grounded on a certain theoretical confusion about sex and gender, but also on the idea that academic writing and ordinary language and experiences are somehow opposed to each other. (In a somewhat oblique way, Chapter 2 in this book is an attempt to undo the second belief; this essay is trying to deal with the first.)

This essay, academic and theoretical as it is, won't tell anyone

---

[11] I discuss this question at some length in Ch. 2, below.
[12] *Ce sexe qui n'en est pas un* (*This Sex Which Is Not One*) is the title of one of Luce Irigaray's most influential books.

what to do about the Taliban. It does show, however, that we do not have to believe that the word 'woman' always carries heavy metaphysical baggage. If I am right about this, then it follows that an anti-essentialist feminist may very well claim that the point of feminism is to make the world a better place for women without being caught in the slightest theoretical contradiction. For me, at least, this is an immensely liberating conclusion. My aim in this essay, then, is to show that the question of what a woman is, is crucial to feminist theory, and that anyone who is willing to think it through once more from the beginning stands to gain a real sense of intellectual freedom.

I. BIOLOGY AND SOCIAL NORMS

> What was decided among the prehistoric Protozoa cannot be annulled by Act of Parliament.
>
>   Geddes and Thomson, 1889

Pervasive Sex

'Sometime in the eighteenth century, sex as we know it was invented', Thomas Laqueur writes in his illuminating study *Making Sex* (149). At this time Western culture was moving from what Laqueur calls a 'one-sex model' to a 'two-sex model' of sexual difference. From Antiquity to the Middle Ages women's anatomy was not seen as inherently different from men's, only as a different arrangement of the same parts: 'all parts that are in men are present in woman', wrote the sixteenth-century doctor Fallopius (Laqueur 97). The vagina was considered an inverted penis, the womb an interior scrotum. Since male and female reproductive organs were not taken to be fundamentally differ-ent, anatomical differences were pictured as hierarchical as opposed to complementary. Man was on top and woman at the bottom of the same scale of values. In this picture, biology or anatomy did not ground the social and cultural differences between the sexes. If the social order was a manifestation of God's plan for mankind, there was no need to appeal to biology to explain why women could not preach or inherit property. As

Laqueur puts it, in this situation gender precedes sex.[13] Although Lacqueur does not say so, the implication is that sexist ideologies based on appeals to what feminists today call gender are no less oppressive than those based on appeals to biological, anatomical, or genetic sex differences.

Under the 'one-sex model' anatomy and biology were ideologically insignificant compared to, say, theology. This changed dramatically with the shift to the 'two-sex model'. In 1913 a British doctor named Walter Heape produced a particularly representative expression of the 'two-sex' view of sexual difference:

> the reproductive system is not only structurally but functionally fundamentally different in the Male and the Female; and since all other organs and systems of organs are affected by this system, it is certain that the Male and Female are essentially different throughout. . . . [They are] complementary, in no sense the same, in no sense equal to one another; the accurate adjustment of society depends on proper observation of this fact (quoted in Laqueur 220).

Science has taken the place of theology or natural philosophy, and biology, as the science of the body, has been drafted into ideological service. Scientific truth, not divine revelation, is supposed to keep women in their place.

I am not turning to Laqueur because I am certain that he is right in his analysis of the history of sex. For all I know, the whole idea of a shift from a 'one-sex' to a 'two-sex model' is wrong. What interests me in Laqueur's fascinating book, however, is the way the 'two-sex model' produces accounts which over and over again picture biological sex as something that seeps out from the ovaries and the testicles and into every cell in the body until it has saturated the whole person. What this shows, to my mind, is that in the nineteenth century, biological sex is pictured as *pervasive*.[14] My

---

[13] '[I]n these pre-enlightenment texts, and even some later ones, *sex*, or the body, must be understood as the epiphenomenon, while *gender*, what we would take to be a cultural category, was primary or "real" ' (8). The formulation is helpful for contemporary readers, but should not be taken to mean that people actually thought in terms of a distinction between sex and gender in pre-modern times.

[14] Laqueur does not use the expression 'pervasive sex': I take responsibility for this interpretation.

claim is not that this was never the case before (I am not a histo-rian and have not done the research to be able to say whether it was or not). My claim, rather, is that precisely at the time that modern feminism is born (in the period stretching from Mary Wollstonecraft through John Stuart Mill to Henrik Ibsen and the first women's movement) it does seem to be the case that sex is pictured as pervasive. Every feminist from Wollstonecraft onwards finds it necessary to oppose this idea. It is in the encounter with the pervasive picture of sex that the need for something like the sex/gender distinction is born.[15]

In the pervasive picture of sex, then, a woman becomes a woman to her fingertips: this is biological determinism with a vengeance. Because sexual desire is considered to trickle out from the reproductive glands, heterosexuality is taken for granted. Pervasive sex saturates not only the person, but every-thing the person touches. If housework, childcare, and selfless devotion are female, heroic exploits are male, and so are science and philosophy. Whole classes of activities are now endowed with a sex. The modern world is a world steeped in sex: every habit, gesture, and activity is sexualized and catego-rized as male or female, masculine or feminine. In the transi-tion to the 'two-sex model', man and woman emerge as two different species.

Strindberg's 1887 play *The Father* provides a vivid example of this way of thinking about sexual difference. An avid reader of contemporary science, Strindberg was particularly well informed about contemporary debates concerning the nature of women and men.[16] In *The Father* man and woman, husband and wife, are two different species, the sexual relationship does not exist, and the truth of sexual difference is a struggle until death, where the most powerful wins:

[15] I am grateful to Chris Vanden Bossche at the University of Notre Dame for helping me to clarify what I want and do not want to use Laqueur for, and to Vigdis Songe-Møller for sharing with me her doubts about Laqueur's validity for Ancient Greek society.

[16] It is no coincidence that the Captain in the play is a scientist, whose work his wife Laura is not only incapable of understanding, but considers as a sign of his madness.

THE CAPTAIN. One last word about reality. Do you hate me?
LAURA. Yes, sometimes! When you are a man.[17]
THE CAPTAIN. This is like race hatred. If it is true that we're descended from apes, then it must have been from two different species. We're simply not like each other, are we?
LAURA. What is all this supposed to mean?
THE CAPTAIN. I realize that in this struggle one of us must go under.
LAURA. Which one?
THE CAPTAIN. The weaker, naturally!
LAURA. And the stronger is right?
THE CAPTAIN. He's always right, since he has the power!
LAURA. Then I'm right![18]

If sexual difference produces two different species, then only power—sexual warfare—will resolve the resulting impasse, Strindberg concludes. Either radical patriarchy or—as Strindberg feared—radical matriarchy would do the trick. The two-sex model, Strindberg realized, cannot produce a relationship between the sexes, at least not if the word 'relationship' implies mutual trust and understanding.

In the picture of sex resulting from the 'two-sex model' any transgression against sexual norms seems 'unnatural'. Since an 'unnatural' man or a woman is no longer a 'real' man or a woman, moreover, different concepts have to be forged to cover the proliferation of new sexual species: Krafft-Ebing's fabulous catalogues of sexual perversions come to mind. Foucault illustrates this logic in his stunning account of the invention of the modern homosexual:

> The nineteenth-century homosexual became a personage, a past, a case history, and a childhood, in addition to being a type of life, a life form, and a morphology, with an indiscreet anatomy and possibly a mysterious physiology. Nothing that went into his total composition was unaffected by his sexuality. It was everywhere present in him: at the root of all his actions because it was their insidious and indefinitely active principle; written immodestly on

---

[17] The play shows that in his relations to his wife, the Captain oscillates between behaving as a phallic, sexual male and regressing to a baby-like state. Laura's 'when you are a man' alludes to her impression that when he isn't a man, he is a baby.

[18] My translation from Strindberg, *Fadren* 72. A somewhat different translation may be consulted in *Strindberg: Five Plays* 35.

his face and body because it was a secret that always gave itself away. It was consubstantial with him, less as a habitual sin than as a singular nature. . . . The sodomite had been a temporary aberration; the homosexual was now a species (43).

The pervasive picture of sex gives rise to essentialism, biologism, accusations of degeneration and 'unnatural' behaviour. It can certainly only consider two sexes. It sexualizes not only the whole person, whether this person is a woman, a man, or a so-called 'pervert', but the whole world of human activities. *This* is the picture of sex that the great majority of contemporary feminists, gays, and lesbians rightly oppose.

When one pictures sex as pervasive, there can be no difference between male and masculine, female and feminine, sex and gender. This would also, incidentally, be true for a pervasive picture of *gender*. As Laqueur's research shows, modern feminist theory was born at a time when sexist ideology often grounded its claims about the subordination of women on appeals to the sciences of the body, particularly biology. This explains why the question of the relationship between nature and social norms has become so important in modern feminist theory. But feminists have no reason to feel more sanguine about ideologies that ground their claims about sexual difference on gender, such as appeals to God's plan for women, or the belief that 'femininity' (whatever this is taken to mean) is eternally subversive because it is eternally 'outside discourse'. Whether it is gender or sex that is pictured as pervasive, the result is an unwarranted sexualization (or 'genderization') of women, and occasionally also of men.[19]

The encounter between the pervasive picture of sex and modern feminism produced the sex/gender distinction and its equivalents. (Here it does not matter what words one uses to express the distinction between these two ways of understanding sexual difference.) Trusting in the authority of science, however, many nineteenth-century biological determinists hoped that the question of women's rights, capacities, and duties could be settled

---

[19] See Sect. V, below, for a more extensive discussion of generalizations about gender.

once and for all. But the more science they read, the less obvious the meaning of the body became. For scientists disagreed about the scientific interpretation of the body, and even more about the correct *social* interpretation of the biological facts established by science (see Laqueur 193): 'The body could mean almost anything and hence almost nothing at all', Laqueur writes (217). Once the body was taken to be meaningful, it became possible for feminists, gays, and others to fight over its interpretation, to dispute just how much or how little meaning the body has in human society. Historically, then, *gender* emerged as an attempt to give to biology what belongs to biology, no more and no less. Gender may be pictured as a barricade thrown up against the insidious pervasiveness of sex.

Biological Determinism

Late nineteenth-century biological determinists drew on the pervasive picture of sex. A quick look at the claims such scientists routinely made about women and men will make it resplendently clear why feminists needed to introduce a distinction between biology and social norms. In 1883 W. K. Brooks, Professor of Biology at Johns Hopkins University, published a book entitled *The Law of Heredity*. The chapter discussing the intellectual differences between men and women was first published in the anti-feminist *Popular Science Monthly* in 1879.[20] Much quoted and much debated, Brooks's views were at the forefront of discussions of biology and women's rights in the last two decades of the nineteenth century.[21] His starting point was the observation that 'among the higher animals . . . the males are more variable than the females' (326). According to Brooks, this 'law is so pronounced and conspicuous that its existence has long been

[20] According to Cynthia Eagle Russett, the editor of the *Popular Science Monthly* scolded people promoting women's rights for their refusal to be guided by science: 'And yet the fundamental questions of this important movement belong solely to scientific investigators' (quoted in Russett 13).

[21] Russett discusses Brooks's influence on G. Stanley Hall, Havelock Ellis, and others (see Russett 92–6).

recognized by all naturalists' (323).[22] This 'fact' can best be explained, he writes, by assuming that the ovum transmits hereditary characteristics and sperm cells transmit acquired characteristics:[23]

> According to this view, the male element is the originating and the female is the perpetuating factor; the ovum is conservative, the male cell progressive. Heredity or adherence to type is brought about by the ovum; variation and adaptation through the male element; and the ovum is the essential, the male cell the secondary factor in heredity. ... Like Aristotle and the ancients, we must believe that the two reproductive elements play widely different parts. Like Bonnet and Haller, we see that the structure of the adult is latent in the egg (84–5).

For Brooks it is obvious that social differences between the sexes are caused by their physiological differences: 'If there is fundamental difference in the sociological influence of the sexes, its origin must be sought in the physiological differences between them' (243).[24] Moving on to the intellectual differences between men and women, he claims that men's brains enable them to grasp the unknown: discoveries, science, the highest artistic and philosophical insights are reserved for them. Women's brains can deal with the known, the ordinary, and the everyday, keep track of traditions and social customs; in short, take care of everything

[22] The variability hypothesis, as it was called, was in fact widely accepted at the time. In *The Descent of Man* (1871) Darwin wrote that 'Numerous measurements were carefully made of the stature, the circumference of the neck and chest, the length of the back-bone and of the arms, in various races; and nearly all these measurements show that the males differ much more from one another than do the females. This fact indicates that, as far as these characters are concerned, it is the male which has been chiefly modified, since the several races diverged from their common stock' (638). Numerous commentators concluded that males were simply 'higher' on the evolutionary ladder than females.

[23] As Brooks himself points out, this theory, which sounds so bizarre to modern ears, positions him 'midway between Darwin's theory of natural selection and Lamarckianism' (80).

[24] He also writes that 'Our examination of the origin and significance of the physiological differences between the sexes, and of the parts which they have taken in the progress of the past, would therefore lead us to expect certain profound and fundamental psychological differences, having the same importance' (257).

that requires 'rational action without reflection' (258). Women preserve the old, men discover the new; 'the ovum is conservative, the male cell progressive'.

Science, Brooks continues, ought to determine social policy concerning women: 'If there is . . . a fundamental and constantly increasing difference between the sexes . . . the clear recognition of this difference must form both the foundation and super-structure of all plans for the improvement of women' (242–3). If his scientific conclusions give comfort to adherents of the status quo, this cannot be helped:

> It is hardly necessary to call attention to the obvious fact that our conclusions have a strong leaning to the conservative or old-fashioned view of the subject,—to what many will call the 'male' view of women. The positions which women already occupy in society and the duties which they perform are, in the main, what they should be if our view is correct; and any attempt to improve the condition of women by ignoring or obliterating the intellectual differences between them and men must result in disaster to the race (263).

Although it is tempting to continue by quoting Brooks's account of women's intellectual inferiority, his gloating over the fact that there has been no female Shakespeare, Raphael, or Handel, or his insistence that women cannot manage intellectual 'reflection', I shall restrain myself, since these themes do not add anything new to his general thesis of male variability and female stability.

Another influential text from the same period is *The Evolution of Sex* by the Scottish researchers Patrick Geddes and J. Arthur Thomson, first published in Britain in 1889. Geddes and Thomson's central claim is that males and females exhibit different 'metabolisms'. Females are 'anabolic', males 'katabolic'; males tend to expend, and females to conserve, energy. Males 'live at a loss', Geddes and Thomson write, 'females . . . live at a profit' (26); or in even more colourful language, males exhibit 'a preponderance of waste over repair' (50). Discussing Brooks's views, they stress that their own thesis is entirely compatible with his: 'The greater variability of the males is indeed natural, if they be the more katabolic sex' (29).

Working their way from a consideration of the adult organism down through the sexual organs and tissues, Geddes and Thomson finally arrive at the sex-cells themselves, or rather at the protoplasm 'that makes them what they are' (81). This induces them to launch into a lengthy discussion of protozoa (unicellular organisms): 'It is among the Protozoa that we must presently look, if we hope to understand the origin and import either of "male and female" or of fertilization' (89). If the protozoa contain the secret of sexual difference, it is because Geddes and Thomson believe that the ovum and the sperm cell *are* protozoa, the only cells in the body that date back to the earliest evolutionary stages. This is how they picture the reproductive cells:

> Just as the ovum, large, well nourished, and passive, is a cellular expression of female characteristics, so the smaller size, less nutritive habit, and predominant activities of the male are summed up in the sperm. As the ovum is usually one of the largest, the sperm is one of the smallest of cells (109).

Geddes and Thomson then drive the point home: 'If the anabolic and katabolic contrast, so plainly seen in the sex-elements, be the fundamental one, we must expect to find it saturating through the entire organism' (130). This is true for all higher animals as well as for humans. The conclusion is inevitable: 'It is generally true that the males are more active, energetic, eager, passionate, and variable; the females more passive, conservative, sluggish, and stable' (270). In other words: the world is full of hungry, lean males in energetic pursuit of large, sluggish females (who, by the sound of it, must be sorely tempted to gobble the little man up for breakfast: there is more than a little fear of the female in this picture).

Geddes and Thomson do not doubt that their theory has clear social and political consequences:

> We have seen that a deep difference in constitution expresses itself in the distinction between male and female, whether these be physical or mental. The differences may be exaggerated or lessened, but to obliterate them it would be necessary to have all the evolution over again on a new basis. What was decided among the prehistoric Protozoa cannot be annulled by Act of Parliament (267).

They deplore the fact that so many contemporary writers completely neglect 'the biological considerations underlying the relations of the sexes' (267). Politics and economics cannot solve the question of the 'subjection of women':

> The reader need not be reminded of . . . the attitude of the ordinary politician, who supposes that the matter is one essentially to be settled by the giving or withholding of the franchise. The exclusively political view of the problem has in turn been to a large extent subordinated to that of economic *laissez-faire,* from which of course it consistently appeared that all things would be settled as soon as women were sufficiently plunged into the competitive industrial struggle for their own daily bread. While, as the complexly ruinous results of this inter-sexual competition for subsistence upon both sexes and upon family life have begun to become manifest, the more recent economic panacea of redistribution of wealth has naturally been invoked, and we have merely somehow to raise women's wages (268).

Giving women the vote, or—even more thoughtlessly—paying them decent wages, are misguided attempts to impose a social order without foundation in nature. Just as Brooks predicts the end of the 'race' if women's position were to change, Geddes and Thomson believe that the 'species' will come to a ruinous end unless women are kept out of economic competition with men.[25]

Although Brooks and Geddes and Thomson harp on different leitmotifs (male variability versus anabolic and catabolic protozoa), the structure of their arguments is remarkably similar:

(1)   the characteristics of the reproductive cells saturate the adult human organism (this is the pervasive—and obviously heterosexist—picture of sex)

AND

(2*a*) biological facts justify social norms;[26]
      or

---

[25] Russett discusses Geddes and Thomson at length (see esp. 89–92), as does Sayers (see 38–50).

[26] By 'social norms' here and in the following I mean 'social norms concerning sex roles and the relationship between the sexes'. I supply six different variations of the three authors' view of the relationship between biological facts and social norms since they seem to wander between all of them without much consistency, often producing circular arguments (first existing social norms are taken to be the aim of evolution, then evolution is used to prove that existing social norms are indeed the result of evolution).

(2*b*) science both can and should tell us what our social norms
        should be;
    or
(2*c*) social norms are expressions of biological facts;
    or
(2*d*) social norms have their cause and origin in nature;
    or
(2*e*) attempts to change the existing social norms will have disas-
        trous consequences for humanity, since they are against the
        natural law (the biological facts);
    or
(2*f*) unless social norms are brought back into harmony with the
        natural law (the biological facts), there will be disastrous
        consequences for humanity.

The claims listed from 2*b* to 2*f* are really just variations on 2*a*, the
idea that *biological facts justify social norms.* In Brooks's and Geddes
and Thomson's texts, this belief draws massive support from the
pervasive picture of sex (claim 1). This picture of sex enables
them to overlook the difference between Plato and the protozoa,
between Raphael and the rhizopods, barnacles, beetles, and
butterflies that provide the evidence for their theses about
human sexual difference. For these writers, a man is essentially an
enormous sperm cell, a woman a giant ovum.

   Biological determinism presupposes a pervasive picture of sex
and considers that biology grounds and justifies social norms:

Biology

↓

Social Norms

There is no distinction between male (sex) and masculine
(gender) or between female and feminine. Whatever a woman
does is, as it were, an expression of the ovum in her. This view,
clearly, is essentialist and heterosexist, and I take as given that all
feminists will want to oppose it.[27] I shall now examine three

---

[27] I am aware of the fact that some late 19th-cent. women tried to ground their
feminism on biological determinism. There are also feminists today who remain
biological determinists. Such feminists usually believe that women's biology make

different ways of responding to the biological determinists' pervasive picture of sex.

II. SEX AND GENDER IN THE 1960S AND 1970S

[I dream of] an androgynous and genderless (though not sexless) society, in which one's sexual anatomy is irrelevant to who one is, what one does, and with whom one makes love.

Gayle Rubin, 1975

Stoller and Rubin

The English-language distinction between the words sex and gender was first developed in the 1950s and 1960s by psychiatrists and other medical personnel working with intersexed and transsexual patients. The transsexuals' dilemma has been summed up as a sense of being 'trapped in the wrong body'. Transsexuals feel that the sex of their body does not correspond to the sex of their mind. Psychiatrists were intrigued by the question of how transsexuals came to develop their sense of belonging to the 'wrong sex'. Once the terms sex and gender had been introduced, doctors could claim that transsexuals suffered from a 'mismatch' between their sex and their gender. This had the advantage of making it look as if the solution to the problem was straightforward. All that needed to be done to cure transsexuals was to bring their sex and their gender into harmonious correspondence with each other by changing the body through surgery and hormone treatment. Why most doctors and all transsexuals consider that the obvious way to achieve this is to change the body and not the mind, is a question I shall not go into here.[28]

Thus, the distinction between sex and gender emerged from a

---

them superior to men, or if not superior, then fundamentally different from men spiritually, mentally, and ethically. They usually wish to inhabit a more 'natural' social order. I do not intend to discuss biological determinist forms of feminism any further in this essay.

[28] I doubt that the distinction between sex and gender actually explains very much about transsexuality, but that is another matter. For a good account of the medicalization of transsexual identity, see Hausman.

concern with individual identity. At its inception, the distinction medicalizes 'sex' and turns 'gender' into a purely psychological category. In 1963 the American psychoanalyst Robert Stoller first formulated a concept of *gender identity* in a paper presented at the 23rd International Psycho-Analytical Congress in Stockholm: 'Gender identity is the sense of knowing to which sex one belongs, that is, the awareness "I am a male" or "I am a female". . . . The advantage of the phrase "gender identity" lies in the fact that it clearly refers to one's self-image as belonging to a specific sex' ('A Contribution' 220).[29] But 'gender identity' is a term concerned only with a person's psychological experience of belonging to one sex or another. By 1968 Stoller had expanded his insights and developed four different concepts:

> I prefer to restrict the term *sex* to a biological connotation. Thus, with few exceptions, there are two sexes, male and female. . . . *Gender* is a term that has psychological or cultural rather than biological connotations. If the proper terms for sex are 'male' and 'female', the corresponding terms for gender are 'masculine' and 'feminine'; these latter may be quite independent of (biological) sex. . . . *Gender identity* starts with the knowledge and awareness, whether conscious or unconscious, that one belongs to one sex and not to the other, though as one develops, gender identity becomes much more complicated, so that, for example, one may sense himself as not only a male but a masculine man or an effeminate man or even a man who fantasies being a woman. *Gender role* is the overt behavior one displays in society, the role which he plays, especially with other people, to establish his position with them insofar as his and their evaluation of his gender is concerned (*Sex and Gender* 9–10).

Although the term 'gender role' soon faded from view in feminist theory, Stoller's other three concepts were quickly appropriated

---

[29] Although John Money and his colleagues coined the phrase 'gender role' as early as 1955 (see Money, Hampson, and Hampson 302), it was Stoller's explicit contrast between sex and gender that fired feminists' imagination. In fact, in 1985, Money polemicized against Stoller's definitions of sex and gender on the grounds that it destroyed his own original concept of 'gender role': 'Its outcome was to restore the metaphysical partitioning of body and mind. Sex was ceded to biology. Gender was ceded to psychology and social science. The ancient regime was restored!' (282).

by feminists. Crucial to Stoller's distinction between sex and gender is the idea that sex belongs to the realm of science, to biology and medicine. Sex is a category that requires scientific description. All the 1960s and 1970s feminist elaborations of the distinction between sex and gender, including that of Gayle Rubin, incorporate this understanding of sex.[30] The 1960s view of sex, then, is clearly at odds with the traditional or pre-feminist meaning of the word in English, where a reference to someone's sex is simply a reference to their being a man or a woman.[31]

When Gayle Rubin, in her path-breaking 1975 essay 'The Traffic in Women', appropriated Stoller's categories for her own feminist purposes, her aim was to develop conceptual tools that would combat sexism by explaining why and how women's oppression was maintained in widely different cultures:

> [Feminists need to] build descriptions of the part of social life which is the locus of the oppression of women, of sexual minorities, and of certain aspects of human personality within individuals. I call that part of social life the 'sex/gender system', for lack of a more elegant term. As a preliminary definition, a 'sex/gender system' is the set of arrangements by which a society transforms biological sexuality into products of human activity, and in which these transformed sexual needs are satisfied (159).

Rejecting the term 'patriarchy' on the grounds that not all sexist systems are ruled by fathers, Rubin nevertheless considers that 'sex/gender system' designates a system that oppresses women. For Rubin, bodily sexual differences and the sex drive are 'biological', the 'raw material' for the production of gender:

> Hunger is hunger, but what counts as food is culturally determined and obtained. Every society has some form of organized economic activity. Sex is sex, but what counts as sex is equally culturally determined and obtained. Every society also has a sex/gender system— a set of arrangements by which the biological raw material of human sex and procreation is shaped by human, social intervention and satisfied in a conventional manner, no matter how bizarre some of the conventions may be (165).

[30] Heinämaa ('Woman—Nature, Product, Style'), Chanter, and Gatens all discuss Stoller's sex/gender distinction.

[31] This, moreover, is also the meaning of *sexe* in French, as Beauvoir's title *Le deuxième sexe* makes clear.

What interests Rubin is not sex, but gender. For her, the fundamental meaning of gender is oppressive social norms: gender is
the oppressive result of a *social* production process.[32] On the
structural level, Rubin takes sex to mean biological sexual differences and gender to mean the oppressive social norms brought to
bear on these differences. This is a classic example of a feminist
rejection of biological determinism. It is important to stress that
on Rubin's definition, gender is always oppressive, that in human
society there can be no such thing as non-oppressive gender
differences.

This assumption has been exceptionally influential in US
feminism. Ideologically, it has been used to justify the idea that
women are above all victims of male power. Perhaps the clear-
est intellectual elaboration of Rubin's view can be found in
Catherine MacKinnon's understanding of what a woman is,
namely the effect of the 'organized expropriation of the sexuality of some for the use of others'.[33] When Judith Butler

[32] Rubin's essay triggered much debate among Marxist and socialist feminists in the 1970s and 1980s. The question was whether her understanding of how
the sex/gender system works was compatible with a Marxist analysis of production, economic relationships, and so on. As recently as 1996, Teresa Ebert
claimed that Rubin's understanding of sex and gender allowed feminists to
'[suppress] any knowledge of the economic relations of production in their
theories of gender and sexuality' (47). It is certainly true that much recent US
feminist work in the humanities has been spectacularly unconcerned by questions of class, economic production, conditions of labour, and so on. Whether
this is a necessary consequence of Rubin's way of thinking about sex and gender,
is a question I shall not venture into here.

[33] MacKinnon writes: 'the organized expropriation of the sexuality of
some for the use of others defines the sex, woman' ('Feminism, Marxism' 2).
I am not implying that Gayle Rubin would necessarily have to agree with such
a radicalization of her own views. The problem with MacKinnon's definition
of woman is that she tries to define woman in a structural way, to make the
concept correspond to the Marxist concept of class. For Marx classes are fully
defined by their antagonism to each other: the working class is per definition
the class that is structurally bound to struggle against the bourgeoisie.
Without the concept of class struggle, there is no proletariat. It hardly seems
satisfactory, however, to define men and women simply in terms of their
structural antagonism to each other. Such a definition makes any hope of
non-patriarchy or reconciliation between the sexes meaningless. Or rather, a
more complex understanding of how the power relations between the sexes

considers sex to be an effect of power, she too becomes one of Rubin's inheritors.[34] While such structural theories of what a woman is enable feminists to produce quite remarkable critiques of sexist ideology and misogynist abuse of power, they have notorious difficulties in explaining what the sexually different body has to do with being a woman, or with women's oppression, and in providing a sufficiently nuanced account of individual subjectivity. Nor are they well placed to provide analyses of power relations more complex than that of domination and subordination.

Although Rubin emphasizes structural social and cultural formations, she also includes personal identity within the sex/gender system. While immensely influential, it would seem that Rubin's attempt to theorize individual subjectivity introduces a number of unacknowledged ambiguities in her understanding of sex and gender. This is how Rubin's argument about individuals goes. All societies turn biological sex into gender in one way or another, she writes: 'Human sexual life will always be subject to convention and human intervention. It will never be completely "natural", if only because our species is social, cultural, and articulate. The wild profusion of infantile sexuality will always be tamed' (199). The individual men and women we meet in everyday life are products of the sex/gender system; no human being exemplifies 'raw' or 'natural' sex.

The problem with this observation is that it makes it all too easy to think of sex as a Kantian *Ding an sich* beyond the reach of

---

actually work, will not be able to use such a definition of gender. In *The Second Sex* Beauvoir compares the oppression of women to that of Jews, Blacks in America, and the proletariat. Unlike MacKinnon she concludes that while the oppression of women shares some features with all of these forms of oppression, it is nevertheless not theorizable in exactly the same terms: 'The proletariat can propose to massacre the ruling class . . . but woman cannot even dream of exterminating the males. The bond that unites [woman] to her oppressors is not comparable to any other. The division of the sexes is a biological fact, not an event in human history. Their conflict has emerged from within a primordial *Mitsein*, and woman has not broken it' (*SS* xxv; *DSa* 19; TA).

[34] See Sect. III, below for an extensive discussion of Butler's work.

ordinary human experience.[35] To say that sex means chromosomal, hormonal, and anatomical sexual differences is perfectly
meaningful. But chromosomes are hardly the *Ding an sich.* Yet, in
poststructuralist sex and gender theory, such statements have
frequently given rise to the idea that there is an alarming conceptual gap between sex (chromosomes, hormones, etc.) and the
body (the concrete, historically and geographically situated
entity) that feminist theory now must bridge. Labouring under
this picture of sex, some feminists seem to believe that as soon as
the body acts, walks, and talks it becomes gender, that is to say an
entity *not* produced by chromosomes, hormones, and so on.
Interpreted in this way, sex becomes a uselessly abstract category,
whereas gender slides towards the traditional prefeminist sense of
sex, and so towards a usage in which the sex/gender distinction is
not operative. Recent poststructuralist theorists relentlessly criticize this understanding of the sex/gender distinction. Yet they
also promote it.[36] Spellbound by this understanding of sex and
gender, they labour to make its abstract and scientistic understanding of sex yield a good theory of the concrete body. As I shall
go on to show, this is a hopeless task.[37]

'Gender is between the ears, sex is between the legs', is a slogan
much used by contemporary transsexuals. In this slogan another
common feminist interpretation of the 1960s sex/gender distinction is at work: sex is the body, gender is the mind.[38] The philosophical and political drawbacks of this reintroduction of the

[35] Rubin herself never explicitly says that sex is 'outside language' or 'outside
history'. Such phrases are nevertheless common—and it has to be said, well-
founded—interpretations of her views. In her pioneering 1984 essay 'Thinking
Sex', Rubin herself criticizes 'The Traffic in Women' for not drawing a distinction between gender and sexual desire (what some would call sexual orientation). On my reading, Rubin is a little too hard on her earlier essay here.

[36] Eve Sedgwick generally refers to 'sex' in its 1960s sense as 'chromosomal
sex' (*Epistemology* 27). She also writes: ' "M. saw that the person who approached
was of the opposite sex." Genders . . . may be said to be opposite; but in what
sense is XX the opposite of XY?' (*Epistemology* 28).

[37] I discuss poststructuralist accounts of sex and gender in Sect. III, below.

[38] Here and in the rest of this essay I will refer to the '1960s distinction' for
short. I really mean to indicate the theories of sex and gender developed on the
basis of Stoller and Rubin's theories, which in fact date back to the 1950s and
find their fullest feminist expression in the 1970s and early 1980s.

body/mind distinction are only too apparent. Entirely divorced from the mind, the body is perceived as a mere object, subject to the mind's decisions, a blank slate on which gender writes its script. In this idealist view, the body (nature) is entirely subordinated to the mind. No contemporary feminist theorists favour this interpretation of the sex/gender distinction, and I will not discuss it further here.[39]

Rubin's pioneering work is more convincing as an analysis of social norms and practices than as a theory of individual subjectivity. In particular, Rubin's understanding of what would count as social liberation for women is suggestive. Armed with much anthropological data, Rubin denies that *any* social configuration of sex is based on or caused by biological facts. Whatever social norms rule the expressions we give to our sex and our sexuality, they are completely arbitrary and usually oppressive to women. Thorough understanding of the social relations of sex and gender will contribute to the feminist task of 'eliminating the social system which creates sexism and gender' (204). But this is not enough:

> I personally feel that the feminist movement must dream of even more than the elimination of the oppression of women. It must dream of the elimination of obligatory sexualities and sex roles. The dream I find most compelling is one of an androgynous and genderless (though not sexless) society, in which one's sexual anatomy is irrelevant to who one is, what one does, and with whom one makes love (204).

In Rubin's utopia gender would disappear. There would be *no* social norms for correct sexual and sexed behaviour. Moving beyond the question of the oppression of women towards a vision of a society where all sexualities may be freely expressed, she embraces a utopia that inspired many 1960s and 1970s critiques of stereotyped images of women.[40] To expect someone to be masculine (which here means 'to conform to socially normative notions of what a man should be like'), just because he is male, or to deny

---

[39] Moira Gatens 1983 essay on sex and gender contains an excellent critique of the body/mind reading of sex and gender.

[40] Mary Ellmann's *Thinking About Women* remains the best and most entertaining example of this trend.

someone the right to behave in 'masculine' ways just because she is female, is to reinforce the sex/gender system. Such stereotyping is oppressive to women, and also, albeit to a lesser degree, to men.[41]

Winning the right to mix and match stereotypes (so that a woman may choose between traditional femininity and traditional masculinity) does not liberate us from gender. When Rubin wishes to 'get rid of gender', she wishes for a society without *any* sexual stereotypes. Gender in her view is a negative term referring to arbitrary and oppressive social norms imposed upon sex and sexuality. While sex and sexuality will always be socialized in some way or other, there is no reason to pretend that the biological differences between men and women furnish the 'natural' organizing principles for that socialization. In so far as the word 'gender' refers to the systematic social organization of sexual difference—the imposition of only two general categories of being as normative for all people—in a non-sexist society gender will simply have to go. In Rubin's utopian world, instead of describing a specific behaviour as masculine or feminine, we would have to come up with more precise descriptions, to consider whether we think of the behaviour as wise, kind, selfish, expressive, or destructive *without* thinking of any of these terms as sex-specific.

In her essay 'Interpreting Gender' Linda Nicholson claims that Gayle Rubin is a 'biological foundationalist' (as opposed to a biological determinist). According to Nicholson, 'biological foundationalism' includes some measure of 'social constructionism', yet it still claims that there are 'real biological phenomena differentiating women and men that are used *in all societies in similar ways* to generate a male/female distinction' (80; my emphasis). Given that Rubin never claims that some aspects of gender are

---

[41] Perhaps one still needs to explain this point: feminists have usually not denied that men too may suffer from a sex/gender system that oppresses women. The point is that since the system fundamentally favours males, for instance by assuring them a better material situation, better working conditions, greater sexual freedom, and so on, it is not necessarily in most men's *interest* to oppose a system that in other ways may weigh heavily on them, for instance because it requires that men live up to stereotypical standards of masculinity.

absolutely invariable in all cultures, this is an unfair description of 'The Traffic in Women'. In fact, Rubin and Nicholson would seem to have a very similar understanding of the role of biological sexual differences. '[T]he position I would like feminists to endorse [is] that biology cannot be used to ground claims about "women" or "men" transculturally', Nicholson writes (89). The only difference between this formulation and Rubin's denial that biology grounds social norms is the word 'transculturally', which is superfluous in this context. To deny that biology grounds social norms *is* to deny that our sexed bodies produce *any* gender norms in whatever context.[42]

Politically, Rubin inherits Simone de Beauvoir's hope for a society where women will no longer be cast as Other. Like Beauvoir's critique of patriarchal femininity, Rubin's critique of gender bears a strong family resemblance to Marxist and socialist critiques of ideology. Gender is ideological in the precise sense that it tries to pass social arrangements off as natural.[43] Common to Rubin and Beauvoir's idea of what a non-oppressive society would look like is the thought that whatever biological differences exist between the sexes, they cannot ground any particular social norms or structures. Any attempt to invoke sex (biological or anatomical sex differences) as a pretext for imposing any specific social arrangement (gender) is ideological and ultimately oppressive. In this theory, a firm line is drawn between biology and social norms:

$$\frac{\text{Biology}}{\text{Social Norms}} \rightarrow \frac{\text{Sex}}{\text{Gender}}$$

---

[42] Nicholson is right to say that some so-called 'social constructionist' theories produce deeply oppressive generalizations about female or feminine difference (see 97). But such oppressive effects will be generated by any theory that reifies femininity or masculinity, regardless of its ideas about the role of biological, anatomical, or genetic sexual differences. If I believe that biological sex differences are an effect of 'regulatory discourses' *and* picture such discourses as all-encompassing, I am going to have just as oppressive a theory of femininity as if I were a biological determinist. I discuss the problems arising from generalizations about femininity in Sect. V below.

[43] I discuss Beauvoir's critique of 'patriarchal femininity' in Ch. 7 of my *Simone de Beauvoir*. Roland Barthes's critique of bourgeois ideology in *Mythologies* is written in the same spirit as Beauvoir's anti-naturalizing critique of sexism.

This figure works well on the general social level. Here 'sex' means something like men and women, or male and female bodies, and 'gender' means general social norms. Yet, as I have shown, Rubin does not fully acknowledge that she also uses sex and gender in a different, and far more problematic, sense. Applied to individual human beings gender appears to mean both individual gender identity and social gender norms, and the meaning of sex emigrates to the far reaches of hormones and chromosomes. Soon theorists following in Rubin's footsteps will think of sex as an ungraspable entity outside history and culture, and of gender as the only relevant term for sexual difference. This appears to leave a gap where the historical and socialized body should be, a gap taken to call out for theorization. But this is a theoretical problem that only arises if one assumes that the sex/gender distinction *must* be the axiomatic starting point for any theory of embodied and sexually differentiated subjectivity. It is this spurious gap that the powerful poststructuralist revision of the sex/gender paradigm steps in to fill.

III. THE POSTSTRUCTURALIST PICTURE OF SEX AND GENDER

> If the immutable character of sex is contested, perhaps this construct called sex is as culturally constructed as gender; indeed, perhaps it was always already gender, with the consequence that the distinction between sex and gender turns out to be no distinction at all.
>
>   Judith Butler, 1990

Sex, Gender, and Sexual Difference

Poststructuralist theorists of sex and gender are unhappy with the way the 1960s understanding of sex and gender accounts for personal identity and the body. They consider, much as I do, that the 1960s understanding of sex easily turns sex into an ahistorical and curiously disembodied entity divorced from concrete historical and social meanings. Their critique of the sex/gender distinction has two major objectives: (1) to avoid biological determinism;

and (2) to develop a fully historical and non-essentialist under-standing of sex or the body. These are aims shared by the great majority of contemporary feminists. The problem with the post-structuralist critique of sex and gender is not its ultimate goal. Rather, my argument is that the goal is not achieved, for two reasons: because the starting point for the poststructuralists' analy-sis is singularly unpromising; and because the theoretical machin-ery they bring to bear on the question of sex and gender generates a panoply of new theoretical problems that poststructuralists feel compelled to resolve, but which no longer have any connection with bodies, sex, or gender. The result is work that reaches fantas-tic levels of abstraction without delivering the concrete, situated, and materialist understanding of the body it leads us to expect.

Before showing how I reach these conclusions, I should stress that my subject in this section is the way the distinction between sex and gender works in poststructuralist feminist theory. I do not pretend to comment on all poststructuralist theory or on all poststructuralist feminist theory. In particular I am not going to analyse the many different ways in which poststructuralists have used the word 'gender'. The most common poststructuralist way of using the word is exemplified in Joan Scott's epochal essay 'Gender: A Useful Category of Historical Analysis'. 'The word [gender] denoted a rejection of the biological determinism implicit in the use of such terms as "sex" and "sexual differ-ence"', she writes (29). Scott's concern is to analyse the historical and social effects of sexual difference. When she calls this subject matter 'gender', she is not necessarily opposing it to 'sex'. In her usage, the word 'gender' does the same work as the French *sexe* and the Norwegian *kjønn*, or the English *sex* in its traditional, pre-1960s meaning. Where Scott writes 'gender', Virginia Woolf would no doubt have written 'sex', and in all probability they would have meant pretty much the same thing.[44] In contempo-rary American academic language, Scott's usage has long since become normative, and I see no reason to deplore this.

The grounds on which Scott chooses 'gender' over 'sex' or

[44] '[I]t is fatal for anyone who writes to think of their sex', Virginia Woolf writes in *A Room of One's Own* (99).

'sexual difference' are nevertheless dubious. It appears that, for her, the word 'gender' in itself signals rejection of biological determinism, whereas the words 'sex' and 'sexual difference' in and by themselves signal acceptance of it.[45] In my view, no one word can serve as talismanic protection against ideological danger. The proof of resistance to biological determinism has to be established in the text as a whole. (Scott herself does so with elegance and verve.) And as soon as opposition to biological determinism has been established, it really does not matter whether one writes 'sex', 'gender', or 'sexual difference'. *The Second Sex* proves that one can be radically opposed to biological determinism without using the word 'gender' once. Conversely, it is obviously easy to say 'gender' and still be a biological determinist. Recent work in sociobiology tends to do precisely this.

In psychoanalytic theory, as opposed to poststructuralist theory, the most widely used concept is sexual difference, not sex or gender. As Moira Gatens has pointed out, the sex/gender distinction is incompatible with the psychoanalytic understanding—be it poststructuralist or not—of sexual difference. The psychoanalytic understanding of the sexually different body offers a challenging alternative to sex and gender thinking. When I started working on this essay, my intention was to include a long section on psychoanalysis. What interests me is the question of what 'femininity' means to different psychoanalytic theorists, and how different psychoanalytic views relate to Beauvoir's understanding of the body as a situation. Unfortunately, I soon realized that these are exceptionally difficult questions, and that I most certainly could not do them justice within the framework of this essay. I will return to them in another context.[46]

So far, I have shown that in Gayle Rubin's work the sex/gender distinction operates on two different levels: on a general social level, where gender becomes synonymous with

---

[45] I am not denying that words such as 'sex' or 'sexual difference' often are steeped in biological determinism, but the same is actually true for gender these days, particularly in everyday American usage. My point is that these words need not have such connotations, and that in some situations they do not have them.

[46] See Ch. 8, below, for a modest first step towards such a project.

social norms or ideology and sex means concrete human bodies; and on an individual level, where gender gets interpreted as personal identity or subjectivity, and sex is imagined to be an elusive entity inside or beyond the actual body. Although it is difficult to imagine a more unpromising point of departure, Butler and Haraway insist on taking the second, highly problematic understanding of sex and gender as the starting point for their attempts to escape identity politics, undo naive conceptions of subjectivity, and develop a concrete, materialist understanding of the body. As I will show, the theoretical difficulties produced by this choice are overwhelming. It is particularly surprising to note that poststructuralists entirely overlook Simone de Beauvoir's originality. They do not discover the enormous differences between *The Second Sex* and the 1960s understanding of sex and gender, and thus fail to appreciate that Beauvoir's understanding of subjectivity and the body offers exactly what they are looking for (see Section IV, below).

Here is a checklist of terms that regularly recur in Judith Butler, Donna Haraway, and Elizabeth Grosz's discussions of sex and gender:

SEX	GENDER
biological	political
natural	cultural
essence	construction
essentialist	constructionist
body	mind
passive	active
base	superstructure
being	doing
substance	performance
fixed	[mobile; variable]
stable	unstable
coherent	non-coherent
prediscursive	discursive
prelinguistic	linguistic
presocial	social
ahistorical	historical

The first thing to be stressed is that poststructuralists are *unhappy* with these dichotomies.[47] They take this binary struc-ture to be inherent in the 1960s understanding of sex and gender, and see their own project as an immense effort to get out of this straitjacket. Judith Butler's project is to make us real-ize that sex is 'as culturally constructed as gender' (*Gender Trouble* 7). In terms of the checklist above, this means that we should realize that sex is as cultural, performative, unstable, discursive (and so on) as gender. In much the same way, Donna Haraway wants to 'historicize and relativize sex' (136), and also frequently refers to the need to deconstruct various binary oppositions relating to sex, gender, and the body:

> In all their versions, feminist gender theories attempt to articulate the specificity of the oppressions of women in the context of cultures which make a distinction between sex and gender salient. That salience depends on a related system of meanings clustered around a family of binary pairs: nature/culture, nature/history, natural/human, resource/product (130).

While this is an accurate account of Gayle Rubin's sex/gender system, Haraway's formulation leaves it unclear whether the terms sex and gender are themselves part of the objectionable 'family of binary pairs'. Poststructuralists certainly often interpret the pair as a variation on clear-cut binary oppositions, such as nature/culture, coherent/non-coherent, stable/unstable, and so on. Yet Gayle Rubin neither thinks of gender as the *opposite* of sex, nor does she define it as the *absence* of sex. The distinction between sex and gender cannot easily be assimilated to the kind of binary opposition that deconstructionists need to work on.

Here one might object that the distinction between writing and speech, which Derrida so memorably deconstructs, is not a binary opposition either. Yet whatever we make of Derrida's analysis of writing and speech, we may agree that these words *are* the key

---

[47] The words listed above are taken from Judith Butler, *Gender Trouble* (6–7, 24–5); Donna Haraway (134–5, 147); and Elizabeth Grosz, *Volatile Bodies* (17–18). I have suggested 'mobile' or 'variable' as the positive opposites of 'fixed'. Both terms are regularly used by poststructuralist theorists of subjectivity, but unlike 'unstable' and 'non-coherent' they do not occur on the pages I consulted.

terms in the field he is dealing with. This is not the case for sex and gender. Many non-English-speaking feminists manage very well without these particular terms, without becoming biological determinists for all that. If we find these words to be particularly troublesome for feminist theory, as many poststructuralist feminists do, the obvious strategy is to look around for a better set of concepts before investing an enormous amount of time and energy deconstructing the bad existing concepts.

The concepts sex and gender represent two different ways of thinking about sexual difference. They do not pretend to explain class, race, or nationality, or anything else. When it comes to thinking about what a woman is, therefore, the sex/gender distinction is woefully inadequate. Many critics appear to believe that a sexed human being is made up of the sum of sex plus gender. From such a perspective it does look as if everything in a woman or man that is not sex must be gender, and vice versa. Suddenly sex and gender start to look like a deconstructable 'pair'. But this analysis forgets that a sexed human being (man or woman) is more than sex and gender, and that race, age, class, sexual orientation, nationality, and idiosyncratic personal experience are other categories that always shape the experience of being of one sex or another.[48]

Whether I consider a woman to be the sum of sex plus gender, to be nothing but sex, or nothing but gender, I reduce her to her sexual difference. Such reductionism is the antithesis of everything feminism ought to stand for. In this context it makes no difference at all whether the woman's difference is taken to be natural or cultural, essential or constructed. All forms of sexual reductionism implicitly deny that a woman is a concrete, embodied human being (of a certain age, nationality, race, class, and with a wholly unique store of experiences) and not just a human

[48] No wonder that Haraway criticizes feminists who think in terms of sex and gender for being unable to include race in the category of gender. We shall only succeed in historicizing 'the categories of sex, flesh, body, biology, race, and nature', Haraway writes, if we ensure that 'the binary, universalizing opposition that spawned the concept of the sex/gender system . . . implodes into articulated, differentiated, accountable, located, and consequential theories of embodiment, where nature is no longer imagined and enacted as resource to culture and sex to gender' (148).

being sexed in a particular way. The narrow parameters of sex and gender will never adequately explain the experience and meaning of sexual difference in human beings. This shortcoming is not repaired by adding on new factors. To think of a woman as sex plus gender plus race and so on is to miss the fact that the experience of being white or black is not detachable from the experience of being male or female.[49]

A major source of confusion in poststructuralist writings on sex and gender is the fact that many critics appear to think of the terms on each side of the checklist (see above) as interchangeable, or rather as one tightly packed bundle of concepts which can never be unpacked. All the terms on the left side of the checklist are projected on to anyone who uses the word sex, all the terms on the right side to anyone who uses the word gender. Particularly widespread is the assumption that anyone who says sex *must* be thinking of it as an essence or a substance, as ahistorical and prediscursive, and so on. There is often the implication that anyone who thinks of biology (or other sciences of the body) as producing valuable and reliable insights must be an essentialist too. In further elaborations, it usually appears that such poststructuralists think of anything natural as stable, fixed, and unchanging, and since sex in their scheme of things is natural, they assume that it follows that sex, unlike gender, is outside history, discourse, and politics. The next step, of course, is to propose various solutions to this 'problem'. The most common suggestion is that 'sex' itself must be considered to be as variable and historical as gender. My point is not that this is false, but that it is a solution to a problem produced by the poststructuralist reading of the sex/gender distinction in the first place.

The idea that sex *must* be ahistorical and outside discourse, for example, is not grounded in an analysis of the concept of sex itself. There is no good reason to assume that someone who thinks that it makes sense to speak of sex as natural must therefore be an essentialist in the bad, metaphysical, and political sense that poststructuralist feminists give the term. The kind of essentialism that

---

[49] Linda Nicholson also discusses the shortcomings of what she calls the 'additive' view of race and gender (see 83).

feminists usually worry about is the kind that claims that women's bodies inevitably give rise to and justify specific cultural and psychological norms. Poststructuralists are right to object to this view, but this is biological determinism, and although Simone de Beauvoir does believe that a woman can be defined by reference to the usual primary and secondary sexual characteristics, it is ludicrous to characterize her (or Gayle Rubin for that matter) as an 'essentialist' in this sense. For Beauvoir, the possession of the usual biological and anatomical sexual characteristics is what makes a woman a woman.[50] But given that she firmly demonstrates that this has no *necessary* social and political consequences, this is a kind of essentialism that has no negative consequences whatsoever for feminist politics. The only kind of essentialism that feminists need to reject is biological determinism.[51]

The fact that the usual understanding of sex often treats the concept as an ahistorical entity is no reason to think that it therefore must be 'outside discourse', or that it must operate as a Kantian *Ding an sich*. If we look at the way feminists use the terms feminine (gender) and female (sex), it is clear that they usually function as two different criteria of selection. Feminists assume that the word 'female' picks out a certain group of people, and that the word 'feminine' will not pick out exactly the same group

[50] It doesn't follow that there will be no ambiguous or difficult cases (see Sect. V, below, for some further discussion of transsexuality).

[51] Gayatri Spivak's famous injunctions to 'take the risk of essence', or to consider the 'strategic use of essentialism' ('In a Word', *Outside* 3–4) may be read in the light of this sentence. Perhaps Spivak may be taken to mean that not all essentialisms are *politically* equally harmful. I think that is right. But if that is so, it follows that there may be cases and situations where essence is no risk at all. Spivak's work on essentialism, particularly in the interview with Ellen Rooney entitled 'In a Word' exemplifies the tension between her allegiance to Derridean deconstruction on the one hand and her admirable grasp of concrete political situations on the other. Spivak's work is a remarkable attempt to hold these two ways of thinking about the world together without falling into theoreticism. The difficulty of the project—the tension between deconstruction and concrete political analysis—surfaces when she asks: 'Is essentialism a code word for a feeling for the empirical, sometimes?' (*Outside* 6), or when she writes: 'if one doesn't . . . consolidate ways of gathering the empirical, antiessentialism versus essentialism can prove a red herring' (*Outside* 7). Spivak's understanding of the relationship between theory and politics in general would be well worth further study.

of people. Why many poststructuralists believe that feminists who use the words in this way secretly consider 'female' the ground and essence of 'feminine' remains a mystery to me.[52]

In such claims there is a pronounced tendency to believe that if we accept that there are biological facts, then they somehow will become the ground of social norms. Consider the common post-structuralist argument that the belief that there are only two sexes, men and women, *must* be heterosexist.[53] This would be true if the speaker making the claim were a biological determinist. Given Rubin's or Beauvoir's—or indeed most feminists'—under-standing of the relationship between biology and social norms, however, this critique makes no sense at all. To deny that biology grounds social norms is to deny that the existence of two biologi-cal sexes justifies any specific socio-sexual arrangements, be they heterosexist or not.[54]

In fact, the idea that there must be something heterosexist about the belief that there are only two sexes presupposes that biology somehow gives rise to social norms. The same is true for the belief that if we can just turn sex into a more 'multiple' or 'diverse' cate-gory than it has been so far, then social norms will be relaxed. This is nothing but biological determinism with a liberal face. Even if we all agreed to have five sexes—Anne Fausto-Sterling has proposed adding 'herms', 'ferms', and 'merms' to the usual two—nothing guarantees that we would get more than two genders, or that we wouldn't be stuck with five sets of oppressive gender norms instead of two.[55] And what are the grounds for believing that a system of three, five, or ten genders (regardless of the number of sexes we decide there are) will be more liberating than two?

Sometimes the argument for a mulitiplicity of sexes is based on the idea that we have to challenge the oppressive binary opposition

[52] I don't mean to say that this usage is unproblematic, just that the problem with it has nothing to do with grounds and essences (see my discussion of femi-nist treatment of words such as 'femininity' and 'masculinity' in Sect. V, below).

[53] See Sedgwick, *Epistemology* 31; Sedgwick, 'Gender Criticism' 276 (essentially a reprint of the same passage); Butler, *Gender Trouble* 22, 33 (*et passim*).

[54] Joan Copjec has given a thoughtful critique of Butler's claims about heterosexism from a Lacanian perspective (see esp. 201–11).

[55] Fausto-Sterling proposes these terms as a way of acknowledging the main forms of intersexuality that naturally occur in human beings (see 21).

man/woman. The assumption is that if we can only show that there are third terms, categories that fall outside the two master terms, then the very meaning of man and woman, male and female will be shaken to the core. One example of this widespread belief may be found in Marjorie Garber's *Vested Interests*, where she claims that transvestism is a sign of a 'category crisis', that is to say that it represents

> a failure of definitional distinction, a borderline that becomes permeable, that permits border crossings from one (apparently distinct) category to another. . . . The binarism male/female . . . is itself put under erasure in transvestism, and a transvestite figure, or a transvestite mode, will always function as a sign of overdetermination—a mechanism of displacement from one blurred boundary to another (16).

Yet a concept ('man', 'woman') that is blurred at the edges is neither meaningless nor useless. Wittgenstein writes:

> One might say that the concept 'game' is a concept with blurred edges.—'But is a blurred concept a concept at all?'—Is an indistinct photograph a picture of a person at all? Is it even always an advantage to replace an indistinct picture by a sharp one? Isn't the indistinct one often exactly what we need?
>
> Frege compares a concept to an area and says that an area with vague boundaries cannot be called an area at all. This presumably means that we cannot do anything with it.—But is it senseless to say 'Stand roughly there'? (*PI* §71).

Hermaphroditism, transvestism, transsexuality, and so on show up the fuzziness at the edges of sexual difference, but the concepts 'man' and 'woman' or the opposition between them are not thereby threatened by disintegration. Nor have all the usual ways of using the words suddenly become impossible: from the fact that the word 'game' doesn't have a clear and essential definition outside every language game, it does not follow that it does not have one within specific language games, nor does it follow that the absence of a clear definition makes the word 'game' more difficult to use, more ambiguous, more unstable, or more transgressive than other words. The existence of hermaphrodites and transsexuals proves that not all human beings can be easily categorized as either male or female, that there will always be ambiguous, unclear, or borderline cases, but I have not noticed that this has made our everyday handling of the terms 'man' and 'woman' more difficult, or the meaning of those words more inherently unstable or obscure. The fact that there are difficult cases doesn't prove that there are no easy ones. If gays, lesbians, transvestites, transsexuals, and intersexed people suffer discrimination in contemporary society, this is the fault of our social norms and ideologies concerning human sex and sexuality, not of the assumption that biologically speaking, there are only two sexes.[56]

If we are serious about denying that biology can justify social norms, it follows that the question of how many sexes there are or ought to be has *no necessary* ideological or political consequences whatsoever. It does not follow, however, that the material structure of our bodies has no impact on our way of being in the world. There is every reason to believe that the world would be vastly different if human beings had three arms and an extra pair of eyes in the back of the head. But bodily structures have no absolute meaning. For Simone de Beauvoir our bodies are an outline or sketch of the kind of projects it is possible for us to have, but it doesn't follow from this that individual choices or social and ethical norms can be deduced from the structure of the human body (see Section IV, below).

In a 1993 interview with Peter Osborne and Lynne Segal, Judith Butler demonstrates just how close the poststructuralist critique of the idea that there are only two sexes comes to biological determinism. Wondering whether Butler doesn't fail to register the 'constraints coming from the body itself', Osborne and Segal ask: 'Why is it that male bodies don't get produced as child-bearing?' (Osborne 112). In her reply Butler speaks of the social ideology that makes women feel they are failures if they do not have children:

> Why shouldn't it be that a woman who wants to have some part in child-rearing, but doesn't want to have a part in child-bearing, or who wants to have nothing to do with either, can inhabit her gender without an implicit sense of failure or inadequacy? When

[56] Suzanne Kessler has written a strong indictment of the thoughtless and ideologically suspect ways in which contemporary medicine treats intersexed infants.

people ask the question 'Aren't *these* biological differences?', they're not really asking a question about the materiality of the body. They're actually asking whether or not the social institution of reproduction is the most salient one for thinking about gender. In that sense, there is a discursive enforcement of a norm (Osborne 113).

Butler is perfectly right to stress that motherhood is a socially constructed institution regularly used to legitimize women's oppression. But her answer says more than this. It makes a second claim, one that I, unlike Butler, think is not necessary to secure the first. For Butler also insists that to define biological sex by reference to testicles and ovaries *is* to enforce the norm that only mothers are 'real women'. The question of biological sex differences is taken to be exactly the same as the question of social ideology ('discursive norms'). But this is precisely the assumption Geddes and Thomson make when they claim that the social roles of the sexes can be read off from the structure of the ovum and the sperm cell. Butler seems to believe that if one takes sexual difference to be determined by reference to the potential reproductive function of the body, then one simply *must* be caught up in repressive sexist ideology. Yet the whole of *The Second Sex* is evidence to the contrary. As a result, Butler ends up implying that most past and contemporary feminists (including Simone de Beauvoir) and just about all medical researchers and biologists are sexist oppressors, just because they accept that there are biological bases for the categorization of human beings into two sexes. Although Butler struggles against the social norm whereas Geddes and Thomson joyfully embrace it, the fundamental logic of their arguments appear to be perilously similar.

I am of course not claiming that poststructuralists working on sex and gender are biological determinists. The widespread tendency to criticize anyone who thinks that biological facts exist for their 'essentialism' or 'biologism' is best understood as a *recoil* from the thought that biological facts can ground social values.[57]

---

[57] In a seminar at UNC-Chapel Hill in Sept. 1996, Anne Balsamo told the audience that after a lecture where she had shown slides of bodies in the process of undergoing various technological interventions, someone came up to her and said: 'But you know, the body is only a *hypothesis.*'

Instead of denying that biological facts ground any such thing, as Beauvoir and Rubin do, poststructuralists prefer to deny that there *are* biological facts independent of our social and political norms.[58] To put this more clearly: I get the impression that post-structuralists believe that if there *were* biological facts, then they would indeed give rise to social norms. In this way, they paradoxically share the fundamental belief of biological determinists (Figure A1). In their flight from such unpalatable company they go to the other extreme, placing biological facts under a kind of mental erasure (Figure A2):

(A1) Since:

$$\text{Biological facts}$$
$$\downarrow$$
$$\text{Social Norms}$$

(A2) Therefore:

$$\sout{\text{Biological facts}}$$
$$\downarrow$$
$$\text{Social Norms}$$

Caught in the fantasy of a nightmarish, immobile, and timeless monster called sex, poststructuralists roll out the heavy theoretical artillery for an all-out counterattack. Against what they take to be the bad 1960s picture of sex, they mobilize their own good 1990s picture of gender. No wonder that so many poststructuralists express their misgivings about the very act of distinguishing between sex and gender. Thus Elizabeth Grosz rightly wants to escape the distinction by turning to theories of the 'lived body' or the 'social body', yet she does so seemingly without any awareness

[58] In the Osborne/Segal interview, Butler gives a fuzzy reply to the question of whether there are biological sex differences or not. On the one hand she '[does] not deny certain kinds of biological differences', on the other she claims that she is 'not sure that [the problematic of reproduction] is, or ought to be, what is absolutely salient or primary in the sexing of the body'. What is remarkable here is that it remains entirely unclear *what* 'kinds of biological differences' Butler accepts, or what *other* criteria for biological sexual differences she might want to propose. In the next sentence, she returns to the idea that reproductive differences are always the effect of social norms. If reproduction is central to the 'sexing of the body', she adds, 'I think it's the imposition of a norm, not a neutral description of biological constraints' (Osborne 113).

that Simone de Beauvoir's concept of the body as a situation provides exactly what she is looking for.[59] Others seek a more radical solution and claim that sex is constructed by gender, or by the same regulatory discourses that produce gender, so that, ultimately, there is no difference between sex and gender; sex turns out to have been gender all along:

(B)

Biological facts ⇔ Social Norms

Sex ⇔ Gender

Because they think that to speak about biological facts is the same as to speak about essences or metaphysical grounds, many poststructuralists believe that in order to avoid biological determinism one has to be a philosophical nominalist of some kind. In their texts, philosophical realism becomes a *politically* negative term. This is obviously absurd. To avoid biological determinism all we need to do is to deny that biological facts justify social values, and even the most recalcitrant realist can do that. In a parallel move, poststructuralists often conflate a nominalist position concerning the *general* relationship between our categories and the world with a *specific political* interpretation of the world. The assumption is always that if only we would become aware of exceptions and hard cases, then we would necessarily be led to question the very meaning of our concepts, politically as well as theoretically. Or to put it the other way round: the assumption is that *political* exclusion is coded into the very concepts we use to make sense of the world. It is this idea that makes some poststructuralists assume that the word 'woman' can never be used in non-ideological ways, that 'woman' *must* mean 'heterosexual, feminine and female'.[60] In this view, all concepts become bundle concepts: mention one word and hosts of others are taken to be implied.

But if political oppression is taken to follow from the fact that every concept draws a boundary, and thus necessarily excludes

---

[59] See Grosz, *Volatile* 18; on Beauvoir see esp. 15–16.

[60] Carrie L. Hull gives a clear, critical account of why Judith Butler thinks that every positive statement will be performative of a political exclusion (see esp. 29–30).

something—i.e. from the very fact that words have a meaning, and that meaning is normative—then it becomes difficult to see what political alternative poststructuralists intend to propose. The incessant poststructuralist invocations of the slippage, instability, and non-fixity of meaning are clearly intended as a way to soften the exclusionary blow of concepts, but unfortunately even concepts such as 'slippage' and 'instability' have fairly stable meanings in most contexts. It follows from the poststructuralists' own logic that if we were all mired in exclusionary politics just by having concepts, we would not be able to perceive the world in terms other than the ones laid out by our contaminated concepts.[61] If oppressive social norms are embedded in our concepts, just because they are concepts, we would all be striving to preserve existing social norms. As a result poststructuralists have difficulty explaining how it can be that a fair number of people *fail* to become 'suddenly and significantly upset' when they encounter phenomena that deviate from conservative (normative) expectations about gender.[62]

Of course language in general and concepts in particular often carry ideological implications. But as Wittgenstein puts it, in most cases the meaning of a word is its use.[63] Used in different situations by different speakers, the word 'woman' takes on very different implications. If we want to combat sexism and heterosexism, we should examine what work words are made to do in different speech acts, not leap to the conclusion that the same word must mean the same oppressive thing every time it occurs, or that

[61]   Diana Fuss exemplifies the belief that there is something *politically* wrong with the very word woman, whether it occurs in the singular or the plural: 'hasty attempts to pluralize do not operate as sufficient defenses or safeguards against essentialism. The plural category "women", for instance, though conceptually signaling heterogeneity nonetheless semantically marks a collectivity; constructed or not, "women" still occupies the space of a linguistic unity' (4). Fuss believes that the very existence of a concept 'woman' or 'women' must be essentializing, exclusionary, and therefore politically oppressive simply by virtue of being a word ('a linguistic unity'). No wonder she argues that we can't ever fully escape essentialism.

[62]   The quotation is from Butler, *Gender Trouble* 110.

[63]   'For a *large* class of cases—though not for all—in which we employ the word "meaning" it can be defined thus: the meaning of a word is its use in the language' (*PI* §43).

words oppress us simply by having determinate meanings, regardless of what those meanings are.[64]

Perhaps Sex Was Always Already Gender?

The subheading is taken from Judith Butler's *Gender Trouble*, and this section will focus on her attempt to show that sex is a cultural construct, the effect of regulatory discourses. Judith Butler has produced by far the most important work on sex and gender in the 1990s. Precisely because her work is such a principled development of poststructuralist thought, it enables me to show why I think alternatives are needed. My analysis of Butler's understanding of sex and gender does not entail a critique of her politics. Butler's important work has given an intellectual voice to gay and lesbian critics. Her critique of heterosexism and homophobia has inspired thousands, and for good reason. Writing as I am in a country where gays and lesbians are shot, tortured, and beaten to death by rabidly homophobic terrorists, I fully realize the importance of Butler's political task. What concerns me in this essay, however, is not Butler's powerful account of heterosexism, homophobia, and of various forms of homosexual and lesbian sexuality, but the question of how she understands sex, gender, and the body. In my view, but possibly not in Butler's, her understanding of the sex/gender distinction and the body does not, or not to any significant extent, ground either her account of sexuality or her politics. In my view, then, Butler's political aims are not

---

[64] As I will show below, for the purposes of understanding how and when the body is political and historical it is not necessary to enter into protracted arguments about the nature of meaning and reference. If I reject the poststructuralist insistence on entering into this problematics when they discuss sex, gender, and the body, it is because I think that certain readings of Wittgenstein propose convincing philosophical alternatives to their post-Saussurean view of language. In his essay 'Wittgenstein on Deconstruction', Martin Stone shows what the differences between Derrida's and Wittgenstein's understanding of language, meaning, and interpretation actually are. I should add that Martin Stone's graduate seminar on Wittgenstein at Duke in the spring of 1997, as well as my many conversations with him about Wittgenstein have been immensely helpful to my work. Over the past few years my understanding of Wittgenstein has also been deepened through discussions with Richard Moran and David Finkelstein.

threatened by my project, which is to show that one may arrive at a highly historicized and concrete understanding of bodies and subjectivity without relying on the sex/gender distinction that Butler takes as axiomatic, and particularly without entering into the obscure and theoreticist debates about materiality and meaning that her understanding of sex and gender compels her to engage with.

In my view, poststructuralist theorists of sex and gender are held prisoners by theoretical mirages of their own making. This becomes starkly evident in Butler's attempt to show that 'sex' or 'nature' or 'biology' or 'the body' is as constructed as gender:

> If the immutable character of sex is contested, perhaps this construct called sex is as culturally constructed as gender; indeed, perhaps it was always already gender, with the consequence that the distinction between sex and gender turns out to be no distinction at all. . . . The production of sex *as* the prediscursive ought to be understood as the effect of the apparatus of cultural construction designated by *gender* (*Gender Trouble* 7).

When sex is seen as a cultural construct, Butler argues, the traditional sex/gender distinction has been undone. Both are now the product of the same discursive norms; sex is not the ground of gender, but the effect of it. This analysis presupposes the 'bad' picture of sex and the 'good' picture of gender discussed above. Anyone who doubts that sex and gender *have* to be described in this way, or anyone who thinks that sex and gender are useless starting points for a theory of the body and subjectivity will find Butler's theoretical exercise empty.

If we enter into the poststructuralist perspective outlined by Butler, it now looks as if we have to solve a new problem. For if sex is as 'discursive' as gender, it becomes difficult to see how this fits in with the widespread belief that sex or the body is concrete and material, whereas social gender norms (discourses) are abstract and immaterial. This is the starting point for Butler's extraordinary attempt, in *Bodies That Matter*, to show by theoretical argument that the body is material and yet constructed. Her major claims concerning the body may be summarized as follows: (1) Essentialists claim that sex determines gender. Butler opposes them by claiming that 'regulatory discourses' determine biological facts: sex is the performative effect of gender. (2) In order to explain how this can be, she concludes that a general theory of 'materiality' is required. (3) Butler then provides one by claiming that matter is an effect of power. (4) This proves that the body is material and constructed, and that it is therefore inside culture, history, and society as well. According to Butler, the body has now been shown to be at once an effect of regulatory norms, concretely material, and fully historical.

I shall take a closer look at some of these arguments. Butler believes that unless she can show that matter (the matter the body is made of) doesn't exist in the form of brute given facts, she will be stuck with an essentialist picture of sex or the body. In her recoil from positivism and biological determinism, she insists that matter cannot possibly be natural or given:

> What I would propose . . . is a return to the notion of matter, not as site or surface, but as *a process of materialization that stabilizes over time to produce the effect of boundary, fixity, and surface we call matter.* That matter is always materialized has, I think, to be thought in relation to the productive and, indeed materializing effects of regulatory power in the Foucaultian sense (*Bodies* 9–10).[65]

By proposing that power produces matter, Butler makes 'power' sound a little like the *élan vital*, or God, for that matter; power becomes a principle that works in mysterious ways behind the veil of appearances.[66] Whether power is of God or man, it does sound as if it ought to be capable of producing any number of differently sexed bodies, and not only two. The question of why we stubbornly think there are only two sexes is not answered by appeals

[65] John McDowell's analysis of the consequences of either denying or accepting the 'myth of the given' might apply to Butler's understanding of the relationship between concepts and world (see John McDowell, esp. chs. 1–2).

[66] I would like to acknowledge here my debt to Sara Danius's instructive essay on the sex/gender distinction in poststructuralist theory. In her essay 'Själen är kroppens fängelse' ('The soul is the prison of the body') Danius discusses Foucault, Laqueur, Butler, and queer theory, and although she is more optimistic about the philosophical value of Butler's arguments than I am, Danius too questions the political value of Butler's understanding of 'materialization' precisely because she can't quite see how the theoretical understanding of matter solves the difficulties that Butler thinks that the distinction between sex and gender produces (see esp. 162–3).

to 'power'. (It remains unclear to me whether Butler thinks that our discursive concepts—'regulatory power'—produce the material world, or whether they just organize it.[67])

A far better starting point would be to ask *when* (under what circumstances) the problem of the 'materiality of the body' might arise. Imagine an inebriated reveller desperately trying to figure out whether those pink elephants really are material. Or a computer specialist who on finding herself face to face with a space invader, starts to wonder whether she really turned off the virtual reality equipment she was testing. The inebriated reveller will perhaps find that the problematic elephants go away when she sobers up, whereas a good night's sleep and a strong cup of coffee will do nothing to solve the other woman's problem. As Stanley Cavell puts it: 'how I make sure is dictated by what I want to know, which in turn is dictated by what special reason there is for raising the question' (*Claim of Reason* 59). Different reasons for raising a question require different kinds of answers.

Butler's reason for asking about the materiality of the body is that her own theoretical description of sex and gender has made this look like a compelling necessity. In the preface to *Bodies That Matter*, Butler writes: 'This text is offered, then, in part as a rethinking of some parts of *Gender Trouble* that have caused confusion' (xii). In *Gender Trouble* Butler claimed that sex was as constructed as gender. In the preface to *Bodies That Matter*, Butler writes that readers of her previous book constantly asked: 'What about the materiality of the body?' (ix). She continues: 'if I persisted in this notion that bodies were in some way constructed, perhaps I really thought that words alone had the power to craft bodies from their own linguistic substance?' (x). *Bodies That Matter* comes across as the author's attempt to deny that she ever denied that the body was material.[68]

Although there clearly are situations in which we need to

---

[67] Sally Haslanger discusses the obscurity of Butler's view at length in her paper 'Natural Kinds'.

[68] In *The Claim of Reason* Stanley Cavell writes: 'And it is startling to remember how many modern philosophers have seemed to be denying the obvious, and then denied they were denying it. Nothing is more characteristic of the skeptic's position' (103).

establish whether a body is material, it is significant that Butler does not mention any. On the contrary, to her, the 'materiality of the body' is a problem situated outside any conceivable situation, an assumption that makes her treat the body as an abstract epistemological object, that is to say that she treats it just like traditional epistemologists treat their 'material objects' (a table, a tomato, a bit of wax, and so on). What she is interested in is 'materiality' in its purest and most general form, not anything specific about any particular body. Stanley Cavell suggests that such an approach turns objects into 'generic objects': 'What is at stake . . . in the object is materiality as such, externality altogether' (*Claim of Reason* 53). The 'materiality of the body' is a problem produced by the poststructuralist picture of sex and gender, not by any concrete question feminists have asked about sex or the body. Ultimately, Butler loses sight of the body that her work tries to account for: the concrete, historical body that loves, suffers, and dies.

One of Butler's attempts to explain the 'materiality' of the body nevertheless deserves some attention, since it relies on one of the most widespread—and most mistaken—poststructuralist arguments around: I am referring to the old cliché about the 'materiality of the signifier'. At one point in *Bodies That Matter*, Butler tries to show that there is no reason to worry that 'linguistic constructivism' turns the body into nothing but a linguistic effect. Because the language in which we speak of the body is material, her argument goes, there can be no opposition between the body and language:

> the materiality of the signifier . . . implies that there can be no reference to a pure materiality except via materiality. Hence, it is not that one cannot get outside of language in order to grasp materiality in and of itself; rather, every effort to refer to materiality takes place through a signifying process which, in its phenomenality, is always already material. In this sense, then, language and materiality are not opposed, for language both is and refers to that which is material, and what is material never fully escapes from the process by which it is signified (*Bodies* 68).

But this is implausible, to say the least. Butler would seem to have been led astray by the assumption that the word 'materiality' means the same thing in relation to language as in relation to the body or other material phenomena. Clearly, signifiers consist of acoustic waves or black marks on a page, and, clearly, nobody would deny that such traces or patterns are material. But Saussure never thought that language was a matter of signifiers alone. Merleau-Ponty tells a good story about this:

> Language takes on a meaning for the child when it *establishes a situation* for him. A story is told in a children's book of the disappointment of a small boy who put on his grand-mother's spectacles and took up her book in the expectation of being able himself to find in it the stories which she used to tell him. The tale ends with these words: 'Well, what a fraud! Where's the story? I can see nothing but black and white!' (*Phenomenology* 401).

In themselves, the black and white patterns on the page signify nothing. It is only by leaving out that which gives our sounds and signs meaning—that is to say, that which makes them *language*—that Butler can persuade herself that she has proved her point. If one really wants to know what makes the body similar to language, or what makes language similar to the body, the answer that both are material is not going to give much satisfaction.

The belief that since language or discourse are material, then any discourse-based theory must be materialist has a long tradition in feminist theory by now. One example that comes to my mind is Elizabeth Grosz's claim that Luce Irigaray's discursive strategies amount to 'a strikingly materialist position, at least insofar as language is regarded as material' (*Sexual Subversions* 241). This is taken to be a conclusive counterargument to my own observation that 'the material conditions of women's oppression are spectacularly absent from [Irigaray's] work' (*Sexual/Textual Politics* 147). The point I was making was that Irigaray spends no time at all discussing the specific ways in which patriarchy oppresses women. To her, both patriarchy and the feminine work in much the same ways in Freud's Vienna as in Plato's Athens. In Grosz's response, clearly, the argument about the materiality of the signifier is at work. But even if language and discourse were material in the sense Butler and Grosz suggest, they surely would not be material in quite the same way as educational institutions, women's wages, women's legal and political status, or women's access to contraception and abortion.[69] The belief that the words 'material' or 'materialist' alone, without further specification, can secure any political claims is destructive to serious discussion of feminist politics.

Butler's intense labours to show that sex is as discursively constructed as gender are symptomatic of the common post-structuralist belief that if something is not discursively constructed, then it must be natural. In keeping with the check-list of terms listed under 'sex' above, nature is taken to be immutable, unchanging, fixed, stable, and somehow 'essential-ist'.[70] It is also assumed that everything cultural is linguistic, discursive, constructed, and so on. When sex is claimed to be 'as constructed as gender', this is an attempt to help nature escape from the tyranny of fixed identities and stable essences. This is also taken to be a radical political claim. The hypothesis is that if something is constructed, then it will be cultural as opposed to natural, and therefore easy to change by political action. But this is a rash conclusion, since it seems far easier to transform a penin-sula into an island or turn a mountain into a molehill than to change our understanding of, say, what is to count as giving direc-tions to a stranger. Furthermore, natural processes are certainly not always calm and stable, but often violent and radically trans-formative. They may be destructive or productive, and—impor-tantly—they do not always resist human intervention.[71] As for the idea that sex is immutable and gender wholly changeable, we should at least note that transsexuals vehemently insist that it is their *gender* that is immutable, and not their sex.

Poststructuralist critics, then, tend to believe that if they can only show that the body or sex is part of discourse, then they have also shown that it is a fully historical phenomenon, situated in the

[69] Comparing Butler's account of materiality to that of Adorno, Carrie Hull concludes that 'Butler *cannot* address social and economic injustice without the addition of materialism to her paradigm' (32). Hull also shows that Butler does not distinguish between different kinds of materiality (see esp. 30).

[70] Kate Soper, *What Is Nature?* gives a good critique of such views. See esp. Ch. 4.

[71] The biologist Helen Lambert reminds us that some biological differences may in fact be changed, and that others can be compensated for by social measures (see esp. 141–5).

realm of power and politics. (This is the effect of taking all the elements in the 'good' 1990s picture of gender to be inter-changeable.) The belief is, in fact, that the first claim (the body is discursive) secures the others, for the usual poststructuralist assumption is that history, politics, power, and discourse are linked in some necessary and intrinsic way.[72] Let us grant, for the sake of the argument, that this may be true on a highly abstract, general level. Yet even so it does not follow that the claim that 'sex is as constructed as gender' thereby becomes meaningful in terms of the politics of everyday life. For we still do not know whether the body is political in the same way that Sinn Fein is political, or in the way that the stock market or Bill Clinton are political, or in some other way altogether. Nor is it clear that the mere invocation of 'history' always secures the desired connection with power and politics. One may, after all, write a fairly adequate history of gold-fish-keeping in America without getting into deep political waters.[73] The general claim that a phenomenon is perceived differently in different historical epochs is not in itself enough to tie that phenomenon to questions of power and resistance. What is missing in so much poststructuralist theory is some awareness of the *specific ways* in which the body may be political and histori-cal and discursive, and so on.

After so many attempts to prove that sex is as discursive as gender, that is to say to prove that 'the distinction between sex and gender turns out to be no distinction at all', as Butler puts it (*Gender Trouble* 7), it is disconcerting to discover that poststruc-turalists still insist that it is politically important, first, to distin-guish between male and masculine, female and feminine, and, second, to accept that these terms vary freely in relation to each

---

[72] Teresa Ebert claims that for Butler power enters into a list of inter-changeable terms: 'through a series of tropic slippages, *power is materiality is discourse is citationality is performativity*' (214).

[73] For the record, I am not claiming that goldfish-keeping could never be politically significant under any historical conditions. Ecological activists might, for all I know, make a very good case for its world-historical consequences. My point is rather that there is a kind of history that isn't always political, or is only ambiguously or innocuously political, or, perhaps, political in an insignificant and uninteresting way. If the goldfish example offends, one might substitute another.

other.[74] In *Gender Trouble* Butler considers male drag shows to be subversive of social gender norms. But, as she herself stresses, any politically or socially subversive effects of male drag shows depend on the contrast ('gender dissonance') between male bodies (sex) and feminine clothes and behaviour (gender). It appears that the original 1960s sex/gender distinction is, after all, quite essential to Butler's political case.[75]

The same tendency to return to the 1960s distinction between sex and gender for political effect is apparent in Butler's discussion of a case where a group of scientists decided to categorize an XX individual as male:

> The task of distinguishing sex from gender becomes all the more difficult once we understand that gendered meanings frame the hypothesis and the reasoning of those biomedical inquiries that seek to establish 'sex' for us as it is prior to the cultural meanings that it acquires. Indeed, the task is even more complicated when we realize that the language of biology participates in other kinds of languages and reproduces that cultural sedimentation in the objects it purports to discover and neutrally describe.
>
> Is it not a purely cultural convention to which [the scientists] refer when they decide that an anatomically ambiguous XX individual is male, a convention that takes genitalia to be the definitive 'sign' of sex? (*Gender Trouble* 109).[76]

---

[74] 'When the constructed status of gender is theorized as radically independent of sex, gender itself becomes a free-floating artifice, with the consequence that *man* and *masculine* might just as easily signify a female body as a male one, and *woman* and *feminine* a male body as easily as a female one' (Butler, *Gender Trouble* 6).

[75] The usual distinction between sex and gender is clearly marked and categorized as politically radical in Butler's account of drag: 'The performance of drag plays upon the distinction between the anatomy of the performer and the gender that is being performed. But we are actually in the presence of three contingent dimensions of significant corporeality: anatomical sex, gender identity, and gender performance ... the performance suggests a dissonance not only between sex and performance, but sex and gender, and gender and performance' (*Gender Trouble* 137).

[76] See also Butler's conclusion concerning this example: 'The desire to determine sex once and for all, and to determine it as one sex rather than the other, thus seems to issue from the social organization of sexual reproduction through the construction of the clear and unequivocal identities and positions of sexed bodies with respect to each other' (*Gender Trouble* 110).

On the one hand Butler's point is that these scientists produce their understanding of sex by reference to cultural conventions of gender; on the other, she seems to imply that there is something scandalous, oppressive, and heterosexist about this.[77] But what else would someone who believes that sex is the effect of gender, of 'regulatory discourses' expect? If sex is and must be an effect of social norms, the scientists simply could not behave any differently. But if, on the other hand, sex (nature) is to be strictly distinguished from gender (cultural norms), then they have indeed behaved objectionably, by imposing their own ideology on scientific research. There is no need to become a 'radical linguistic constructivist' to reach this conclusion: Simone de Beauvoir as well as Gayle Rubin would have been perfectly capable of producing a succinct critique of sexist scientific practices.[78] Insofar as poststructuralist work on sex and gender denounces the 1960s understanding of sex and gender while relying on the same distinction for political effects, it is deeply incoherent.

Gender, Performativity, Subjectivity

Perhaps the most famous claim in poststructuralist understanding of sex and gender is Judith Butler's contention that gender is performative (see *Gender Trouble* 25, 141). Sometimes this has been taken to mean that we are all constantly performing our gender, in a way that produces either sex or gender identity, or both. At other times critics speak of the 'performance of gender' and actually mean performances on stage or screen. Expressions such as

[77] Butler introduces the case by quoting feminist researchers who have attacked these scientists for displaying 'cultural prejudice [and] gendered assumptions about sex', adding—somewhat confusingly, but clearly critically—that 'the [scientists'] concentration on the "master gene" suggests that femaleness ought to be understood as the presence [*sic!*] or absence of maleness or, at best the presence of a passivity that, in man, would invariably be active' (*Gender Trouble* 108 and 109).

[78] In fact, feminists from Ruth Bleier (*Science and Gender*) to Evelyn Fox Keller (*Reflections on Gender and Science*) and Sandra Harding (*The Science Question in Feminism*), just to mention a few, have done fundamental work on sexism in science precisely by drawing on the usual sex/gender distinction. Harding and O'Barr (eds.), *Sex and Scientific Inquiry* remains a valuable starting point for further inquiry into feminist critiques of science.

'gender performativity' or just 'performativity' abound in contemporary literary criticism and theory, and innumerable confusing claims have been made about the relationship between 'performativity' and the work of J. L. Austin on the one hand and Jacques Derrida on the other.[79] I shall not venture into this theoretical wilderness. Nor will I spend any time wondering what 'gender' means in this context (social norms? personal identity? the compulsory internalization of norms?). Instead I shall work from the assumption that when a critic speaks of 'gender performativity' she intends to oppose 'gender essentialism'; that against the being of sex, she is asserting the doing of gender. To say that one performs one's gender is to say that gender is an act, and not a thing.[80] As Judith Butler acknowledges, this is an idea that has close affinities with Sartre and Beauvoir's thought. For the French existentialists, our acts do indeed define us, we are what we do.[81] There is a sense, then, in which 'gender performativity' is a 1990s way of speaking of how we fashion ourselves through our acts and choices. On this interpretation, the claim that we all perform our gender might mean, for example, that when a man behaves in ways that are socially acceptable for men, then he feels more convinced than ever that he is a 'real' man. It might also mean that if the man behaves in idiosyncratic ways, he helps to transform our previous understanding of how men behave. More generally, we might conclude that 'gender performativity' means that when most people behave according to certain gender norms, this ensures that the norms are maintained and reinforced. On this interpretation, Judith Butler inherits Simone de Beauvoir's understanding of how sexual difference is produced. The important difference is that Butler translates Beauvoir's anti-essentialism into the conceptual register of sex and gender. To

---

[79] See Sedgwick, 'Queer Performativity' 1. For an incisive critique of the poststructuralist reading of J. L. Austin, see Timothy Gould, 'The Unhappy Performative'. Poststructuralists usually draw on Derrida's reading of Austin in *Limited Inc.* For a philosophical critique of Derrida's reading of Austin, see Cavell, *A Pitch of Philosophy*, Ch. 2.

[80] See Sedgwick, 'Queer Performativity' 2.

[81] See Butler, *Gender Trouble* 112 for the recognition that for Beauvoir woman is a 'becoming'.

speak about gender as something we *do*, rather than as something we *are*, may not be an entirely new idea, but it is a good one, and I have no difficulty in understanding its appeal.[82]

Unfortunately, from my point of view, Judith Butler struggles to free herself from her existentialist heritage. She would resist my interpretation of performativity on the grounds that it presupposes a 'doer behind the deed', an agent who actually makes choices. Shifting her ground from Sartre to Foucault, Butler insists that 'Gender is performative insofar as it is the effect of a regulatory regime of gender differences in which genders are divided and hierarchized under constraint. ... There is no subject who precedes or enacts this repetition of norms.'[83] Whatever we make of this, it is clear that gender performativity is a term designed to ensure that we don't think of identity and subjectivity as something that precedes social norms. But why do we have to make a choice between a 'discursive' and 'prediscursive' subject? Beauvoir, for one, would resist the dichotomy proposed by Butler. Lived experience, she would say, is an open-ended, ongoing interaction between the subject and the world, where each term continuously constructs the other.

In spite of her attempts to free herself from identity politics, it appears that, for Butler, the question of gender remains intrinsically bound up with the question of identity. In fact, poststructuralists regularly denounce any belief in a 'coherent inner self' or in 'coherent categories called women and men' as theoretically unsound and politically reactionary.[84] According to some critics, if we think of the self as coherent, stable, or in any way unified, we will fall back into the bad picture of sex, and therefore somehow become unable to resist racism and capitalism. Politically speaking,

---

[82] In the USA, West and Zimmerman's essay 'Doing Gender' made a similar point in 1987.

[83] 'Critically Queer' 21. Butler continues in this way: 'performativity is a matter of reiterating or repeating the norms by which one is constituted: it is not a radical fabrication of the gendered self. It is a compulsory production of prior and subjectivating norms, ones which cannot be thrown off at will, but which work, animate, and constrain the gendered subject, and which are also the resources from which resistance, subversion, displacement are to be forged' ('Critically Queer' 21–2). This essay was reprinted in *Bodies That Matter* 223–42.

[84] The quotations come from Haraway, 'Gender' 135, 147.

these are puzzling claims, since the whole liberal tradition and indeed the Marxist humanist tradition, with their antediluvian views on individual agency, freedom, and choice, were quite capable of fighting racism, sexism, and capitalism before post-structuralism came along.

On the theoretical level it is necessary to ask whether different pictures of subjectivity and identity actually have any necessary relationship with different theories of sex and gender. The answer seems to be yes in only one case, that of the pervasive picture of sex. Brooks and Geddes and Thomson imagine that a woman is saturated through and through by her womanness. In this picture a woman is reduced to nothing but sexual difference ('a giant ovum', Beauvoir writes). There seems to be no opportunity here for thinking that a woman's social class, race, nationality, or age might profoundly affect her way of being a woman. The poststructuralist critics are right, therefore, to assume that biological determinism is intrinsically bound up with a stable, unitary, coherent, fixed, immobile (and so on) picture of subjectivity. What they overlook is that no particular understanding of subjectivity or identity follows from the fact of *denying* that biological facts justify social norms. Beauvoir and Carol Gilligan both reject biological determinism, but they have very different views of subjectivity and consciousness. To Beauvoir consciousness is not a unified, coherent, and stable entity; yet Gilligan, who carefully distinguishes between sex and gender in the 1960s way, seems to imagine the female subject in much the same terms as traditional liberal humanists do.[85]

Liberation, Subversion—Same Thing?

Poststructuralists usually consider emancipation and liberation unfortunate Enlightenment terms, and believe that Foucault's denunciation of the 'repressive hypothesis' about sex shows that we can never speak of oppression and liberation without revealing that we actually believe in a true human nature shackled and bound by social norms. For them, anyone speaking of women's liberation must believe that it consists in letting our true, essential sexual

[85] For the existentialist understanding of consciousness, see Howells. See also Gilligan.

nature shine forth unfettered by social norms. Yet feminists rang-
ing from Simone de Beauvoir to Juliet Mitchell have believed that
oppression is a concrete historical situation that it is in our interest
to change. Once the unfair, unjust, and exploitative conditions in
question have been eliminated, it is quite justified to speak of liberation: no metaphysics about true nature needs to be implied.

Poststructuralist theorists of sex and gender, however, prefer to
think in terms of *subversion* of dominant social norms. Since we
cannot escape power, we can only undermine it from within. For
this reason they have often invoked the male drag artist as a
particularly subversive figure. By parodying dominant gender
norms, he shows them up as conventional and artificial, and thus
enables us to maintain a critical or ironic distance to them. Unlike
Gayle Rubin, poststructuralists do not explicitly dream of a society without gender; rather, they seem to hope that greater freedom or justice or happiness will arise when we are able freely to
mix and match socially normative concepts of masculinity and
femininity as we like. Perhaps the idea is that this will eventually
so weaken the impact of the dominant social norms that gender
might ultimately wither away after all. Politically, the hopes and
aspirations of Simone de Beauvoir, Gayle Rubin, and the poststructuralist theorists of sex and gender do not seem to be all that
different. It would seem that we all wish for a society unmarred by
repressive norms legislating politically correct sexuality and
gender behaviour for women and men. Poststructuralists have yet
to show how their politics (as opposed to their theory) differ from
that of their feminist predecessors.

Imprisoned in their own theoretical framework, poststructuralist theorists of sex and gender have largely forgotten that the
distinction was supposed to carry out a specific task, namely that
of opposing biological determinism (which includes the essentialism and heterosexism produced by the pervasive picture of
sex). On my analysis, poststructuralists have yet to show what
questions concerning materiality, reference, essence, realism,
nominalism, and the inside and outside of discourse have to do
with bodies, sex, or gender, or with biology and social norms. In
short, I find poststructuralist work on sex and gender to be
obscure, theoreticist, plagued by internal contradictions, mired

in unnecessary philosophical and theoretical elaborations, and dependent on the 1960s sex/gender distinction for political effect.[86] As for the positive objectives that the poststructuralists wish to achieve, Simone de Beauvoir achieved them first, and with considerably greater philosophical elegance, clarity, and wit.

IV. 'THE BODY IS A SITUATION': SIMONE DE BEAUVOIR

The body is not a thing, it is a *situation*: it is our grasp on the world and a sketch of our projects.

Simone de Beauvoir, 1949

The Body as an Object and the Body as a Situation

'The body is a situation', Simone de Beauvoir writes in *The Second Sex*. I now want to show that this is not only a completely original contribution to feminist theory, but a powerful and sophisticated alternative to contemporary sex and gender theories. Let me stress that Beauvoir's claim is that the body *is* a situation. Some critics have taken this to mean that 'the physical capacities of either sex gain meaning only when placed in a cultural and historical context'.[87] But this is to miss the point, to reduce Beauvoir's claim that the body *is* a situation back to the more familiar idea that the body is always *in* a situation. For Beauvoir these are different claims, equally important and equally true, but not reducible to one another.[88] For Beauvoir, the body

---

[86] 'Theoreticism' refers to the belief that theoretical correctness somehow guarantees political correctness.

[87] I am quoting Julie Ward. Her sentence continues as follows: 'this, I argue, is what Beauvoir means by saying that the body is to be seen as a *situation*' (225).

[88] My assumption is that I do not need to explain the claim that the body is *in* a situation all that thoroughly, since most feminists are familiar with this kind of argument. What requires investigation, is the claim that the body *is* a situation. In this section I shall therefore emphasize the phenomenological philosophy that underpins Beauvoir's claim. As I will try to make clear in the text, it should nevertheless be understood throughout that, for Beauvoir as for Merleau-Ponty, the phenomenological experience of the body is always historically situated, always engaged in interaction with ideologies and other social practices. In *Sex and Existence* Lundgren-Gothlin makes the case for Beauvoir's historical understanding of 'situation' with great clarity.

perceived as a situation is deeply related to the individual woman's (or man's) subjectivity.[89]

In the first chapter of *The Second Sex* Simone de Beauvoir asks what a woman is. In the next chapter she turns her attention to attempts to answer by pointing to women's biological and anatomical differences from men. This chapter has been severely criticized by contemporary feminists: 'in turning (apparently at Sartre's suggestion) to an examination of the biological differences between the sexes, [Beauvoir] adopts something of an essentialist view of biology', one critic writes (Evans 61–2). Nothing could be further from the truth. There is no evidence that Sartre directed Beauvoir to write about biology. Moreover, it is in the chapter on biology that she first claims that the sexed body is a situation. In fact, this is a claim specifically designed to *refute* the kind of biological determinism espoused by scientists such as Brooks and Geddes and Thomson. This is how the chapter begins:

> Woman? [*La femme?*] Very simple, say the fanciers of simple formulas: she is a womb, an ovary; she is a female [*femelle*]—this word is sufficient to define her. In the mouth of a man the epithet *female* [*femelle*] has the sound of an insult, yet he is not ashamed of his animal nature; on the contrary, he is proud if someone says of him: 'He is a male!' The term 'female' [*femelle*] is derogatory not because it grounds [*enracine*] woman in nature, but because it imprisons her in her sex; and if this sex seems to man to be contemptible and inimical even in harmless animals, it is because of the uneasy hostility stirred up in him by woman. Nevertheless he wishes to find in biology a justification for this sentiment. The word *female* [*femelle*] brings up in his mind a saraband of imagery— a vast, round ovum engulfs and castrates the agile spermatozoon; the monstrous and swollen termite queen rules over the enslaved males; the female praying mantis and the spider, satiated with love, crush and devour their partners . . . (*SS* 3; *DSa* 35; TA).

This passage may seem puzzling to some readers. Why does Beauvoir leap to the conclusion that to be called a female must be an insult? Why does the word female conjure up in her mind

---

[89] I want to signal here that in *The Second Sex* Beauvoir also defines the body as *background*. See Ch. 2, below for a discussion of this understanding of the body.

pictures of insatiable and monstrous termites and spiders? In English, this does sound somewhat exaggerated; in French, the passage depends for its effect on the distinction between *femme* and *femelle*, a distinction that is not fully conveyed by the words *woman* and *female*. Although both the English *female* and the French *femelle* designate 'the sex which can bear offspring, or produce eggs', *female* refers to 'women, girls, and animals', as opposed to *femelle*, which refers exclusively to animals: its meaning is 'she-animal', not 'human female'. Precisely because of its association with she-animals, *femelle* is regularly used as a pejorative term for woman. In French, Beauvoir's point is clear: by refusing to reduce the woman (*femme*) to the she-animal (*femelle*), she takes a strong stance against the misogynist ideology which can only picture a woman as a monstrous ovum. Her imagery is a send-up of the pervasive picture of sex.

Beauvoir in fact discusses many of the theses put forward by Brooks and Geddes and Thomson, usually without quoting any particular source for them. Janet Sayers writes that Geddes and Thomson's book was quickly translated into French, and that their arguments turn up in A. J. E. Fouillée's *Tempérament et caractère selon les individus, les sexes et les races* from 1895 (see Sayers 41). Beauvoir comments directly on Fouillée's theses:

> In his book *Le tempérament et le caractère*, Alfred Fouillée undertakes to found his definition of woman *in toto* upon the ovum and that of man upon the spermatozoon; and a number of supposedly profound theories rest upon this play of doubtful analogies. It is a question to what philosophy of nature these dubious ideas pertain; not to the laws of heredity, certainly, for, according to these laws, men and women alike develop from an ovum and a sperm. I can only suppose that in such misty minds there still float shreds of the old philosophy of the Middle Ages which taught that the cosmos is an exact reflection of a microcosm—the ovum is imagined to be a female homunculus, the woman a giant ovum . . . (*SS* 14; *DSa* 47–8; TA).

After refuting the claims put forward by biological determinists, Beauvoir describes the facts of female sexual and reproductive development.[90] Overall, she concludes that women's role in the

---

[90] She tends to interpret them from a Hegelian perspective. For two serious, but divergent, accounts of Beauvoir's understanding of Hegel, see Lundgren-Gothlin, *Sex and Existence*, esp. 53–82, and Bauer, esp. Chs. 3–6.

reproduction of the species is more onerous, more time-consuming, and more dangerous than men's. A man can father a hundred children without any physical damage to himself, a woman cannot even have ten children without running considerable risks of lasting physical impairment and even death. For Beauvoir, such biological facts are 'extremely important. In the history of woman they play a part of the first rank and constitute an essential element in her situation' (*SS* 32; *DSa* 71). Her conclusions are nevertheless strikingly different from those of Brooks and Geddes and Thomson:

> But I deny that [the biological facts] establish for her a fixed and inevitable destiny. They are insufficient for setting up a hierarchy of the sexes; they fail to explain why woman is the Other; they do not condemn her to remain in this subordinate role for ever (*SS* 32–3; *DSa* 71).

How can Beauvoir maintain both that biology is extremely important to women's situation and that it is not destiny? To answer this question, we need to consider Beauvoir's existentialist understanding of what a human being is:

> But man is defined as a being who is not given, who makes himself what he is. As Merleau-Ponty very justly puts it, man is not a natural species; he is a historical idea. Woman is not a fixed reality, but rather a becoming, and it is in her becoming that she should be compared with man; that is to say her *possibilities* should be defined. . . . [A]s viewed in the perspective that I am adopting— that of Heidegger, Sartre, and Merleau-Ponty— . . . the body is not a thing, it is a *situation*: it is our grasp on the world and a sketch [*esquisse*] of our projects (*SS* 34; *DSa* 73; TA)[91]

To say that 'woman is not a fixed reality' is to say that as human beings (and unlike animals) women are always in the process of

---

[91] The published English translation of the last sentence is particularly egregious: '[Le corps] est notre prise sur le monde et l'esquisse de nos projets', Beauvoir writes. '[The body] is the instrument of our grasp upon the world, a limiting factor for our projects', Parshley translates, thereby introducing (1) the wholly erroneous idea of the body as an *instrument* for a grasp, rather than as the 'grasp [*prise*]' itself; and (2) the idea of the body as a *limitation*, as something that necessarily hampers our projects. Both thoughts correspond to the traditional picture of a consciousness inhabiting the body, but this, precisely, is the picture Beauvoir wants to resist.

making themselves what they are. We give meaning to our lives by our actions. Only death puts an end to the creation of meaning. As the famous existentialist slogan has it: 'Existence precedes essence'. For Beauvoir and Merleau-Ponty, human transcendence—human freedom—is always incarnated, that is to say that it always presents itself in the shape of a human body. My body is a situation, but it is a fundamental kind of situation, in that it founds my experience of myself and the world. This is a situation that always enters my lived experience. This is why the body can never be just brute matter to me. Only the dead body is a thing, but when I am dead I am lost to the world, and the world is lost to me: 'The body is our general medium for having a world', Merleau-Ponty writes (*Phenomenology* 146).

I just used the term *lived experience*. This is a central existentialist concept. The situation is not coextensive with lived experience, nor reducible to it. In many ways 'lived experience' designates the whole of a person's subjectivity. More particularly the term describes the way an individual makes sense of her situation and actions. Because the concept also comprises my freedom, my lived experience is not wholly determined by the various situations I may be a part of. Rather lived experience is, as it were, sedimented over time through my interactions with the world, and thus itself becomes part of my situatedness.

Beauvoir and Merleau-Ponty do not deny that there is anything object-like about my body.[92] It is quite possible to study it scientifically, to measure it, to predict how it will react to antibiotics, and so on. Both Beauvoir and Merleau-Ponty are happy to accept scientific data in their analyses of the body. Yet, for them, scientific methodology cannot yield a valid philosophy of human existence.

---

[92] Sara Heinämaa's useful account of Beauvoir's view of the body stresses that Simone de Beauvoir's phenomenological understanding of the body falls outside the parameters of the sex/gender distinction, since it doesn't consider the body as an object (see 'Woman—Nature, Product, Style'). Following Sonia Kruks's lead, Heinämaa also reminds us of Merleau-Ponty's importance for Beauvoir, who actually reviewed the *Phenomenology of Perception* in the second issue of *Les temps modernes* in Nov. 1945. See Kruks, 'Simone de Beauvoir: Between Sartre and Merleau-Ponty'; Kruks, 'Simone de Beauvoir: Teaching Sartre about Freedom'; and Heinämaa, 'What Is a Woman?', as well as 'Woman—Nature, Product, Style'.

In *Phenomenology of Perception,* Merleau-Ponty denounces what he
calls the 'objective' way of looking at the world, exemplified by
science on the one hand and common sense on the other. In
turning the world into an object, the 'objective' perspective
represses the fact that human consciousness is part of every
human experience:

> Obsessed with being, and forgetful of the perspectivism of my
> experience, I henceforth treat it as an object and deduce it from a
> relationship between objects. I regard my body, which is my point
> of view upon the world, as one of the objects of that world. My
> recent awareness of my gaze as a means of knowledge I now
> repress, and treat my eyes as bits of matter. . . . I now refer to my
> body only as an idea. . . . Thus 'objective' thought . . . is formed—
> being that of common sense and of science—which finally causes
> us to lose contact with perceptual experience, of which it is never-
> theless the outcome and the natural sequel (70–1).

By placing 'objective' in inverted commas, Merleau-Ponty indicates that *he* doesn't believe that the scientific (or the common-
sensical) point of view is 'objective' in the positivist sense of
bearing no trace of the human consciousness that produced it.
On the contrary, even scientific research presupposes human
experience:

> I am not the outcome or the meeting-point of numerous causal
> agencies which determine my bodily or psychological make-up. I
> cannot conceive myself as nothing but a bit of the world, a mere
> object of biological, psychological or sociological investigation. I
> cannot shut myself up within the realm of science. All my know-
> ledge of the world, even my scientific knowledge, is gained from
> my own particular point of view, or from some experience of the
> world without which the symbols of science would be meaningless.
> . . . Scientific points of view, according to which my existence is a
> moment of the world's, are always both naive and at the same time
> dishonest, because they take for granted, without explicitly
> mentioning it, the other point of view, namely that of conscious-
> ness, through which from the outset a world forms itself round me
> and begins to exist for me (viii–ix).

To say that science presupposes a human perspective is not to
reject its insights about the human body, but rather to reject

scientism, positivism, empiricism, and other would-be 'objectivist' world-views. This is why Merleau-Ponty feels free to draw copiously on psychological and biological research concerning perception and brain functioning.

The body, then, does not carry its meaning on its surface. It is not a thing, but a situation. In *Being and Nothingness* Sartre claims that all human beings are always situated—*en situation*, as he puts it. The concept of the *situation* deserves a more thorough discussion than I can give it here. Sartre devotes over a hundred pages to it in *Being and Nothingness*. Merleau-Ponty understands it, after Sartre, as an irreducible category between subjectivity and objectivity. For Sartre, Beauvoir, and Merleau-Ponty, the concept of the situation is crucial, since they need it in order to avoid dividing lived experience up in the traditional subject/object opposition.[93] For Sartre my class, my place, my race, my nationality, my body, my past, my position, and my relationship to others are so many different situations.[94] To claim that the body *is* a situation is not the same thing as to say that it is placed *within* some other situation. The body both is a situation *and* is placed within other situations. For Sartre, a situation is a structural relationship between our projects (our freedom) and the world (which includes our bodies). If I want to climb a crag, my situation is my project as it exists in the encounter with the brute facticity of the crag. In this view, the crag alone is not a situation. My situation is not *outside* me, it does not relate to me as an object to a subject; it is a synthesis of facticity and freedom. If your project is to climb, and my project is to enjoy the mountain views, then the very same crag would present itself to you as being easy or difficult to scale, and to me as 'imposing' or 'unremarkable'. Faced with the same crag, our situations would be different because our projects are different. We are always in a situation, but the situation is always part of us.

To claim that the body is a situation is to acknowledge that the meaning of a woman's body is bound up with the way she uses her freedom. For Beauvoir, our freedom is not absolute,

93 For an illuminating discussion of the successes and failures of the concept in the works of these writers, see Kruks, *Situation*.

94 See *Being and Nothingness* 619–707; *L'être et le néant* 538–612.

but situated. Other situations as well as our particular lived experience will influence our projects, which in turn will shape our experience of the body. In this way, each woman's experience of her body is bound up with her projects in the world. There are innumerable different ways of living with one's specific bodily potential as a woman. I may devote myself to mountain climbing, become a ballet dancer, a model, a nurse, or a nun. I may have lots of sexual relations or none at all, have five children or none, or I may discover that such choices are not mine to make.

Many critics of Beauvoir would disagree with my analysis. In their view, Beauvoir sees the female reproductive body as inherently oppressive. In an interesting essay on Beauvoir and Hegel, Catriona Mackenzie considers that Beauvoir's understanding of the body forces us to accept the conclusion that 'the reproductive body must be denied' (156). I do not want to contest the idea that Beauvoir herself was highly ambivalent about mothers, motherhood, and pregnancy. In my view, almost all her texts, including *The Second Sex*, are haunted by a destructive mother imago.[95] Yet whenever Beauvoir's unconscious horror of the mother surfaces, far from spelling out the inner logic of her argument it places her understanding of the body as a situation in contradiction with itself. For the logic of her argument is that greater freedom will produce new ways of being a woman, new ways of experiencing the possibilities of a woman's body, not that women will for ever be slaves to the inherently oppressive experience of childbearing. At the end of *The Second Sex* Beauvoir writes: 'Once again, in order to explain her limitations it is woman's situation that must be invoked and not a mysterious essence; thus the future remains largely open. . . . The free woman is just being born' (*SS* 714–15; *DSb* 640–1). In a non-sexist future, women's freedom will lead to changes we cannot even imagine: 'New relations of flesh and sentiment of which we have no conception will arise between the sexes' (*SS* 730; *DSb* 661). Beauvoir's belief in social and individual

---

[95] I discuss the negative mother imago in Beauvoir's texts at length in my *Simone de Beauvoir* (see esp. Chs. 4, 6, and 8).

transformation is the logical outcome of the double claim that the body *is* a situation and that it always is *in* a situation, not of the belief that women will always be oppressed by their reproductive capacities.[96]

Some critics gloss Beauvoir's claim that the body is a situation by saying that for her, 'the body is a social construction'.[97] Without a clearer understanding of what 'social construction' means I can't say whether this is a helpful formulation. If 'social construction' is no more than convenient shorthand for 'non-essentialist', then Beauvoir's understanding of the body as a situation counts as 'constructionist'. Insofar as Beauvoir's understanding of situation includes the freedom of the subject, it clashes with the extreme determinism of some contemporary ideas of how 'social construction' works. When it comes to the body, 'social construction' is a nebulous concept which there is no reason to prefer to Beauvoir's precisely defined and highly productive concept of situation.

When Beauvoir writes that the body is not a thing, but a situation, she means that the body-in-the-world that we are, is an embodied intentional relationship to the world.[98] Understood as a situation in its own right, the body places us in the middle of many other situations. Our subjectivity is always embodied, but our bodies do not only bear the mark of sex. In *Black Skin, White Masks* (1952) Frantz Fanon analyses race as a bodily situation, drawing on exactly the same concepts as Beauvoir, and in

[96] In her well-known essay 'French Feminism Revisited' Gayatri Spivak rightly stresses that 'Beauvoir sees the Mother as a situation' (*Outside* 149). In fact, most of the chapters of the second volume of *The Second Sex* are devoted to a different situation. Thus the chapter entitled 'The Mother' describes different women's reactions to the situation of motherhood, the chapter entitled 'The Married Woman' discusses different ways of living the experience of marriage, and so on.

[97] I am quoting Julie Ward's valuable essay on 'Beauvoir's Two Senses of Body' (231).

[98] In her valuable essay 'Throwing Like a Girl', Iris Marion Young combines Merleau-Ponty and Beauvoir's analysis of the body to explore a certain 'feminine' style of orienting the body in space. Echoing Beauvoir, Young stresses that a woman under patriarchy often ends up living her body *as* a thing (see esp. 150).

Phenomenology of Perception Merleau-Ponty discusses class as a historical and bodily situation (see 442–50).[99]

'The body is to be compared, not to a physical object, but rather to a work of art', Merleau-Ponty writes (*Phenomenology* 150). Perceived as part of lived experience, the body is a style of being, an intonation, a specific way of being present in the world, but it does not for that reason cease to be an object with its own specific physical properties. Considered as a situation, the body encompasses both the objective and the subjective aspects of experience. To Merleau-Ponty and Beauvoir, the body is our perspective on the world, and at the same time that body is engaged in a dialectical interaction with its surroundings, that is to say with all the other situations in which the body is placed. The way we experience—live—our bodies is shaped by this interaction. The body is a historical sedimentation of our way of living in the world, and of the world's way of living with us.[100]

The body matters to Simone de Beauvoir. If I have to negotiate the world in a crippled body or sick body I am not going to have the same experience of the world or of myself as if I had a healthy or particularly athletic body. Nor will the world react to me in the way it would if I had a different body.[101] To deny this is to be guilty

[99] The achievement of Simone de Beauvoir consists in having shown that bodily sexual difference makes the body a potentially different situation for men and women. (I write 'potentially different' because Beauvoir does not believe that sexual differences always and everywhere matter more than other situations: she does not have a pervasive picture of sex.) Unfortunately neither Fanon (who writes after her) nor Merleau-Ponty (who writes before her) manage to discuss sexual difference as a situation that interacts with that of race and class. For a brief comparison of Fanon and Beauvoir, see my *Simone de Beauvoir*, Ch. 7.

[100] As we have seen, Beauvoir's understanding of the body is explicitly and obviously phenomenological. I am therefore struck by the fact that Elizabeth Grosz, who in *Volatile Bodies* devotes a whole chapter to Merleau-Ponty, in the subsection entitled 'Feminist Phenomenology?' makes no reference at all to Simone de Beauvoir (103–7).

[101] The medievalist Caroline Bynum complains that feminists nowadays reduce the body to sexual difference: 'an extraordinarily large amount of [the] recent discussion of the body is in fact a discussion of sex and gender'. One recent book on theology and the body, she notes, 'devotes only about seventeen pages to what was surely, in earlier times, theology's major preoccupation with bodies: suffering and death' (5). As my examples show, Beauvoir's understanding of the body would not lead to this problem.

of idealist subjectivism. To assume that the meaning of a sick or a healthy body is written on its surface, that it is and will be the same for all human beings, is to fall prey to empiricism or what Merleau-Ponty calls 'objectivism'.[102] As Fanon has shown, the same logic applies to the difference between a black body and a white body.

Although our biology is fundamental to the way we live in the world, biological facts alone give us no grounds for concluding anything at all about the *meaning* and *value* they will have for the individual and for society. At the same time, however, biological facts cannot be placed outside the realm of meaning. For Beauvoir and Merleau-Ponty, the human body is fundamentally *ambiguous*: it is subject at once to natural laws and to the human production of meaning, and it can never be reduced to either one of these elements. Because the body is neither pure nature nor pure meaning, neither empiricism nor idealism will ever be able to grasp the specific nature of human existence. When Merleau-Ponty claims that 'Man is a historical idea' he is not trying to disavow nature, but rather to expand our understanding of what nature is. Instead of accepting the scientistic and empiricist concept of nature, he wants to stress that nature also belongs to the order of meaning. 'Man is a historical idea' means that our nature is to be historical. As Merleau-Ponty goes on to say:

> Everything is both manufactured and natural in man, as it were, in the sense that there is not a word, not a form of behaviour which does not owe something to purely biological being—and which at the same time does not elude the simplicity of animal life, and cause forms of vital behaviour to deviate from their pre-ordained direction, through a sort of *leakage* and through a genius for ambiguity which might serve to define man (189).

Following Merleau-Ponty and Sartre, Beauvoir repeatedly stresses that biological facts cannot ground human values:

[102] Merleau-Ponty's discussion of 'objective' thought occurs in the context of his effort to put shortcomings of subjectivism as well as of objectivism behind him: 'We cannot remain in this dilemma of having to fail to understand either the subject or the object. We must discover the origin of the object at the very center of our experience; we must describe the emergence of being and we must understand how, paradoxically, there is *for us* an *in-itself* (*Phenomenology* 71).

But in truth a society is not a species; for it is in society that the species realises itself as existence—transcending itself toward the world and toward the future. Its ways and customs cannot be deduced from biology, for individuals are never abandoned to their nature; rather they obey that second nature which is custom, in which the desires and fears that express their ontological attitude are reflected.[103] It is not merely as a body, but rather as a body subject to taboos, to laws, that the subject becomes conscious of himself and attains fulfillment [*s'accomplit*]—it is with reference to certain values that he valorizes himself. To repeat once more: physiology cannot ground any values; rather, the facts of biology take on the values that the existent bestows upon them (*SS* 36; *DSa* 76; TA).

Beauvoir makes a number of claims amounting to a flat rejection of the theses of the biological determinists:

(1) sex is not pervasive: a woman is not a giant ovum;
(2) biology (science) cannot justify social norms;
(3) social norms are not the expression of biological facts;
(4) social hierarchy (subjection, oppression) can never be explained or justified by biology.

Beauvoir's rejection of biological determinism resembles Gayle Rubin's distinction between gender as social norms and sex as the concrete human body. Beauvoir's understanding of individual subjectivity, on the other hand, is vastly different from sex and gender theories. First of all, it never occurs to her that an individual human being can be divided into a natural and a cultural part, in the way suggested by the sex/gender distinction. Merleau-Ponty actually spells this point out with particular clarity when he writes that 'It is impossible to superimpose on man a lower layer of behaviour which one chooses to call "natural", followed by a manufactured cultural or spiritual world' (189). That Beauvoir shares this point of view becomes clear in the very last lines of her chapter on biology:

Thus we shall have to view the facts of biology in the light of an ontological, economic, social and psychological context. The

---

[103] In French: *leur attitude ontologique*. The English text, unfortunately, translates this as 'their essential nature', thus giving rise to many misunderstandings.

enslavement of the female to the species and the limitations of her various powers are extremely important facts; the body of woman is one of the essential elements in her situation in the world. But that body is not enough to define her; it does not gain lived reality [*réalité vécue*] unless it is taken on [*assumé*] by consciousness through activities and in the bosom of a society. Biology is not enough to give an answer to the question that is before us: why is woman the *Other?* We need to find out how nature has been taken up [*reprise*] in her throughout the course of history; we need to find out what humanity has made of the human female [*la femelle humaine*] (*SS* 37; *DSa* 77; TA).[104]

In this passage Beauvoir makes the following claims: (1) biological facts only take on meaning when they are situated within economic, social, and psychological contexts; (2) biological facts are nevertheless important elements in women's situation; (3) biological facts alone cannot define a woman; (4) the body alone does not define a woman, on the contrary, she needs to make it her own, turn it into 'lived reality',[105] a process that is always accomplished in interaction with the woman's socially situated, conscious choices and activities; and (5) biology cannot explain the social subordination of women.

When Beauvoir writes, 'But that body is not enough to define her,' she means to reject the biological determinist theories of

[104] This passage sounds very different in Parshley's translation. Failing to grasp Beauvoir's syntax and philosophical vocabulary, he translates 'Mais ce n'est pas non plus lui [le corps] qui suffit à la définir, il n'a de réalité vécue qu'en tant qu'assumé par la conscience à travers des actions et au sein d'une société' as 'But that body is not enough to define her as a woman; there is no true living reality except as manifested by the conscious individual through activities and in the bosom of society'. It is clear that Parshley reads Beauvoir's 'il [ce corps] n'a de réalité' as 'il n'y a de réalité', and doesn't understand the idea that consciousness must 'shoulder' or 'take on' the body for it to become part of lived experience. The last sentence in French contains the phrase 'savoir comment en elle la nature a été reprise au cours de l'histoire'. This gets translated as 'discover how the nature of woman has been affected throughout the course of history'. No wonder so many Anglophone readers of *The Second Sex* have felt that Beauvoir's understanding of the body is incoherent, or worse.

[105] Let me note that although Beauvoir here uses the expression *réalité vécue*, elsewhere she writes about *expérience vécue*: the body gains lived reality when it becomes (part of) lived experience.

sexual difference she has spent most of the chapter discussing. The formulation 'not enough' signals that she also means to reject purely idealist constructions of what a woman is. The female body is a necessary part of the definition of 'woman', but to take it to be sufficient to define the meaning of the word is to fall back into 'objectivism'. The difference between the body considered as a situation and the body considered as an object is not homologous with that between sex and gender. We are, rather, dealing with two different *perspectives* on the body: the empiricist or scientistic perspective on the one hand, and the phenomenological on the other. The implication is that we have to choose between them. The one cannot somehow be added on to the other without forcing us into an unsatisfactory see-saw movement between empiricism and idealism, or between objectivism and subjectivism. As Merleau-Ponty reminds us, it makes no sense to think of human beings as consisting of two superimposed layers, one which we choose to call 'natural' and another that we consider 'cultural' or 'spiritual'. For Beauvoir and Merleau-Ponty, then, the body perceived as an object is *not* the ground on which the body as a situation is constructed; a woman is *not* the sum of the 'objective' and the situational perspective on the body. For Beauvoir, a woman defines herself through the way she lives her embodied situation in the world, or in other words, through the way in which she makes something of what the world makes of her. The process of making and being made is open-ended: it only ends with death. In the analysis of lived experience, the sex/gender distinction simply *does not apply*.[106] I shall now go on to show that the opposition between 'essentialism' and 'constructionism' that has plagued contemporary feminist theory in the 1980s and 1990s does not apply either.

One Is Not Born a Woman: Biology and Lived Experience

'One is not born, but rather becomes, a woman', Beauvoir writes. Many contemporary feminists have assumed that this means that Beauvoir is opposing sex to gender, or biological essence to social

---

[106] On this point, I agree completely with Sara Heinämaa (see 'Woman— Nature, Product, Style').

construction. This is not the case. Anyone who tries to read *The Second Sex* through the lens of the sex/gender distinction is bound to misunderstand Beauvoir. Judith Butler's 1986 commentary on Beauvoir's famous sentence is a good example of such a misreading:

> 'One is not born, but rather becomes, a woman'—Simone de Beauvoir's formulation distinguishes sex from gender and suggests that gender is an aspect of identity gradually acquired. The distinction between sex and gender has been crucial to the long-standing feminist effort to debunk the claim that anatomy is destiny; *sex* is understood to be the invariant, anatomically distinct, and factic aspects of the female body, whereas *gender* is the cultural meaning and form that that body acquires, the variable modes of that body's acculturation. . . . Moreover, if the distinction is consistently applied, it becomes unclear whether being a given sex has any necessary consequence for becoming a given gender. The presumption of a causal or mimetic relation between sex and gender is undermined. . . . At its limit, then, the sex/gender distinction implies a radical heteronomy of natural bodies and constructed genders with the consequence that 'being' female and 'being' a woman are two very different sorts of being. This last insight, I would suggest, is the distinguished contribution of Simone de Beauvoir's formulation, 'one is not born, but rather becomes, a woman' ('Sex and Gender' 35).

In this passage, Butler shows herself to be an extremely acute reader of Beauvoir's phenomenological feminism, but her close affinities with Beauvoir are, as it were, derailed by Butler's fundamental commitment to the sex/gender distinction. Beauvoir's view would presumably be that the category of 'sex' is scientistic, and therefore useless as an explanation of what a woman is. From a Beauvoirean perspective, then, the trouble with the sex/gender distinction is that it upholds the 'objective' or 'scientific' view of the body as the ground on which gender is developed. To consider the body as a situation, on the other hand, is to refuse to break it down into an 'objective' and a 'subjective' component; we don't first consider it scientifically, and then add cultural experience. For Butler in 1986, sex or the body is an object, for Beauvoir 'sex' could only be seen as the philosophically misguided act of perceiving the body as an object.[107]

Rejecting biological determinism (anatomy is destiny), Butler denies that the objectively described ('factic') body gives rise to values. On this point, she follows Beauvoir. When Butler conceives of gender as a category that does *not include* the body, however, she loses touch with Beauvoir's category of 'lived experience'.[108] As a result, she is left with only one way of conceptualizing the body, namely as sex. In order to avoid biological determinism, Butler is then forced to claim that a woman is gender, and that the category of gender varies freely in relation to a narrowly scientistic understanding of sex. In Butler's picture of sex and gender, sex becomes the inaccessible ground of gender, gender becomes completely disembodied, and the body itself is divorced from all meaning.

For Beauvoir, on the other hand, the body is a situation, and as such, a crucial part of lived experience. Just as the world constantly makes me, I constantly make myself the woman I am. As we have seen, a situation is not an 'external' structure that imposes itself on the individual subject, but rather an irreducible amalgam of the freedom (projects) of that subject and the conditions in which that freedom finds itself. The body as a situation is the concrete body experienced as meaningful, and socially and historically situated. It is *this* concept of the body that disappears entirely from Butler's account of sex and gender.

---

[107] As Mary McIntosh has pointed out, Butler's use of the word 'gender' in relation to a number of French thinkers (including, I should add, Beauvoir and Wittig) is not very helpful: 'I find Butler's use of the sex/gender distinction confusing. This distinction . . . does not sit well with any of the French work that Butler engages with. Those writers in the French tradition who have problematized the category of "woman" have not used the term gender. What they have done is to question whether the biological category "woman" has any stable social significance, not to question the biological category as such' (McIntosh 114).

[108] Heinämaa's 'What Is a Woman?' convincingly demonstrates that Judith Butler misreads Beauvoir by reading her through the lens of the traditional understanding of sex and gender. Her 'Woman—Nature, Product, Style' argues that Beauvoir's phenomenological understanding of the body cannot be reduced to the common feminist sex/gender distinction. If she means that the sex/gender distinction is not at work *inside* Beauvoir's concepts of 'lived experience' or 'body as situation', I agree with her.

Butler returns to Beauvoir's famous sentence in *Gender Trouble* (1990). She writes that 'it follows that *woman* itself is a term in process, a becoming, a constructing that cannot rightfully be said to originate or to end' (*Gender Trouble* 33). This strikes me as a good interpretation of Beauvoir's view. But then Butler continues:

> As an ongoing discursive practice, it [the term *woman*] is open to intervention and resignification. Even when gender seems to congeal into the most reified forms, the 'congealing' is itself an insistent and insidious practice, sustained and regulated by various social means. It is, for Beauvoir, never possible finally to become a woman, as if there were a *telos* that governs the process of acculturation and construction. Gender is the repeated stylization of the body, a set of repeated acts within a highly rigid regulatory frame that congeal over time to produce the appearance of substance, of a natural sort of being (*Gender Trouble* 33).

The slippage from Beauvoir's 'woman' to Butler's 'gender' is obvious. Here Butler leaps from the thought that for Beauvoir, a woman is always becoming, always in the process of making herself what she is, to the rather different idea that, for Beauvoir, a woman must therefore be *gender*, that is to say, an 'ongoing discursive practice', a continuous production of a 'congealed' social form.[109] Butler and Beauvoir are both anti-essentialist. But whereas Beauvoir works with a non-normative understanding of what a woman is, Butler thinks of a woman as the ongoing production of a congealed ideological construct. For Butler a woman is gender, and gender is simply an effect of an oppressive social power structure. In short, Butler's concept of gender does not encompass the concrete, historical and experiencing body. This is a particularly clear example of the way in which Butler inherits Gayle Rubin's understanding of gender as an intrinsically oppressive social construct.[110]

Whereas Butler finds oppressive social norms at work in the

---

[109] We might note that for Beauvoir, a woman is not a particularly incomplete term: if a woman is in continuous process, it is because *all* human beings are. Since nothing (with the exception of death), could count as 'completion' for an existentialist, the claim that all human beings are 'incomplete' doesn't actually have much force.

[110] See my discussion of Rubin's work in Sect. II, above.

very concept of woman, Beauvoir takes the female body as a non-normative starting point for her phenomenological analysis of what a woman is. By 'non-normative' I mean that Beauvoir considers that only the study of concrete cases—of lived experience—will tell us exactly what it means to be a woman in a given context. For her it is impossible to derive the definition of 'woman' from an account of social norms alone, just as it is impossible to derive the definition of 'woman' from an account of biological facts alone. Butler's understanding of gender as an effect of power ends up reducing 'woman' to 'power'. This is why it becomes impossible for her and her followers to imagine that the word 'woman' could ever be used in ways that fail to reproduce oppressive power structures. In such an analysis 'power' is opposed to 'sex' or 'the body' and the result is a theory of 'woman' that is structurally similar to the transcendental idealism Beauvoir and Merleau-Ponty want to avoid. Or in other words, for Butler 'power' functions as the secret principle of all meaning, just as 'spirit' does for an idealist philosopher. In short, taking woman to mean gender, Butler thinks of the female body as sex, and assumes that there is a radical divorce between sex and woman/gender. It is *this* move that effectively exiles sex from history and society in Butler's work. However much Butler analyses women and men, she will never believe herself to be saying anything at all about sex, or about the body. For Beauvoir women exist, for Butler they must be deconstructed.[111]

As a result of her understanding of sex, Butler ends up arguing that Beauvoir thinks that anyone—regardless of whether they have a penis or not—can become a woman. This is simply not the case. For Beauvoir, a woman is someone with a female body from beginning to end, from the moment she is born until the moment she dies, but that body is her situation, not her destiny.

---

[111] Butler's belief that 'woman' or 'women' must be deconstructed is everywhere apparent: 'the category of women does not become useless through deconstruction, but becomes one . . . which stands a chance of being opened up, indeed of coming to signify in ways that none of us can predict in advance', she writes in *Bodies* (28–9). Beauvoir would say that because we define ourselves through our existence, all human beings are in principle unpredictable as long as they live. Only death deprives us of the possibility of change.

For Beauvoir people with female bodies do not have to fulfil any special requirements to be considered women. They do not have to conform either to sexist stereotypes, or to feminist ideals of womanhood. However bizarrely a woman may behave, Beauvoir would not dream of denying her the name of woman. The logic of Butler's argument, on the other hand, implies that someone who does not behave according to the dominant 'regulatory discourse(s)' for femininity, is not a woman. To behave like a woman comes to mean 'to behave like an effect of patriarchal power'. In this way the term 'woman' is surrendered to the patriarchal powers feminists wish to oppose. The fact that Beauvoir refuses to hand the concept of 'woman' over to the opposition, is precisely what makes *The Second Sex* such a liberating read. Here, finally, is a book that does not require women somehow to prove that they are 'real' women, to prove that they can conform to someone else's criteria for what a woman should be like.

I want to bring out the implications of Beauvoir's views by turning to the passage where she makes her most famous claim:

> One is not born, but rather becomes, a woman [*femme*]. No biological, psychological, or economic destiny defines the figure that the human female [*la femelle humaine*] acquires in society; it is civilization as a whole that develops this product, intermediate between male and eunuch, which one calls feminine [*féminin*]. Only the mediation of another [*autrui*] can establish an individual as an *Other*. In so far as he exists for himself, the child would not be able to understand himself as sexually differentiated. In girls as in boys the body is first of all the radiation of a subjectivity, the instrument that accomplishes the comprehension of the world: it is through the eyes, the hands, and not through the sexual parts that children apprehend the universe (*SS* 267; *Dsb* 13; TA).

In this passage, Beauvoir is not distinguishing between sex and gender but between *femme* and *femelle*, between human and animal, between the world of values and meaning (lived experience) and the scientific account of our biology (the 'objective' view of the body). The female of the human species, Beauvoir claims, cannot be understood simply as a natural kind, as a *femelle*; it is by virtue of being *human* that she is a product of civilization. In Beauvoir's reminder that a child explores the world with her whole body, and not with the sexual parts alone, we find another echo of her refusal to consider a woman a giant ovum or a monstrous vagina. If sex is not pervasive, sexual difference does not saturate a woman through and through. Rather, our lived experience encompasses bodily sexual difference, but it is also built up by many other things that per se have nothing to do with sexual difference.

If a little girl reads a book about birds, this is not in itself a sexed or gendered activity: any child can read about birds. The beauty of Beauvoir's theory is that she does not have to claim that the reading takes place in a disembodied space. She would insist on the fact that the situation of the reading is the little girl's body. Even if the girl's experience of reading initially is no different from that of her little brother, depending on the social context there is a greater or smaller chance that the gaze of the Other will fall differently on the spectacle of a little girl reading as opposed to the spectacle of a little boy reading. Some girls may not be treated differently from boys in such a context, but others will, and from such different experiences the girls' different relationship to boys and books will be forged.

'One is not born, but rather becomes, a woman': the woman that I have become is clearly not just sex. To think so, is to fall back on the pervasive picture of sex. A pervasive picture of gender, on the other hand, would be no better. The woman I have become is more than just gender, she is a fully embodied human being whose being cannot be reduced to her sexual difference, be it natural or cultural. I have said that for Beauvoir only people with female bodies become women. Writing in 1949, she does not mention sex-change operations. There is fascinating work to be done on the question of what Beauvoir's phenomenological perspective would have to say about the lived experience of trans-sexuals (see Section V, below, for some discussion of this.) Here I shall just note that nothing in Beauvoir's view commits her to claiming that there are no unclear cases, or that no human baby was ever miscategorized at birth, and thus brought up to become a woman regardless of its XY chromosomes. To repeat a point I have made before: the existence of hard cases does not necessarily change our perception of the easy ones.

Beauvoir does not deny that our biology fundamentally shapes the human world. But to say so is not to reduce social life to biological facts. It means, rather, that as long as technology has not made the usual method of human reproduction obsolete, the biological requirements of pregnancy, childbirth, and childcare will have to be accommodated within any social structure. In this sense, sex is different from both race and class. We can very well imagine societies in which race and class no longer exist as social categories, but it is impossible to imagine a society that has ceased to acknowledge that human babies are helpless little creatures. It follows from Beauvoir's analysis that although our biology forces us to organize human societies with child-rearing in mind, it does not impose any *specific* way of doing this.[112] There is nothing to prevent us from placing an extremely high or an extremely low social value on the task. We may assign it to any social group we like, make it the task exclusively of people with brown eyes, or of people between the ages of 40 and 50, or of anyone living in Manchester or Minnesota. What we may *not* do, is to claim that it follows from the fact that women give birth that they should therefore spend twenty years of their lives doing nothing but child-rearing. One might just as well claim that since men impregnate women, they should spend the rest of their lives looking after their offspring. Although our biology places certain limitations on culture, our specific cultural arrangements cannot be read off from our biology.

For Beauvoir, then, the question is not how someone of any sex becomes a woman, but what values, norms, and demands the female human being—precisely because she is female—comes up against in her encounter with the Other (society). In order to understand what it means for the individual woman to encounter the Other, we must investigate her concrete lived experience. It is no coincidence that the sentence 'One is not born, but rather becomes, a woman' introduces the volume of *The Second Sex* that bears the title 'Lived Experience'.

---

[112] Terry Eagleton puts a similar point very nicely: 'It is important to see . . . that we are not "cultural" rather than "natural" creatures, but cultural beings by virtue of our nature, which is to say by virtue of the sorts of bodies we have and the kind of world to which they belong' (*Illusions* 72–3).

Sex and Gender in Beauvoir?

In her pioneering essay on gender, Donna Haraway writes that 'Despite important differences, all the modern feminist meanings of gender have roots in Simone de Beauvoir's claim that "one is not born a woman" ' (131).[113] This can be a misleading statement unless one is firmly aware of what the differences are. Although no feminist draws a clearer line between biology and social norms than Simone de Beauvoir, the concepts of sex and gender cannot be superimposed on her categories. Given the vast proliferation of 'gender theory' in contemporary feminism, gender itself has become a concept that defies easy definition.[114] The word is nevertheless mainly used in two different ways: to refer to 'sexual stereotypes' or 'dominant gender norms', or to an individual's qualities and ways of being ('gender identity'). The figures below summarize the difference between various sex/gender theories and Beauvoir's categories:

(1960**s:**)

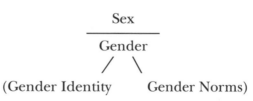

The mainstream model of sex and gender corresponds neatly to nature and culture, biology and social norms. Beauvoir's categories, on the other hand, cannot be reduced to such binary opposites:

(Beauvoir:)
> Body as object
> Body as situation
> Lived experience (subjectivity)
> Myths of femininity (ideology; norms)
> Sex (the fact of being a man or a woman)

---

[113] See also Haraway 133 and 147–8.

[114] In a talk entitled 'Disembodying Race and Gender' given at Duke University in Mar. 1996, Sally Haslanger made an interesting contribution to a clarifying analysis of gender and race.

To Beauvoir, the category of the body perceived as an object is 'objectivist' and 'scientific'. For this reason this category resembles the 1960s understanding of sex. We have seen that Beauvoir rejects this category as a useless starting point for any attempt to understand what a woman is. To consider the body as a situation, on the other hand, is to consider both the fact of having a specific kind of body and the meaning that concrete body has for the situated individual. This is not the equivalent of either sex or gender. The same is true for 'lived experience' which encompasses our experience of all kinds of situations (race, class, nationality, etc.), and is a far more wide-ranging concept than the highly psychologizing concept of gender identity. Beauvoir's 'myths of femininity' closely resemble the concept of gender stereotypes or norms.[115] Roland Barthes uses the same meaning of 'myth' in *Mythologies*. I take this to be an entirely social category, with strong family resemblances to the Marxist concept of ideology. When Gayle Rubin writes that she wishes for a society without gender, I assume that she means a society without oppressive stereotypes of femininity and masculinity, not a society without the lived experience of sexual difference. In short, Beauvoir's concepts are capable of drawing more nuanced and precise distinctions than the sex/gender distinction can provide.

A comparison of the two sets of categories also reveals that the 1960s concept that is most foreign to Beauvoir's thought is that of gender identity. In *The Second Sex*, Beauvoir never discusses identity because she thinks of the individual's subjectivity as interwoven with the conditions in which she lives. To analyse lived experience is to take as one's starting point the experiencing subject, understood as always situated, always embodied, but also as always having a dimension of freedom. Subjectivity is neither a thing nor an inner, emotional world; it is, rather, our way of being in the world. Thus there can be no 'identity' divorced from the world the subject is experiencing. To speak of a generalized 'gender identity' is to impose a reifying or objectifying closure on

[115] This category requires some updating. We would probably want to add 'and masculinity', and explore its relationship to a concept such as ideology. The title of the first volume of *The Second Sex* is 'Les faits et les mythes': 'Facts and Myths'.

our steadily changing and fluctuating experience of ourselves in
the world. If we use the words 'femininity' and 'masculinity' to
designate anything other than sex-based stereotypes, we may find
that we have locked ourselves into precisely such a reified concept
of gender.[116]

Beauvoir believes that the fact of being born with a female body
starts a process which will have specific, yet unforeseeable consequences. Each woman will make something out of what the world
makes out of her: this phrase captures at once a sense of limitations and a sense of freedom. To Beauvoir the relationship
between one's body and one's subjectivity is neither necessary nor
arbitrary, but contingent.[117] If we want to understand what a
woman is, generalizations about sexual difference will never be
enough, whether this is understood in terms of sex, gender or
both. Instead Beauvoir invites us to study the varieties of women's
lived experience. One aspect of that lived experience will be the
way in which the individual woman encounters, internalizes, or
rejects dominant gender norms. But this encounter is always
inflected by the woman's situation, and that means by her
personal and idiosyncratic history as this is interwoven with other
historical situations such as her age, race, class, and nationality,
and the particular political conflicts in which she may be involved.

Beauvoir's conceptual distinctions are more nuanced and carry
out more work than the usual feminist distinction between sex and
gender, and they do their work with greater finesse and sophistica-
tion. Rejecting the pervasive picture of sex, Beauvoir does not
reduce the *femme* to the *femelle*, does not consider that a woman can

---

[116] I return to this point in some detail at the end of this essay.

[117] Moira Gatens's excellent essay on sex and gender makes the point that a
psychoanalytic understanding of the body casts the relationship between the
body and the psyche as contingent: 'it is also clear that there is a contingent,
though not arbitrary, relation between the male body and masculinity and the
female body and femininity. To claim this is neither biologism nor essentialism
but is rather to acknowledge the importance of complex and ubiquitous
networks of signification to the historically, psychologically and culturally variable
ways of being a man or a woman' (*Imaginary Bodies* 13). This contrasts with the
widespread poststructuralist belief that if something isn't necessary, then it must
be arbitrary. (I have also noticed, in some recent theoretical contexts, a confusing tendency to take the word 'contingent' to *mean* 'arbitrary'.)

only be defined within the narrow semantic register of sex, sexuality, or sexual difference. For Beauvoir, a woman is a human being as much as she is a woman: women too embody humanity. Because Beauvoir's theory denies that biological differences justify social norms, there is no risk of biological determinism. By considering the body as a situation, *The Second Sex* lays the groundwork for a thoroughly historical understanding of the body, one that steers clear of the Scylla of empiricism as well as the Charybdis of idealism. By stressing the oppressive function of sexual ideology and social norms, *The Second Sex* develops a devastating critique of sexism. By stressing the fact that women's freedom and agency only rarely disappear entirely, even under severely oppressive conditions, Beauvoir produces a powerful vision of liberation: Beauvoir's women are victims of sexism, but potential revolutionaries too. Her feminism, like that of Gayle Rubin, is emancipatory. By accepting that bodily differences of all kinds contribute to the meaning of our lived experience, Beauvoir indicates that she has a proper respect for biology and other sciences of the body: she is not against science, but against scientism. Beauvoir's account of woman as an open-ended becoming gives us the tools we need to dismantle every reifying gender theory. In short, because it rejects both biological determinism and the limiting distinction between sex and gender, *The Second Sex* provides a brilliant starting point for future feminist investigations of the body, agency, and freedom.

V. DOES IT MAKE A DIFFERENCE? SEX, GENDER, AND THE LAW

In the law a constant stream of actual cases, more novel and more tortuous than the mere imagination could contrive, are brought up for decision—that is, formulae for docketing them must somehow be found.

J. L. Austin, 1956[118]

Nothing will help us more to get clear on a subject than 'cases [imagined] with vividness and fullness', J. L. Austin writes (198). In

---

[118] The quotation comes from the essay with the wonderful title 'A Plea for Excuses' (186).

the last main section of this essay I want to ask what a discussion of concrete cases can tell us about the body, sex, and gender. I shall use as my examples a few cases that have been brought forward by two feminist lawyers working on sex and gender, namely Mary Ann Case who takes a 1960s view of gender, and Katherine Franke who works with the poststructuralist picture of sex.[119] Their discussions will be contrasted with my own, Beauvoir-inspired perspective.

As American legal theorists Case and Franke have to propose solutions that will work with the wording of current US law. Their project is to show how the law can be made to yield a fair treatment of women and sexual minorities. Whatever their own views on sexual difference may be, their essays would not be taken seriously by other lawyers if they failed to remain responsive to the way American law is currently practised and understood. I am not bound by such concerns. In drawing attention to some of the theoretical and political implications of Case and Franke's analyses of sex and gender in the law, I am implicitly commenting on the way US law makes feminists think about sexual difference.

How would the law have to change to take account of a Beauvoirean feminist perspective? This is a fascinating question, but it is not one that I have the competence to answer. The answer would in any case be different in different legal systems. At one point below I question employers' right to fire or promote whoever they want. American law might find it harder to accommodate such ideas than the law in, say, Scandinavia, which traditionally has provided quite extensive protection of workers' rights.[120] My thoughts about a few legal cases are no more than an invitation to a conversation. Further discussion, whether of the same cases, or of different cases in different contexts, would be an immensely helpful contribution to the project of developing a feminist theory inspired by *The Second Sex.*

[119] Although Franke does discuss gender to some extent, Case does not focus on sex. I am grateful to Professor Katharine Bartlett at Duke Law School for drawing my attention to the essays by Franke and Case, and also for helping me to see more clearly what feminist legal theorists (as opposed to an ordinary feminist theorist such as myself) try to do.

[120] On this point, Katharine Bartlett's comments on a draft of this paper were immensely helpful to me.

Discrimination on the Basis of Sex

US anti-discrimination law states that it is unlawful to discriminate against someone 'on the basis of sex'. Here the word sex is used in its traditional pre-1960s sense: it means 'because of being a man or woman'. The law is intended to protect us from discrimination based solely on our *status* as male or female. 'What was decided among the prehistoric Protozoa cannot be annulled by Act of Parliament', Geddes and Thomson wrote (267). It seems almost too obvious to mention, but the very fact of *having* legislation outlawing sex discrimination means that the law is not committed to biological determinism. If someone wanted to fire me from my job at Duke University on the grounds that my female biology makes me unsuited to intellectual work, Geddes and Thomson would not object to the principle of it, but contemporary US law most certainly would. The introduction of anti-sex-discrimination legislation in the United States represented a major victory for feminists who deny that biology grounds social norms.[121]

The traditional sense of sex invoked by US law is not necessarily complicit with sexual conservatism. In the traditional sense, sex does not mean just chromosomal and hormonal sexual differences, it means the fact of being a man or a woman. '[I]t is fatal for anyone who writes to think of their sex', Virginia Woolf writes (*Room* 99). For Woolf as for Beauvoir it is self-evident that men and women are always situated in a particular time and place. Used in this sense, sex does not necessarily refer to some ahistorical entity. It does not prevent us from denying that biology grounds social norms, nor does it commit us to any particular view of what a man or a woman is. As Simone de Beauvoir's usage shows, the traditional meaning of sex does not oblige us to define a woman as someone who is female, feminine, and heterosexual. More open than the 1960s understanding of the term, the traditional meaning of sex has the advantage of not forcing us to classify every ordinary action or

---

[121] The question of whether the courts accept *some* biologically based generalizations about women and men remains open. Katherine Franke writes: 'We have inherited a jurisprudence of sexual equality that seeks to distinguish, as its primary function, inaccurate myths about sexual identity from true—and therefore prepolitical—characteristics of sex that are factually significant' (29).

quality as belonging either to sex or to gender. If I lose my job
because I am a woman it would in most cases be a complete waste
of time to try to decide whether I lost my job because of my sex or
because of my gender.

Among US lawyers there is currently some confusion of usage
concerning sex and gender. Although the majority of courts
speak of discrimination on the basis of *sex*, the US Supreme Court
Justice Ruth Bader Ginsburg usually speaks of discrimination on
the basis of *gender*. For her, this is not a conceptual distinction, but
a matter of convenience:

> [Ginsburg] stopped talking about sex discrimination years ago. . . .
> [S]he explained that a secretary once told her, 'I'm typing all
> these briefs and articles for you and the word sex, sex, sex, is on
> every page. Don't you know those nine men [on the Supreme
> Court], they hear that word and their first association is not the
> way you want them to be thinking? Why don't you use the word
> "gender"? It is a grammatical term and it will ward off distracting
> associations'.[122]

When she says 'gender', Ginsburg in fact means sex in the traditional sense. Many legislators now follow her example. Thus the
Pentagon's 'Don't ask, don't tell' policy on homosexuality states
that it will discharge members of the military who marry or
attempt to marry 'someone of the same gender'.[123] In the United
States, this usage is becoming increasingly accepted in everyday
life, where all sorts of forms and questionnaires routinely require
us to tick the box for male or female gender. Everyday references
to gender to mean 'sex' or 'the fact of being a man or a woman'
are now too numerous to count.[124] Ginsburg's secretary surely

---

[122] An interview with Justice Ginsburg, as quoted by Case (10).

[123] 'Sexual orientation will not be a bar to service unless manifested by homosexual conduct. The military will discharge members who engage in homosexual conduct, defined as a homosexual act, a statement that the member is
homosexual or bisexual, or a marriage or attempted marriage to someone of the
same gender' (quoted in Parker and Sedgwick, 'Introduction' 5).

[124] One recent handbook on non-sexist usage summarizes this usage as
follows: 'The terms *sex* and *gender* . . . are often used synonymously in contemporary writing to denote biological femaleness or maleness (with *gender* seen by
some as merely a way to avoid the word *sex*, which also designates, of course,
sexual intercourse and related activities)' (Frank and Treichler 10).

provides the major explanation for this: in the latest puritanical backlash, the very word 'sex' appears to have gained porno-graphic connotations. Insofar as the new usage simply substitutes 'gender' for 'sex' in the traditional sense, it does not owe much to the feminist understanding of the sex/gender distinction.[125] Just as one cannot assume that someone who refers to a person's 'sex' means to espouse biological essentialism, one cannot assume, either, that someone who refers to a person's 'gender' means to reject biological determinism.

The question of what sex or gender means in US courts is complicated by the fact that one of Justice Ginsburg's more conservative colleagues on the Supreme Court, Justice Antonin Scalia, insists on distinguishing between sex and gender. In a 1994 minority opinion Scalia wrote:

> Throughout this opinion, I shall refer to the issue as sex discrimi-nation rather than (as the Court does) gender discrimination. The word 'gender' has acquired the new and useful connotation of cultural and attitudinal characteristics (as opposed to physical characteristics) distinctive to the sexes. That is to say, gender is to sex as feminine is to female and masculine to male.[126]

The case in question was one where the prosecution in a paternity suit had used peremptory challenges to eliminate men from the jury. Scalia's point was that the case should be considered one of sex (and not gender) discrimination because it did not involve 'peremptory strikes exercised on the basis of femininity and masculinity (as far as it appears, effeminate men did not survive the prosecution's peremptories)'.[127] Any teacher of women's stud-ies might agree. Scalia's discovery of the sex/gender distinction nevertheless produces new legal ambiguities. Does he believe that the law makes it illegal to discriminate on the basis of *gender* as well as of sex? Does he still think of sex as the fact of being a man or a woman? Or would he accept that sex means chromosomes

---

[125] Some speakers may of course have a vague idea that gender somehow is a 'more feminist' *word* than sex, but this does not necessarily change the way they use it. See also my discussion of Joan Scott's use of the word gender in Sect. III, above.

[126] Quoted in Franke 9 (also in Case 12).

[127] Scalia, quoted in Case 12.

and hormones and nothing else? To judge from the example
Scalia gives—*men* were struck off the jury regardless of their
gender—I would say he still assumes that sex means 'the fact of
being a man or a woman', but the text does not explicitly address
the issue.[128] The fact that such questions of interpretation arise all
the way up to the US Supreme Court, shows that the question of
what exactly sex discrimination means is far from settled.

Poststructuralism, Sex Discrimination, and the Sex of Transsexuals

Katherine Franke is a poststructuralist feminist lawyer. Her essay
on why the law should not distinguish between sex and gender is
based on the assumption that sex means 'body parts' or 'chromosomes' and that such things are entirely natural, completely
outside society and culture.[129] She declares that it is oppressive
and essentialist to 'conceive of sex biologically—to carve up the
population into two different kinds of people' (92). Since sex is
natural, whereas all discriminatory practices per definition are
social, there is no such thing as *sex* discrimination:

> When women are denied employment, for instance, it is not
> because the discriminator is thinking 'a Y chromosome is neces-
> sary in order to perform this kind of work.' Only in very rare cases
> can sex discrimination be reduced to a question of body parts (36).

If *sex* discrimination does not exist, there is no point in distinguishing between sex and gender. What there is, and what the law
should recognize, Franke claims, is *gender* discrimination.

   In order to fend off the 'ludicrous' and 'absurd' idea that there
is a biological foundation to sex discrimination, Franke denies that
biological facts are relevant to any human activity whatsoever.[130]
To her, any acknowledgment of biological sexual differences *must* give

---

[128] According to both Franke and Case, Scalia's opinion does not spell out his
views on discrimination on the basis of gender (see Case 12; Franke 9–10).

[129] Attributing her own interpretation of sex to Scalia, Franke takes him to
mean that 'gender-based distinctions are *not* what "discrimination on the basis
of sex" was intended to reach' (9–10). Franke cites no evidence in support of her
interpretation that Scalia intends to exclude gender. Mary Anne Case does not
think that Scalia's distinction is necessarily ominous (see Case 4).

[130] See Franke 31 ('absurdity'); 40 ('indeed almost ludicrous').

rise to socially oppressive norms. Sexual equality jurisprudence in America, she writes, has accepted 'a fundamental belief in the truth of biological sexual difference' (3), and is therefore contradictory. 'How can the Court at once tolerate sexual differentiation and proscribe sexual discrimination?', Franke asks (31). The alternative is to think of biological differences as an '*effect* of normative gender ideology' (2).[131] In her poststructuralist recoil from the bad picture of sex, she recommends that we proceed as if bodies did not exist. Bodies should simply 'drop out of' the legal picture.[132]

There is an obvious tension between Franke's unproblematic use of the words women and men, and her resolute denial that the population consists of two biologically different kinds of people, namely women and men. At times she appears simultaneously to deny and affirm that sexism consists in the oppression of women just because they are (biological) women:

> Women who are sexually harassed in the workplace do not experience discriminatory harm because of their biology but because of the manner in which sex is used to exploit a relationship of power between victim and harasser. This relationship of power is based either upon supervisor/subordinate roles or upon cultural gender roles which encourage men to use sex to subordinate women. Biology has absolutely nothing to do with either one of these material grounds for workplace sexual harassment (91).

Franke is making two fundamental assumptions. First, that sex *must* mean biology, which must mean essence, nature, and ground, which can have nothing to do with social practices; and, second, that a 'man' or a 'woman' is nothing but gender. Women and men are best understood not as bodies, but as the 'congealed ideological constructs' conjured up by Judith Butler. The question of why we persist in thinking in terms of two sexes and not one or ten remains unexplored.

---

[131] 'Ultimately', Franke writes, 'there is no principled way to distinguish sex from gender, and concomitantly, sexual differentiation from sexual discrimination' (5). She also writes that 'By accepting [biological sexual differences], equality jurisprudence reifies as foundational *fact* that which is really an *effect* of normative gender ideology' (2).

[132] '[E]quality jurisprudence must abandon its reliance upon a biological definition of sexual identity and sex discrimination and instead . . . adopt a more behavioral or performative conception of sex' (8).

Franke's attitude to the sex/gender distinction is as inconsistent as that of other poststructuralists. Although the title of her essay claims that the 'central mistake of sex discrimination law [is] the disaggregation of sex from gender' (1), she is not actually against distinguishing between sex and gender at all. What she is against, is the belief that sex *determines* gender, and what she explicitly wants to escape is the 'death grip that *unifies* sex and gender' (90; my emphasis). Hers is a case against the pervasive picture of sex, and against biological determinism, but not against the distinction between sex and gender. In practice, Franke distinguishes between male and masculine, female and feminine, and even hails as 'revolutionary' the attempt to create 'the cultural conditions for masculinity to be separated from maleness and be remapped onto the female body' (87). This is the equivalent of Judith Butler's celebration of the subversive potential of men in drag.[133] When pushed to make a concrete political or legal claim, the poststructuralist theorist finds herself returning to the 1960s distinction between sex and gender that she otherwise denounces. When Mary Ann Case denounces 'gender conformity', which she defines as the belief that one's gender and one's sexual orientation *must* correspond to one's sex, she is saying exactly the same thing as Franke when she criticizes the belief that sex determines gender.[134] On this point, then, Franke's political argument is exactly the same as that of just about every other contemporary feminist.

Much of Franke's essay is devoted to extensive discussion of the dilemmas of transsexuals.[135] In the case known as *Ulane* v. *Eastern Airlines* (1984 and 1985), the plaintiff had been hired as a male pilot by Eastern Airlines. Here is Franke's account of the case:

> Ulane later took a leave of absence to undergo sexual reassignment surgery and was fired by Eastern when she returned to work as a woman. She then filed a Title VII [employment-related] sex discrimination action against her employer, alleging that she 'was fired by Eastern Airlines for no reason other than the fact that she ceased being a male and became a female' (Franke 33).

---

[133] This claim is made in the context of a discussion of Shannon Faulkner's brief attendance at the Citadel. I shall return to this case below.

[134] I discuss Case's views below.

[135] Franke prefers to speak of 'transgendered people' (see 32–3 n. 130).

The court dismissed Ulane's claim, reasoning that

> it is unlawful to discriminate against women because they are women, and against men because they are men. . . . [E]ven if one believes that a woman can be so easily created from what remains of a man, that does not decide this case. If Eastern had considered Ulane to be female and had discriminated against her because she was female . . . then the argument might be made that Title VII applied (cited in Franke 33).

Franke does not provide a clear discussion of this case, but the drift of her argument is that the court was wrong to dismiss Ulane's claim, and in particular wrong not to accept that Ulane had become a woman: '[on a foundational level, they all [all courts] embrace an essentially biological definition of the two sexual categories' (35).

But, as the court indicated, Ulane's problem would not necessarily have been solved if the court had thought of her as a woman, rather than as a strangely equipped man. She wasn't fired, one might argue, because of her *status* as male or female, but because she had undergone a sex-change operation (i.e. because of something she had *done*, rather than something she *was*). To this one might object that the fact of submitting to surgery is virtually part of the definition of the term 'transsexual'. It may seem just as plausible to claim that Ulane was dismissed for *being* a transsexual as to say that she was dismissed for *having* a sex-change operation. This argument implicitly recommends that transsexuals should be considered neither male or female, but a third (or third and fourth) sex. The court seems to have recognized this option, since it adds that 'if the term "sex" . . . is to mean more than biological male and biological female, the new definition must come from Congress' (cited in Franke 33). As US law currently stands, however, there is no protection for transsexuals qua transsexuals.[136]

Many transsexuals, however, do not want to be recognized *as* transsexuals. What they want is to have their *new* sex recognized by the law.[137] This seems to be Franke's view too. Let us assume for

[136] So far at least, nothing indicates that US law, or indeed any country's law, has developed a coherent doctrine concerning sex change (see Rogers).

[137] An increasing number of transsexuals disagree with this, however. Sandy Stone and Kate Bornstein both make powerful cases for their right to be recognized as *transsexual women*.

the moment that Ulane's sex was not in doubt, and that all parties agreed to consider her a bona fide woman. In order to get protection under the law, Ulane would then have had to show that she was fired because of being a woman. But if she was fired not for *being* a woman, but for the *act* of changing her sex in order to *become* one, general recognition of her new sex would still not advance her case. What I am trying to show is that if we believe that transsexuals should be protected under sex discrimination law, there is no need first to dismiss the belief that there are biological differences between men and women. After all, transsexuals themselves go to painful lengths to acquire the sex organs of the 'target sex'.[138] Rather than denouncing the belief in biological sex differences, Franke ought to denounce the belief that the very fact of wanting a sex-change operation is a symptom of the kind of mental instability that makes one unsuitable for a responsible job.

Let us suspend legal and political disbelief for a moment, and assume that US legislators had just happily voted to amend current Title VII (employment related) law to the effect that nobody should be discriminated against 'because of his sex *or because of changing his sex*'.[139] Depending on the circumstances of her case, the new wording might have saved the unfortunate Ulane. The new wording does not require us to reject the traditional meaning of sex, or to accept that sex is an effect of the performance of gender. Nor does the distinction between sex and gender come up. In this case, there is no necessary link between our political aim (recognition of the rights of transsexuals) and

---

[138] Some poststructuralists have concluded that it follows that drag artists are radical and transsexuals are conservative, or, in somewhat attenuated terms, that drag artists are 'queer' (they unsettle categories), whereas transsexuals risk turning themselves into 'essentialists'. In an essay on Leslie Feinberg's fine novel *Stone Butch Blues*, Jay Prosser writes: '[In *Stone Butch Blues*] becoming fully one sex is mythicized as rightful and crucially inextricable from transsexual identity; the trope of a gendered home structures the transsexual story. In spite of the difference of its story line, *Stone Butch Blues* participates in this transsexual version of the narrative of gendered belonging and becoming which it can't quite give up in a distinctly unqueer fashion. . . . Transsexuality is a narrative of essentialist constructionism . . .' (491).

[139] I use 'his' here, because that is the wording of the law.

our beliefs about biological facts. In the case of *Ulane* v. *Eastern Airlines*, poststructuralist theory seems to make no difference at all.

But Franke is not mainly concerned with transsexuals filing Title VII cases. Her most detailed discussion of the situation of transsexuals focuses on cases involving marriage, divorce, and alimony. Her principal case is the famous British case known as *Corbett* v. *Corbett* (1971), concerning the marriage between Arthur Corbett, who had at times considered himself a male transvestite, and April Ashley, a male-to-female transsexual. They courted each other for three years, and were married in Gibraltar in September 1963. '[T]hey separated after only fourteen days', Franke writes, 'in part because Corbett was unable fully to consummate the marriage' (44).[140] Corbett challenged the legal validity of the marriage. The main question to be decided was whether April Ashley was a woman at the time of the marriage. If she was not, the marriage was never valid, and no divorce would be necessary; if she was, usual divorce proceedings would have to be undertaken.[141]

To make a long story short: in 1971 Judge Ormrod ruled that April Ashley was born male, and that subsequent surgery and hormone treatment failed to change this fact.[142] Franke denounces this as 'biological essentialism' (50), and at the end of her paper she concludes that 'Ultimately, sexual equality jurisprudence must abandon its reliance upon biology in favor of an underlying fundamental right to determine gender independent of biological sex' (99). Taken in the poststructuralist spirit in which it is written, this means that courts should accept that someone's gender *is* their sex, that the performance of gender produces sex, and that no biological facts can override this

[140] Franke adds her own analysis of what destroyed the relationship of this couple: 'And so the couple split, the normalizing and liberalizing effect of the institution of marriage having destroyed the fantasy that had made the relationship initially so powerful for both parties' (44).

[141] Needless to say, the court and all the parties in this 1960s case took for granted that a married couple had to be of different sex.

[142] 'The correct criteria for "womanness" should be "the chromosomal, gonadal and genital tests. . . . [But] the greater weight would probably be given to the genital criteria than to the other two"' (Franke 46).

conclusion. Applied to the case of *Corbett* v. *Corbett*, it follows that because April Ashley 'performed her gender' to perfection, the court should accept that she was a woman. (According to the medical experts in the case, Ashley had 'remarkably good' female genitals, and there was no physical impediment to full penetration.) Franke's argument assumes that the claim that gender is performative secures the conclusion that transsexuals should *always* be legally recognized as being their 'target sex'.

To accept that anyone who performs femininity is a woman, is to blur the difference between a woman who performs femininity, a man (drag artist or cross-dresser) who does it, and a transsexual who has changed his or her body in order to achieve a more convincing 'performance'. Is the 'gender' performed really the same in each case? Even if we assume that these three people all perform the same script (which is by no means a foregone conclusion), does a different body really make no difference at all as to the effect of the performance? Fortunately there is no need to make a final decision about the performativity or otherwise of sex and gender in order to accept the claim that male-to-female transsexuals should be legally recognized as women. All that is required is that we deny that biology grounds social norms. It is neither politically reactionary nor philosophically inconsistent to believe both that a male-to-female transsexual remains a biological male *and* that this is no reason to deny 'him' the legal right to be reclassified as a woman. This would be in keeping both with Gayle Rubin's wish to get rid of social gender norms, and with Beauvoir's emphasis on women's (and men's) freedom to define their sex as they please.

Some judges—including Judge Ormrod—have decided that whatever some people get up to with their bodies, the sex assigned at birth remains the only sex of the person unless there is evidence that a mistake has been made. This corresponds exactly to the views of some feminist and lesbian activists, particularly with regard to male-to-female transsexuals who claim that they are lesbians and wish to participate in lesbian women-only organizations and meetings. Some lesbians are adamant that the male-to-female transsexual remains a male, who insofar as he is trying to infiltrate lesbian organizations, is no better than a fifth columnist, an agent of homophobic patriarchy.[143] In all these cases the question at stake is the same: when deciding what sex someone is, how much importance are we to attach to genital surgery and hormone treatment—to body parts—and how much to a person's lived experience?

Some courts have decided that while individuals have a legitimate right to have their wish to *pass* as a man or a woman accepted by society, and so allow transsexuals to change their first names and get a new driver's licence, it doesn't follow that they actually *have changed* their biological sex. They cannot marry a 'same-sex' partner, or change their birth certificates.[144] Many transsexuals consider that this produces a completely absurd situation, since the same person now has documents declaring him or her to be male in some cases and female in others. I imagine that many judges and radical lesbians would agree with Franke that what is needed is a clear-cut decision about the person's sex, whether this is taken to be based on biology or performativity. But this is not an obvious conclusion.

Let us imagine that I wake up tomorrow with a fully male body, but with exactly the same memories and life experiences as I have today. Would I then be a man? First of all, we need to note that this question is formulated in a way that tempts us to think that there must be something deeply mysterious and difficult about the answer, that to find an answer requires some special insight into what it means to *be* a man or a woman, in some *deep* sense. The belief is that no ordinary considerations could possibly help us to answer the question.[145] Moreover, we may be inclined to

---

[143] See e.g. Janice Raymond, *The Transsexual Empire* and Christine Burton, 'Golden Threads'. For vociferous counterarguments, from a broadly poststructuralist perspective, see Sandy Stone, 'The Empire Strikes Back', and Kate Bornstein, *Gender Outlaw*. Leslie Feinberg's interesting new book *Transgender Warrior* shows discontent with the poststructuralist paradigm, and lack of certainty about possible alternatives.

[144] Franke quotes one decision that granted a petition to change an obviously male name to a female one, but then added that 'the order shall not be used or relied upon by petitioner as any evidence or judicial determination that the sex of the petitioner has in fact been changed' (54).

[145] My analysis here is inspired by Martin Stone's 'Focusing the Law'. Drawing on Wittgenstein, Stone shows that the temptation to invest certain questions or expressions with a mysterious strangeness leads us away from the ordinary and everyday and towards metaphysics (see esp. 44–57).

think that the question has to be settled once and for all by a clear
yes or no. This is where Simone de Beauvoir teaches us to think
differently. As she points out, it is the Other who assigns my sex to
me. We cannot determine someone's sex in abstraction from any
human situation. If I lived in perfect isolation from all other
human beings, I would never even know what sex I was.

If we assume, for the sake of the argument, that my new male
body was perfect, right down to the XY chromosomes, to insist
that I was still simply a woman would be somewhat odd.[146] It is not
enough to think of oneself as a woman in order to become one.
Like most of us, Beauvoir would presumably take someone with a
male body to be a man, unless she had good reason to think
otherwise. Confronted with my case, she would, I imagine, agree
that my brand-new male body represented a radical change of
situation for me. The unsuspecting world would see nothing but
a man wherever I turned up, and I would be treated accordingly.
If, from old habit, I still tried to use the women's toilets, for
instance, I would surely be shown the door. Under the circumstances, it is difficult to see that there would be anything wrong in
this. For the purpose of using public toilets I would definitely be
a man. (This is not to claim that the current sex segregation of
public toilet facilities should be maintained for ever.) A different
situation might produce a different answer to the question of
what my sex was. If I were asked to speak at a women-only conference, it would seem unfair to exclude me on the grounds that I
no longer was a woman. Should all my female experiences and
work on feminist theory count for nothing just because I had
woken up to find myself equipped with a penis? And what if some
committee needed expertise on sex changes? Would I not be
perfectly entitled to claim that I was an ex-woman, a member of
the select group of people who have changed their sex? Over time
my new situation would affect my general sense of identity. I

---

[146] This is precisely the problem that confronts the protagonist of Angela
Carter's profound novel *The Passion of New Eve* (1977). Having been transformed
into a perfect woman, Evelyn/Eve has to learn through experience what it might
mean to be a woman in different situations. At the end of the novel, Eve has
become a woman, and for Carter that means no more and no less mythological
than any other incarnation of femininity.

would steadily gain more male experiences, yet for a very long time (and possibly always), I would have to consider the answer to the question of which sex I belonged to, as relatively open to variation.

On my reading of feminist theory, poststructuralists and other sex/gender feminists have failed to address the question of transsexuals adequately because they have no concept of the body as a situation, or of lived experience, and because they tend to look for one final answer to the question of what sex a transsexual is. Moreover, because they tend to understand sex as a matter of a few narrowly defined biological criteria, they forget that the meaning of the words man and woman is produced in concrete human situations. That is, feminists and transsexuals have overlooked the fact that what counts as being a woman for the purpose of marriage is not necessarily the same thing as what counts as being a woman for the purpose of participating in a lesbian activist group. To ask courts to have a clear-cut, all-purpose 'line' on sex changes is to ask them *not* to engage in new interpretations of the purpose of the different human institutions and practices which are brought into conflict by the arrival of transsexuals. I can't see how this could be in the interest either of feminists or of transsexuals.

All this, of course, leaves the question of whether April Ashley should be considered a man or a woman at the time of her marriage to Arthur Corbett unresolved. The fact is that I find it extremely difficult to come up with an answer. A closer reading of the case nevertheless provides some revealing information. First of all, Judge Ormrod stresses over and over again that he is only concerned with determining the sex of April Ashley for the purposes of marriage: 'The question then becomes', he writes, 'what is meant by the word "woman" in the context of a marriage, for I am not concerned to determine the "legal sex" of the respondent at large' (106).[147] Judge Ormrod, in my view, is clearly right to frame his decision in this narrow way. By asking 'what is April Ashley's sex for the purposes of marriage?' he helps us to see that the ideological difficulties arising from his decision have

---

[147] The legal reference to this British case is *Corbett* v. *Corbett* [1971]: 83–119.

little to do with the way he thinks about sex, and rather more to do with the way he thinks about marriage. Let us accept that a British court in 1971 had to define marriage as a relationship between a man and a woman. But even given this assumption, Judge Ormrod's understanding of what matters in a marriage is, to say the least, contentious. 'Marriage is a relationship which depends on sex and not on gender', he writes (107):

> Having regard to the essentially hetero-sexual character of the relationship which is called marriage, the criteria [of April Ashley's sex] must, in my judgment, be biological, for even the most extreme degree of transsexualism in a male or the most severe hormonal imbalance which can exist in a person with male chromosomes, male gonads and male genitalia cannot reproduce a person who is naturally capable of performing the essential role of a woman in marriage (106).

This raises the delicate question of exactly what the 'essential role of a woman in marriage' is, and what the difference between performing it 'naturally' or in some other way might be. My impression is that Judge Ormrod takes the fundamental purpose of marriage to be procreation. In order to procreate one needs a real vagina, as opposed to 'an artificial cavity': 'When such a cavity has been constructed in a male, the difference between sexual intercourse using it and anal or intra-crural intercourse is, in my judgment, to be measured in centimetres' (107). But if the decisive criterion for being a woman for the purposes of marriage is the ability to be able to reproduce 'naturally', then infertile or post-menopausal women, or women born without a vagina do not qualify as women for the purposes of marriage. A question mark must also be raised about women who get married without the slightest intention of having children. If we take Judge Ormrod's understanding of marriage to imply, at the very least, the requirement that there has to be vaginal sexual intercourse, whether it has a chance of leading to reproduction or not, then married couples who prefer not to indulge in this activity, for one reason or another, also need to ask themselves whether they are genuinely married.

Judge Ormrod took a view of marriage consonant with that of the Catholic Church. He would not have needed to wait for the gay marriage debates of the 1990s to find alternative views. In his 1643 tract on divorce, Milton writes: 'God in the first ordaining of marriage taught us to what end he did it, in words expressly implying the apt and cheerful conversation of man with woman, to comfort and refresh him against the evil of solitary life, not mentioning the purpose of generation till afterwards, as being but a secondary end in dignity . . .' (183). Although Milton's editors note that 'conversation' in 1643 signified intimacy and/or cohabitation, I think Milton is saying that there is no intimacy, and therefore no marriage, without loving and joyful conversation between the spouses. As Ibsen's *A Doll's House* (1879) teaches us, if the criterion for a genuine marriage were 'apt and cheerful conversation', then few could claim to be married. When Nora discovers that she has never really known her husband, that Thorvald is not the hero she took him to be, she says: 'In that moment I realized that for eight years I have been living here with a strange man, and that I have had three children—. Oh, I can't bear to think of it! I could tear myself to bits and pieces' (85; my translation). Nora's conclusion is that regardless of their lawfully wedded legal status, and regardless of the fact that they have fulfilled the injunction to procreate, the two of them have never actually been married at all. Her famous exit line insists precisely on this point. She would only ever come back, she says, if 'our life together could become a marriage' (86). If we want to determine whether April Ashley was a woman for the purposes of marriage, we may want to leave questions of identity and essence behind and instead ask what it might mean to be married in contemporary Western society.

Against Femininity: Gender, Stereotypes, and Feminist Politics

Mary Ann Case's thoughtful analysis of gender and the law provides an exemplary starting point for further exploration of feminist gender theory. Case's essay 'Disaggregating Gender from Sex and Sexual Orientation: The Effeminate Man in the Law and Feminist Jurisprudence' is interesting both because it brings the concept of gender to bear on legal cases, and because it uses the concept in a way that is representative for feminist theory and criticism in the United States.[148]

Case's main concern is the fate of traditionally feminine qualities in present-day society. '[W]omen in this society are ... moving closer to the masculine standard, and ... are rewarded for so doing', she writes (29). Current interpretation of the law has permitted discrimination against the 'stereotypically feminine, especially when manifested by men, but also when manifested by women' (3). This amounts to permitting *gender* discrimination (as opposed to *sex* discrimination), that is to say discrimination that favours the 'masculine over the feminine rather than the male over the female' (33). Case shows that courts consistently favour employers who refuse to hire or promote someone who is too 'feminine', whether that person is male or female. It follows that both feminine women and effeminate men have a hard time making their Title VII claims heard. Because many courts confuse gender (effeminacy) and sexual orientation or desire (homosexuality), effeminate men suffer doubly from the present law.[149] Although the law may protect us against gender discrimination, it extends no such protection to homosexuals. A man fired because he wears an earring to work may have standing to claim sex discrimination, but if the same man also turns out to be gay he may have no recourse. In keeping with the feminist wish to analyse sexuality as an issue separate from gender and sex, Case concludes that we need a separate law for claims based on sexual orientation.

It is against this background that Case turns to her major case study: *Price Waterhouse* v. *Hopkins* (1989). This is a rather unusual case, in that it expands the standards for what is to count as discrimination on the basis of sex. So far, it has only rarely been taken as a precedent by other courts. In 1982 Ann Hopkins sued

---

[148] When it comes to gender, Franke agrees with Case's analysis whenever they discuss the same case. I therefore make no further reference to Franke's essay in this section.

[149] 'Thus, discriminating against the effeminate man may be overdetermined, and effeminacy conflated with gayness' (54).—Case tends to use 'feminine' about women and 'effeminate' about men. I am not sure how to take this usage.

the accounting firm of Price Waterhouse for not promoting her to a partnership on the grounds that she did not behave in a feminine fashion. Case writes:

> Ann Hopkins was the only woman among eighty-eight persons considered for partnership. . . . She had at that point worked at the firm for five years, and she had 'generated more business for Price Waterhouse' and 'billed more hours than any of the other candidates under consideration' that year. The Policy Board . . . recommended that Ann Hopkins's candidacy be placed on hold. . . . Both her supporters and her detractors in the partnership, as well as her clients, described Hopkins as manifesting stereotypically masculine qualities, for better and for worse. She was praised for, among other things, a 'strong character, independence and integrity', 'decisiveness, broadmindedness, and intellectual clarity' and for being 'extremely competent, intelligent', 'strong and forthright, very productive, energetic and creative' (41–2).

Other partners took a different view of the same aspects of Hopkins's personality:

> One partner described her as 'macho'; another suggested that she 'overcompensated for being a woman'; a third advised her to take 'a course at charm school.' Several partners criticized her use of profanity; in response, one partner suggested that those partners objected to her swearing only 'because it's a lady using foul language' . . . [T]he man who . . . bore responsibility for explaining to Hopkins the reasons for the Policy Board's decision . . . delivered the *coup de grace:* in order to improve her chances for partnership, [he] advised, Hopkins should 'walk more femininely, talk more femininely, dress more femininely, wear make-up, have her hair styled, and wear jewelry' (42).

In 1989 the Supreme Court found that to refuse to promote a 'masculine' woman accountant unless she became more 'feminine' was prohibited sex discrimination. Justice Brennan wrote for the majority: 'As for the legal relevance of sex stereotyping, we are beyond the day when an employer could evaluate employees by insisting they matched the stereotype associated with their group' (quoted by Case 95).

According to Case, Ann Hopkins was not refused promotion because of her sex, but because of her gender. *Hopkins* shows that

the courts accept that sex discrimination includes gender discrimination. Case concludes that there is no need to add the word 'and
gender' to existing sex discrimination law (see Case 4). Yet she still
finds a problem in *Price Waterhouse* v. *Hopkins.* The court seems to
have accepted that Hopkins needed to display stereotypically
'masculine' traits in order to do well at her job; the 'gendering' of
the job was not questioned at all.[150] Would a traditionally feminine
woman have recourse under the law if she were fired for not being
aggressive *enough?* '[A]n unquestioning acceptance of the current
gendered requirements for most jobs hurts women', Case writes.
(46). At first glance, her point seems valuable. If putting 'masculine' job requirements in place enables employers to fire traditionally 'feminine' women, then feminists should surely demand
that the employers demonstrate why 'feminine' qualities will not
be just as effective when it comes to getting the job done.

The more I consider Case's arguments, however, the more her
understanding of gender (an understanding US law no doubt
obliges her to work with) appears problematic to me. As we have
seen, Case herself characterizes the following list of Hopkins's
qualities as 'masculine': strong character, independence,
integrity, decisiveness, broad-mindedness, intellectual clarity,
extreme competence, intelligence, strength, forthrightness,
productivity, energy, and creativity.[151] But all of my women friends
display some or all of these traits, and it has never occurred to me
to consider them 'masculine' for all that. (I don't think of them
as 'feminine' either.) Why does Case concur in labelling all these
characteristics masculine? Does she want to challenge job descriptions that require decisiveness, intellectual clarity, energy, and
creativity on the grounds that traditionally feminine women have
none of these qualities?

When Case speaks of gender, she usually means sex-based

---

[150] Part of the reason why Hopkins won her case was actually that the firm
placed her in an impossible double bind: she was effectively asked to tread an
impossibly narrow line between being masculine enough to do her job well and
feminine enough to conform to some of the partners' aesthetic requirements of
a woman.

[151] See the quotation from Case 41–2 given above. I have rewritten some of
the adjectives as nouns, and removed superfluous conjunctions.

stereotypes. Her admirable research provides expert guidance on what these are. Drawing on the so-called Bem Sex-Role Inventory (BSRI), Case lists a number of adjectives that psychologists and other researchers regularly consider coded masculine and feminine in contemporary American culture:[152]

MASCULINE	FEMININE
aggressive	affectionate
ambitious	cheerful
analytical	childlike
assertive	compassionate
athletic	flatterable
competitive	gentle
dominant	gullible
forceful	loyal
independent	sensitive
individualistic	shy
self-reliant	soft-spoken
self-sufficient	sympathetic
strong	tender
	understanding
	warm
	yielding

Another 'femininity scale' lists the following items:

FEMININITY
emotional
gentle
kind
understanding
warm
able to devote oneself completely to others
helpful to others
aware of others' feelings.

No wonder that Case concludes that 'There can be, I would contend, a world of difference between being female and being

---

[152] See Case 12, including n. 20.

feminine' (11).[153] Adamantly opposed to 'gender conformity', Case insists that we should not expect sex to determine gender or sexual orientation.[154] Among feminists of all persuasions today this is a completely uncontroversial position.[155] To a Beauvoirean feminist, however, Case's *conclusion* is not uncontroversial at all. Her aim is to 'focus attention on the reasons why the feminine might have been devalued in both women and men . . . to protect what is valuable about the traditionally feminine without essentializing it, limiting it to women, or limiting women to it' (105). I take this to require that we *show* what is valuable about traditional femininity. In order to do so we need some general criteria for what is to count as 'valuable'. It would also seem arbitrary to refuse to assess traditional masculinity according to the same criteria, first because we might find something valuable there too, and second because we can't very well let traditional stereotypes of femininity determine what phenomena feminists should investigate. If we decide that it is valuable to be 'helpful to others' (just to take one item from the femininity scale), then it surely must be valuable for men as well as for women.

If we grant these claims, then the question of why we would still want to label the fact of being 'helpful to others' *feminine* becomes urgent. If we still intend to call qualities such as 'tenderness', 'warmth', and 'loyalty' feminine, how do we expect to get rid of the idea that they have or ought to have some special connection with women? If we believe that such qualities have no intrinsic or necessary, but only an ideological, connection with women or female bodies, what reason do feminists have for continuing to call them feminine? Would this not imply that sex determines gender after all? (This is where the spectre of 'gender conformity' returns to haunt us.)

[153] The preceding scale is quoted by Case as the 'femininity scale' of Spence, Helmreich and Stapps's 1974 Personal Attributes Questionnaire (PAQ). See Case 13 and n. 24.

[154] Judith Butler's critique of the belief that there must be 'coherence and continuity among sex, gender, sexual practice and desire' is entirely in keeping with Case's critique of 'gender conformity' (see *Gender Trouble* 17).

[155] As I have shown above, Katherine Franke is utterly in agreement with the critique of 'gender conformity', and the same, I imagine, would be true for Simone de Beauvoir.

Even if we make every effort to distinguish between female and feminine, sex and gender, the problem does not go away. Let us say that I declare that to me, 'feminine characteristics' only mean those characteristics conventionally categorized as feminine, not an eternal feminine essence. This amounts to saying that, ultimately, the word feminine has no necessary relation to the word female.[156] I obviously have the right to define my terms any way I want, but I ought not to be surprised if people fail to get my point. The problem is that once I have said that 'feminine' does not *have to* mean 'pertaining to women', or 'associated with females', it becomes difficult to explain what it *is* supposed to mean. If I speak of a 'feminine mind', and stress (*a*) that both men and women can have this kind of mind, and (*b*) that in a just world women will not have it more often than men, then what exactly am I talking about? Why can't I just *say* 'a subtle mind', 'a forceful mind', or whatever it was that I meant? The only useful answer is that when I say a 'feminine mind' I am referring to some stereotype attributed to women by a certain social group at a certain time. To make myself understood, I shall have to specify what the relevant associations to the word are. A retired woman officer interviewed on National Public Radio about what it was like to join the US Army in 1957 told the journalist: 'I didn't mind when they said I couldn't do this or that because I was too short, or because my eyesight was not good enough, but I always protested when they said I couldn't do something because I was a woman, or because they didn't have enough lavatories.'[157] This woman drew exactly the same distinction I am trying to draw between unwarranted generalizations about women and attention to individual specificity. Like Simone de Beauvoir this woman demonstrates that one does not need to imagine that only people situated entirely beyond sexism, in a space outside our common sexist history, could possibly manage to break the hold of sexist ways of speaking.

[156] Feminists have made a similar criticism of the claim put forward by some Lacanians, namely that the phallus has absolutely nothing to do with the penis. 'Why call it phallus, then?' is the logical reply. To my mind the Lacanians who accept that the phallus does have *something* to do with the penis are on stronger ground than those who don't.

[157] I heard this interview on Sunday 18 Oct. 1997.

If I say 'a woman's mind' or a 'womanly mind' the same questions arise as in the case of 'a feminine mind'. On the other hand, none of this implies that I shouldn't use the word *woman* when I need it. I can happily speak of Simone de Beauvoir as an intellectual *woman*, and of her 'femaleness' or 'femininity' (*féminité* in French, *kvinnelighet* in Norwegian) when I mean the simple fact of being a woman, not some phenomenon that is taken to be an inexorable consequence of this fact. The word 'woman' (or 'women') does not commit me to any specific view as to what women should be like. The problems only start if, like so many critics, we feel compelled to refer to Beauvoir's 'masculine intelligence' or 'feminine anxiety'. The term 'male-identified' is just as ideologically loaded, since it too implies that Beauvoir fails to live up to some stereotypical standard of femininity. But why should feminists want to uphold *any* standard of femininity? There are many good reasons to criticize Beauvoir. But such criticism can only be effective if it formulates specific charges: in my own book on Beauvoir I have claimed, among other things, that she idealizes men; that her fear and loathing of her own mother resurfaces in her theory; that she generalizes more than her own theory would seem to allow her to do; that her use of the concept of 'immanence' is philosophically unsatisfactory. To replace such specific criticisms by general references to Beauvoir's failure or success in conforming to more or less elaborate notions of femininity and masculinity is to contribute to the production of sexist ideology.

'Feminine' and 'masculine' are excellent terms of critique, but I would hesitate to use them positively, to take them as guidelines for my own work. So far at least, it looks as if even the most unsexist search for 'femininity' in literature, film, or other cultural phenomena ends up producing fairly predictable clichés. Seen in the light of such considerations the psychoanalytic concept of femininity becomes terribly difficult to categorize. Should I consider it simply as another reified ideological generalization? Or is it a serious attempt to understand what it might mean to be a woman in the modern world? As Freud himself puts it: 'It is essential to understand clearly that the concepts of "masculine" and "feminine", whose meaning seems so unambiguous to ordinary people, are among the most confused that occur in science' (*Three Essays, SE* 7: 219 n). What phenomenon is a psychoanalyst trying to account for when she speaks about femininity? To what question is 'femininity' the answer? Can all psychoanalytic theorizing about femininity be written off as so much ideological nonsense? Or is that an unfair generalization? There are clear parallels between Freud's case histories and Beauvoir's phenomenological descriptions in *The Second Sex* of the situation of married women, young girls, prostitutes, and so on. Would it be true to say that psychoanalytic theory is simply trying to understand and describe the psychological effects of living in the world in a female body? If so, is the body a situation for Freud as for Beauvoir? But in that case, how general are psychoanalytic accounts of femininity supposed to be? Are they examples of phenomenological descriptions or normative moralizing? And what are we to make of the many different psychoanalytic accounts of femininity, not least those produced by women analysts from Karen Horney, Joan Rivière, and Helene Deutsch to Juliet Mitchell, Françoise Dolto, and Julia Kristeva? Any feminist reassessment of psychoanalytic theory will require answers to such questions, and all I am capable of saying here is that the task of providing them will not be easy.

Beauvoir's denunciation of femininity as a patriarchal concept is a critique of ideology. As such it is still as valid as when it was written. Regardless of whether we believe that masculinity and femininity are manifestations of deep sexual essences or the products of dazzling discursive performances, the very fact of continuing to label qualities and behaviours as 'masculine' and 'feminine' will foster sex-based stereotypes. In *this* context the essence/construction or sex/gender opposition is irrelevant.[158] What I am criticizing here, then, is the belief that the sex/gender

---

[158] French and Norwegian do not have two words for 'feminine': *kvinnelig* and *féminin* mean both 'female' and 'feminine'. Feminists who generalize about *féminité* or *kvinnelighet* encounter exactly the same problems as those who generalize about femininity. The difference is that the speaker cannot assume that the very word she uses automatically signals opposition to biological determinism. This may either make her more careful to specify exactly what she means, or completely oblivious to the whole question.

distinction somehow protects us against oppressive generalizations about sexual difference. The only thing it is designed to
protect us against is biological determinism. This it does quite
efficiently. In contemporary English, feminists are right to think
that although a 'female mind' and a 'feminine mind' may refer to
exactly the same awful beliefs, the two expressions *may* still signal
a different attitude to biology.[159] Oppressive generalizations,
however, are not only produced by the likes of Geddes and
Thomson. Contemporary feminist gender theory runs a close
second when it comes to contributing to our general stock of
nonsensical ideas about 'femininity'.

Here is one example. The Virginia Military Institute (VMI) and
the Citadel are two state-funded military-style American colleges
that until 1996 steadfastly refused to admit women. When they
were sued by rejected female candidates, both schools proposed
to set up new, parallel institutions for women. These would offer
a more 'feminine' leadership training, which although different
in style, would be equal in quality to the training received by the
men. In 1996 the US Supreme Court decided that the proposed
parallel institutions for women did not offer equal educational
opportunities. The schools would have to admit women or lose
their state funding. Case, who was writing before this opinion was
handed down, considers that it would be acceptable to open up
the VMI and the Citadel to members of either sex 'who are appro-
priately gendered, thus both masculine men and masculine
women could attend VMI or the Citadel, while [the parallel insti-
tutions] could admit those of both sexes more suited to or
attracted by a more feminine approach' (105). She is surely right
to say that this would be compatible with current US law. My question, which Case may not be free to address in the context of a
legal essay, is whether this really is desirable feminist politics.

Imagine a scenario in which two schools specializing in 'leadership' are open to both sexes. One school provides a stereotypically 'masculine' education, the other a stereotypically 'feminine'

---

[159] Many speakers of English do not try to distinguish between female and
feminine. In order to find out what words such as feminine and female mean in
a given case, we need to analyse the whole speech act that produced them (to
consider what was said when, to paraphrase J. L. Austin).

education. At the same time, young men and women are classified as being either 'gendered masculine' or 'gendered feminine'. As a result of the classification they will be encouraged to apply to the relevant institution. It is difficult to understand why this will not reinforce stereotypes of femininity and masculinity. Do feminists really want to strengthen the belief that the world contains only two, clearly separable styles of gendered behaviour? (In my experience, even under patriarchy most men and women do not conform to one of two gender stereotypes.) What is feminist about having a system of feminine schools training people of both sexes to become kind and helpful to others, and masculine schools training them to become aggressive, dominant, and competitive? Do we want *anyone* to be trained in any of these ways? How could such institutions avoid reifying and perpetuating the very sex-based stereotypes feminists have argued against for centuries?

For more than twenty years now feminist theorists have characterized women as relational, caring, and nurturing; as mumbling and incoherent; or as always seething with feminist rage, just to mention a few well-known leitmotifs. Since nothing distinguishes them from traditional stereotypes, such 'gender theories' are all too easy to appropriate for sexist purposes. Carol Gilligan's research opposing a masculine 'ethics of justice' to a feminine 'ethics of care' is a good example of this. In the cases against the Citadel and VMI her research was used by the *defence*, in spite of Gilligan's protestations that she in no way intended her research to support all-male institutions.[160] The American broadcasting network NBC drew on the same kind of theories when it planned its condescending, vacuous, and self-styled 'feminine' coverage of the 1996 Summer Olympics. Specially designed to appeal to women, the resulting programming was long on tear-jerking profiles of athletes overcoming everything from cancer to criminal grandparents, and short on actual sports

---

[160] Case is sensitive to the problems raised by Gilligan's theories, but, again, considers that as long as one stresses that one speaks of gender and not sex (masculine and not male), this is not a serious obstacle to agreeing with Gilligan, who did file a brief *against* the all-male schools, protesting against the way they used her research (see Case 98 and n. 345 and 346).

coverage.[161] I hope that the feminist future does not lie with gender stereotypes, however influential they may currently be.

So what is the alternative? Let me suggest that we reconsider Simone de Beauvoir's distinction between detrimental social norms ('myths') incarnated in other people and in institutions, and the individual human being's lived experience. Case writes that she does not 'have as a normative goal the preservation of gender any more than its abolition'.[162] Here it is not clear what gender means: is it stereotypes or lived experience? The same ambiguity runs through all contemporary 'gender theories'. Feminists want to get rid of stereotypes, but nobody has ever proposed giving up lived experience. Sexist ideology attempts to reduce our lived experience to two simple sex-based categories. Beauvoir teaches us that to accept such categorization is alienating and destructive of freedom.[163]

The accountancy firm Price Waterhouse wanted Ann Hopkins to go to 'charm school' before making her a partner. The US Supreme Court found that this was unacceptable, and rightly so. Under contemporary social conditions I have no doubt that male partners in an accountancy firm would be far more likely to require a potential female colleague to be charming than a man. In the social context where the requirement was made, 'charm' was indeed gendered feminine. Yet it is also true that in present-day society 'charm' is not in fact a characteristic that is unique to women, nor one that somehow makes a man less masculine were he to display it. Feminists are not well advised to encourage the belief that there is something particularly feminine about charm. Instead of protecting stereotypically feminine values we should argue that to require an *accountant* to be charming is an irrelevant job requirement, regardless of the sex of the accountant.

    [161] In a scathing *New Yorker* review of NBC's coverage, David Remnick writes: 'In fact, the NBC creed does not depart so much in spirit from a range of feminist theories about differences in gender and narrative' (27). Then follow references to Carol Gilligan, Tania Modleski, and Hélène Cixous (27–8).

    [162] Case 76 n. 258.

    [163] For a more thorough analysis of Beauvoir's concept of alienation, see ch. 6 of my *Simone de Beauvoir*.

Case proposes a strategy in which feminists ask the courts to protect traditionally feminine qualities in men as well as women. To my mind this will have the reactionary effect of forcing more courts, and more people generally, to classify more actions and behaviours as either masculine and feminine. In the attempt to avoid gender stereotyping we will produce more of it. In employment cases, it seems that feminists can only escape this vicious circle by proposing that we should be protected under the law against employers who fire *anyone* (man, woman, gay, heterosexual, transsexual, black, white, working class, disabled, and so on) for reasons that have nothing to do with the requirements of the job. Instead of protecting traditional femininity just because it happens to be traditional femininity, feminists should challenge all unreasonable job requirements. (I realize that US law such as it is today may not allow this.) I agree with Case that it is difficult to believe that an accountant really needs to be 'aggressive' and 'abrasive' to get her job done, I just don't think it will advance our case to harp on the idea that to be aggressive and abrasive is 'unfeminine'. Nor should we go along with the idea that any quality that is not feminine must be masculine. The world is full of more interesting adjectives.

It is by no means certain that it makes sense to try to separate Hopkins's gender from her sex. Feminists have known for years that the same qualities are perceived differently in men and women.[164] It is impossible to categorize any specific quality as masculine or feminine without 'objectifying' it, Beauvoir would say. To imagine that I can determine what counts as feminine in isolation from any particular human situation, is to reify 'femininity'. This is why the lists of 'gender characteristics' quoted above look so absurd. When I meet a charming man or a charming woman, I am incapable of separating the quality of their charm from the fact that the charm comes from a man or a woman. In itself charm is neither feminine nor masculine, neither female nor male. This is what Beauvoir means when she says that the body—the sexually different

---

[164] Case is very well aware of this: 'The same degree of masculinity and femininity is read quite differently in a man and in a woman, as Ann Hopkins learned to her cost' (23).

body—is a fundamental human situation. The meaning of my charm cannot be determined by reference to my body alone, but nor can it be assessed without taking my body into account.[165] The problem with so many contemporary gender theories is that they take a number of qualities that, at best, have been associated with a specific group of women at a specific time and turn them into reified stereotypes, in effect creating new social norms for women to be oppressed by. No wonder such theories are eagerly seized upon by sexists looking for simple solutions to difficult questions.

Because it can refer to 'social stereotypes' or 'dominant gender norms' as well as to an individual's qualities and ways of being, the very word gender lends itself to such reification, in a way that Simone de Beauvoir's distinction between 'lived experience' and 'myths' does not. Ultimately, I think we should follow Gayle Rubin's suggestion and stop thinking in terms of gender altogether. To me, that means trying to produce a society without sexist ideology or gender norms, without oppressive myths of masculinity and femininity. It does not mean that we should stop thinking of the sexually different human body as a fundamental situation that tends to leave its trace on the meaning of our words and actions.[166] The old choice between sameness and difference does not apply here. *The Second Sex* doesn't ask us to choose between a society with or without sexual difference but between one with or without sex-based oppression.

AFTERWORD: THE POINT OF THEORY

In this paper I have asked whether the sex/gender distinction is helpful to a project shared by most contemporary feminist theorists, namely the wish to elaborate a concrete, historically

---

[165] As discussed above (Sect. IV), *within* the category of the body as a situation, or the category of lived experience, Beauvoir does not distinguish between sex and gender.

[166] 'Beauvoir's final message is that sexual difference should be eradicated and women must become like men', Tina Chanter writes (76). That such a good reader of Irigaray can be such a bad reader of Beauvoir indicates that like so many other contemporary feminists, Chanter does not take Beauvoir seriously as a philosopher.

grounded and socially situated understanding of what it means to have a human body. I have shown that the distinction usually dissolves into a scientistic understanding of 'sex' and an idealist understanding of 'gender', and that although poststructuralist sex and gender theorists strive to overcome this problem, they remain caught in the see-saw between scientism and idealism set up by their own understanding of the distinction. By turning to the phenomenological approach of Merleau-Ponty and Beauvoir, I hope to have shown that there are ways to answer the question 'What is a woman?' that escape the constraints both of the sex/gender distinction and the essence/construction opposition. By reflecting on what it means to say that the body is a situation, I have shown that for Beauvoir the question of what a woman is can never have just one answer. *The Second Sex* shows us that what it means to be called a woman, or to call oneself a woman, is a question that cannot be settled once and for all.[167] There is, then, no reason to believe that the word woman is always inherently metaphysical or essentialist. 'In a *large* class of cases . . . the meaning of a word is its use' (*PI* §43).

Poststructuralist theorists declare that the relationship between sex and gender is arbitrary, usually because they see this as the only alternative to the idea that sex necessarily determines gender. Against this, I have claimed that the best defence against biological determinism is to deny that biology grounds or justifies social norms. If we consistently deny this, we do not have to assume that the idea that there are only two sexes must be steeped in sexism and heterosexism. This is not to deny that invocations of nature usually come wrapped up in sexist or heterosexist ideology. To show that ideology is at work in such contexts remains a necessary feminist task. But to claim that sexist and heterosexist ideology often seeks to justify its claims by naturalizing them—by representing social relations as if they were given in nature—is precisely to assume that there is nothing in nature that actually justifies the ideological claims of biological determinists. To be even more precise: my argument is *not* that there is nothing in

---

[167] I investigate some situations in which Beauvoir calls herself a woman, or imagines being called one by others in Ch. 2, below.

nature (i.e. that we have to deny the existence of biological facts), but that whatever there is in nature (whatever facts we may discover about human biology and genetic structure) is never going to justify any *particular* social arrangement. Even if we assume that there are only two sexes, this is no reason not to construct a society with three or five or ten genders, or indeed without gender at all. Or in other words, on my understanding of what the biological facts are, we can never get rid of sex, but we can certainly hope to produce societies that either multiply or eliminate gender. This, precisely, is the logical consequence of denying that biology justifies social norms. The power of the sex/gender distinction is that it is one way of saying precisely this. What the sex/gender distinction does not provide, however, is a good theory of subjectivity or a useful understanding of the body.

Instead of speaking in terms of sex and gender, I have found it useful to speak in terms of bodies and subjectivity. What Merleau-Ponty and Beauvoir show is that the relationship between body and subjectivity is neither necessary nor arbitrary, but contingent. For these thinkers the body is fundamentally ambiguous, neither simply subject to the natural laws of cause and effect that science might uncover, nor simply an effect of consciousness (or of power, ideology, or regulatory discourses, for that matter). When Merleau-Ponty writes that 'man is a historical idea and not a natural species', he does not mean to say that human bodies are not natural at all, but rather that our nature is to be historical beings. His project is to expand our understanding of nature, to wrench it away from the deadening hand of positivism and scientism by showing that in so far as the human body is concerned, one can draw no clear-cut line between that which belongs to the realm of nature and that which belongs to the realm of meaning. This is what he means when he speaks of the *ambiguity* of human existence. On this account, the human body is neither sex nor gender, neither nature nor culture. To say that my subjectivity stands in a contingent relationship to my body is to acknowledge that my body will significantly influence both what society—others—make of me, and the kind of choices I will make in response to the Other's image of me, but it is also to acknowledge that no specific form of subjectivity is ever a necessary consequence of having a particular body.

No theory of bodies and subjectivity is of any use if it does not yield significant understanding of concrete cases. To challenge the ideas in this essay, it would be useful to see if they would help to understand transsexuality. Transsexuals are usually defined as persons who feel that their sex does not correspond to their gender, and who wish to undergo hormone treatment and surgery in order to align their sex with their gender. As I have shown, the sex/gender distinction was first invented by medical personnel working with transsexuals and intersexed persons. The distinction emerged in the 1950s and early 1960s in response to the new medical technologies developed after World War II (hormone treatment, new and improved techniques of plastic surgery). Thus the very existence of the concept of the 'transsexual' depends on a distinction I think is useless for the understanding of lived experience. What would happen if one tried to understand transsexuality in completely different terms?

This is a more contentious question than it might seem. For the very language of sex and gender is a language that implies that sex is a matter of body parts, and that gender is 'everything else'. This language produces a picture of human bodies and subjectivity that makes it appear meaningful to call a certain number of medical procedures a sex change. Many transsexuals fear that unless one accepts the standard definitions of sex and gender and also believes that the relationship between sex and gender is absolutely arbitrary, it will become impossible to justify their demand for surgical transformation of the body. My critique of the sex/gender distinction, on the other hand, makes the very meaning of the term *sex change* problematic. When the sex/gender distinction disappears, it is no longer obvious what one desires when one desires a sex change. It does not follow, of course, that so-called sex-change operations are unjustified. What their purpose and meaning might be, would precisely be the subject of a phenomenological account of transsexuality.

The method such an account would employ would have much in common with Simone de Beauvoir's method in *The Second Sex*. One would have to study historical and legal material in order to establish what social norms and expectations transsexuals encounter, read fiction and watch films to discover something about the cultural signification of sex changes, and examine medical material in order to understand what interventions a sex change requires, and what the medical consequences actually are. Psychoanalytic and psychiatric case studies would be central to the project. Perhaps most important of all would be autobiographies, memoirs, and other texts written by transsexuals, as well as interviews and conversations with them. It goes without saying that the differences between transsexuals, transvestites, and other transgendered people would need to be taken into account. Such an investigation might help explain why it is that the number of people who want to change their sex is steadily increasing. If one could understand what the wish to become a woman represents for someone who started out in life as a man, one would perhaps also understand why it is that so many women never wish to change their sex. In short, a serious attempt to understand the transsexual's project and situation in the world would provide a deeper understanding than a purely theoretical essay like this one of what it means to claim that the sexed body is a situation.

I just mentioned psychoanalytic theory and case studies as a valuable source of insight about transsexuality. Among transsexuals, however, there is considerable hostility towards psychoanalysis. I suspect that some transsexuals' worries are based on the fact that, like existentialism, psychoanalysis has no use for the sex/gender distinction. The fear is that any psychoanalytic account of the desire to change one's sex *must* lead to the conclusion that transsexuality is a psychiatric condition, and that all that is required to make the transsexual 'normal' is a good bout of analytic therapy. I don't think this is necessarily the case.[168] In general, transsexual arguments against psychoanalysis are similar to feminist arguments against psychoanalysis, and I shall not go into them here.

---

[168] Even Catherine Millot, a French psychoanalyst highly sceptical of the transsexual's claim to have a firm and non-contradictory gender identity, does not doubt that surgical interventions can have psychological effects: 'Gabriel's [Gabriel is the pseudonym of a female-to-male transsexual] operations seem in any case to have modified his subjective position. . . . The possibility of intervention in the real having effects on the symbolic plane cannot be excluded' (135–6).

Just as I have not engaged with psychoanalysis in this paper, I have not discussed sexuality in the sense of sexual desire or sexual orientation. This is because I consider the relationship between the body and sexuality to be as contingent as the rest. Neither heterosexuality nor homosexuality is inscribed in the structure of our bodies. Even if scientists were to find the infamous 'gay gene', it would not follow that everyone who had it would choose the same sexual practices, or that sexuality would have the same meaning for them. This is what Merleau-Ponty means when he says that the body—including our genes and chromosomes—is fundamentally ambiguous. Precisely because Beauvoir stresses over and over again that biology provides no foundation for social norms, her understanding of the body provides no justification for sexual bigotry and oppressive gender norms.

Since heterosexism and homophobia are the effects of social norms for sexuality and sexual practices, it makes a great deal of sense to consider such questions under the rubric of 'gender', as long as we are aware that 'gender' here means 'social norms', 'ideology', 'power', or 'regulatory discourses', and that such terms do not tell us all that much about bodies. That an individual's encounter with such social norms has consequences for the way she will experience her body and for the kind of subjectivity she will develop is precisely Beauvoir's and Merleau-Ponty's point. But their point is also that different individuals will respond in different ways to the same coercive pressure. Freud could have said the same thing. To put this in Beauvoir's terms: although social norms concerning sex and sexuality are of crucial importance to the formation of a given person's subjectivity, an account of such norms and regulations will not in itself explain that person's lived experience. We are continuously making something of what the world continuously makes of us: our subjectivity is always a becoming that neither precedes nor follows from the encounter with the Other.

When Beauvoir says 'I am a woman', she is not saying that she is a creature that in every respect conforms to the dominant gender norms of her society. She is making the verb signify existence, and existence is always a becoming, a process that only comes to an end in death. To say that existence precedes essence is not to say that it replaces or obliterates it. 'I am a woman' also means 'There are women in the world, and I am one of them'.[169] Given that existence precedes essence, however, the fact that I am a woman does not tell you what kind of a woman I am. Stereotyping of any kind is incompatible with Beauvoir's understanding of what a woman is. The opposition between identity and difference is not central to Beauvoir's feminism; the concepts of freedom, alienation, and oppression are. Beauvoir's fundamental value is not identity, but freedom, and for Beauvoir freedom is a universal value: if it is good for women and feminists, it is because it is good for everyone.

In my discussion of poststructuralist sex and gender theory I have not been trying to contest the political aims of the theorists in question: my argument is, on the contrary, that those aims appear to be compatible with those of non-poststructuralist feminists from Beauvoir to Rubin. For this very reason it becomes important to challenge the theoreticism of poststructuralist feminist theory, that is to say the belief that certain theoretical positions function as guarantees of one's radical political credentials. The poststructuralist theorists who appear to believe that a general account of meaning or reference (interpretivism, realism, nominalism, etc.) *must* have a necessary set of political implications have yet to make a convincing case for their claims. They also have yet to show why questions of materiality and the inside and outside of discourse must be settled in the correct way in order to enable us to make politically acceptable claims about bodies, sex, and gender. The attempt to lay down theoretical requirements for what politically 'good' theory *must* look like regardless of the actual situation in which one is trying to intervene, is idealist and metaphysical to the core.

The point of doing a critical analysis of some of the presuppositions of poststructuralist thinking about sex, gender, and the body is to free us (I mean anyone who has ever been caught up in it, including myself) from a theoretical picture that tells us how things *must* be, and so blinds us to alternative ways of thinking. One such picture is the idea that we *must* think in terms of the

---

[169] I return to this claim in Ch. 2, below.

sex/gender distinction as soon as we are interested in questions of sexual difference. What I have done here is to show that in the case of a question that truly matters to me, namely 'What is a woman?', there are good reasons to consider alternatives to the sex/gender distinction. I have not tried to lay down some *other* set of requirements for how things must be. In particular, I have not suggested—and I do not think—that the sex/gender distinction is always useless. On the contrary, I think it is useful when it comes to opposing biological determinism à la Geddes and Thomson, for example. Others may be able to show that it also excels in other, specific contexts.

For Wittgenstein, the role of philosophy is to be therapeutic, to produce a diagnosis of the theoretical pictures that hold us captive, not in order to refute them, but in order to make us aware of other options: 'A *picture* held us captive. And we could not get outside it, for it lay in our language and language seemed to repeat it to us inexorably' (*PI* §115). The aim of his own thought is to reach 'perspicuous representation [*übersichtliche Darstellung*]' (*PI* §122). Once we see things clearly, Wittgenstein believes, all specifically philosophical problems fall away. 'For the clarity that we are aiming at is indeed complete clarity. But this simply means that the philosophical problems should completely disappear' (*PI* §133). Here it may be useful to recall that Wittgenstein thinks of a philosophical problem as a question that arises when we are lost in a kind of linguistic fog. What characterizes such questions is that they have no satisfactory answer because they have no clear meaning (see *PI* §5). Wittgenstein pictures the clearing of the fog as an intellectual liberation: we are released from the linguistic shackles that hold us captive. There is no loss here, since all that has disappeared is nonsense. Once we manage to escape from the picture that held us captive, we are released from the futile task of trying to answer questions that can have no answers because they do not make sense. Rather than solving the problem we struggled with, Wittgenstein's therapy makes it fall away. We see, as it were, that the problem was the way we posed the problem. Once we realize this, it is pointless to remain obsessed with the old problem. We find that we are free to ask new questions. To anyone who has experienced the effects of psychoanalysis, Wittgenstein's account of how philosophical therapy works will sound quite familiar.

Yet Wittgenstein does not believe that the fog can be cleared once and for all. New situations and new confusions will always arise. There will always be a need for philosophical therapy. This means that in the very act of asking a new question we risk succumbing to new confusions, to lock ourselves up in new prison-houses of language. The task is always to try to produce language that makes sense as opposed to what Wittgenstein calls 'language on holiday', that is to say, language that does no work for us (see *PI* §38).[170] The way I understand Wittgenstein, this task is at once intellectual and ethical; it is always with us; it can never be done once and for all. Serious intellectual work would seem to have much in common with housework.[171]

It would be nice if 'feminist theory' could eventually come to mean a kind of thought that seeks to dispel confusions concerning bodies, sex, sexuality, sexual difference, and the power relations between and among women and men, heterosexuals and homosexuals. Such theory would aim to release us from the metaphysical pictures that hold us captive, and so return our words to the sphere of the ordinary, that is to say the sphere in which our political and personal struggles actually take place. 'What *we* do is to bring words back from their metaphysical to their everyday use' (*PI* §116). Such a course of philosophical therapy would help feminist critics and theorists not to get lost in meaningless questions and pointless arguments, and enable us instead to raise genuine questions about things that really matter.

---

[170] Specialized languages—those of chemistry and infinitesimal calculus, for example—are part of ordinary language. Such languages are to be pictured as 'suburbs of our language', Wittgenstein writes in a passage where he likens our language to an 'ancient city': 'a maze of little streets and squares, of old and new houses, and of houses with additions from various periods; and this surrounded by a multitude of new boroughs with straight regular streets and uniform houses' (*PI* §18). I discuss the meaning of 'ordinary language' more fully in Ch. 2, below.

[171] New paths seem to have led me back to an old idea. In the introduction to my *Simone de Beauvoir* I also compare my intellectual approach to housework (see 8).

'I Am a Woman':
The Personal and the Philosophical

If any individual—Samuel Pepys or Jean-Jacques Rousseau, mediocre or exceptional—reveals himself with sincerity, almost everyone is called into question. It is impossible to shed light on one's own life without at some point illuminating the life of others.

Simone de Beauvoir[1]

All the philosopher, this kind of philosopher, can do is to express, as fully as he can, his world, and attract our undivided attention to our own.

Stanley Cavell[2]

INTRODUCTION

'I now tend to think that theory itself, at least as it is usually practiced, may be one of the patriarchal gestures women *and* men ought to avoid', Jane Tompkins writes in 'Me and My Shadow', her controversial defence of the inclusion of the personal in literary criticism (122). I am writing this essay because I am a woman and a feminist who has written and intends to continue to write theory. If I were to accept Jane Tompkins's view, I would have to give up writing theory altogether.[3] 'But Tompkins is just

I am grateful to Stanley Cavell for his generous response to this essay. Terry Eagleton, Hazel Rowley, Kate Soper, Martin Stone, and Lisa Van Alstyne also provided valuable last minute feedback.

   [1] I have translated Beauvoir's 'tout le monde, plus ou moins, se trouve mis en jeu' as 'almost everyone is called into question' (*PL* 10; *FA* 1; TA).

   [2] 'Aesthetic Problems of Modern Philosophy', in *Must We* 96.

   [3] The title of this essay is 'The Personal and the Philosophical'. It could just as well have been called 'The Personal and the Theoretical'. The former is more suitable for the second half dealing with Simone de Beauvoir, the latter would

an anti-intellectual', some would surely say, 'why do you want to take her so seriously?'

Tompkins's point of view cannot be dismissed out of hand. In different ways and different formulations, her worries about the oppressive effects of theory are shared by a large number of literary critics. Postmodern theory declares that all knowledge is situated or 'located', tied to specific subject positions, imbricated in particular contexts of power, subversion, and resistance.[4] Summarizing the dominant trend, David Simpson writes that the 'contemporary notion [is] that all knowledge claims must be accompanied by or seen as consisting in a rhetoric of speaking personally and saying where one is coming from' (78). Most critics link the demand for subjectivity to a general postmodern scepticism about claims to objective knowledge. Given the postmodern understanding of what knowledge is, how can I pretend to make 'objective' or 'universal' statements? How can I possibly imagine that I am speaking for anyone but myself? On the other hand there is no such thing as a theoretical statement that does not lay claim to general validity. The claim that 'knowledge is always situated' is itself as universalizing and generalizing as the claim that 'knowledge is never situated'. The universalism of theory is not undermined by producing theory that universalizes the local, the specific, and the subjective. This essay is an attempt to think through the relationship between the personal (subjectivity) and theory. I hope that this investigation will help me to find a way to write theory without neglecting or repressing the claims of the personal, the local, and the specific, but also without dismissing or diminishing the claims of the impersonal, the objective, and the universal.

---

fit the first half better. For the purposes of my project in this essay, there is no important distinction to be drawn between the two terms. I think of what I write as 'theory'. At the same time, a lot of the texts I am inspired by and learn from, not least those of Simone de Beauvoir, are conventionally known as 'philosophy'.

4 I use the term 'postmodern theory' fairly loosely. I just mean various kinds of recent theories that tend to stress that knowledge is local, specific, subjective, relative, and so on.

The questions of subjectivity and the locatedness of knowledge are central in the postmodern tradition. Yet postmodern theory generalizes as much as the theories it wishes to supplant. Moreover, much contemporary theory often gives the impression of preaching to the converted. Descartes, who starts from first principles, is more fun to read, not to mention a genuine Enlightenment thinker such as Rousseau with all his universalist pronunciations. Such texts invite passionate reactions, comments, and critical discussion in a way that much recent theory often does not. Reading the section devoted to Sophie in *Émile*, for example, everyone in my class instantly understood why it inspired Mary Wollstonecraft to write *Vindication of the Rights of Woman*. Our own reactions to Rousseau helped us not only to get something out of his text, but to read Wollstonecraft's writing with deeper understanding as well. What characterizes both Rousseau and Wollstonecraft is their passionate engagement in the questions they explore. Engagement is always personal. If there is no engagement in the writing, it is difficult to produce engagement in the reader, and without engagement there is usually little thought and no political commitment. If one wants to find out how to write theory in a way that acknowledges the claims of the personal, questions about philosophical or theoretical tone, style, and voice are going to be as important as questions about 'speaking position' or 'location' or 'where one is coming from'.

Like other theorists, I have no wish to write in a way that is falsely universalizing, exclusionary, arrogant, and domineering. Yet the fact remains that it is impossible to write theory without generalizing and universalizing. Is it possible to write theory in a way that overcomes the apparent conflict between the general and the particular, the third person and the first person? How do I write theory in a personal voice? How do I write theory without losing myself and alienating my readers in the process?

Because my focus is on theory, I am not going to discuss interesting recent attempts to produce new kinds of personal memoirs and intellectual autobiographies such as my colleague Alice Kaplan's *French Lessons* or Deborah McDowell's *Leaving Pipe*

Shop.[5] And although theory is produced in all kinds of disciplines, I am going to stick to a loosely defined field stretching from literary theory to philosophy.[6] This may sound unduly conservative. Am I not imprisoning myself in traditional disciplinary thinking? Have I no understanding of the need to cross and break up generic and disciplinary boundaries? Do I really believe that there is no 'theory' in an autobiography? Think of St Augustine! Clearly, literary and autobiographical work offer thoughtful analyses of philosophical and theoretical questions. I regularly teach Ibsen's *A Doll's House* alongside Hegel on women and Milton on divorce, precisely because each text, regardless of genre, is at work on the same set of problems. This can be done,

---

[5] I see Carolyn Steedman's *Landscape for a Good Woman* as a more explicitly theoretical kind of book than the two I mention here. I want to acknowledge the importance of Steedman's attempt to write on the margins of autobiography, history, and psychoanalysis in order to understand the factors that shaped her own life and that of her mother. Her book was an inspiration for my very different attempt to understand the making of Simone de Beauvoir as an intellectual woman. My question in this essay, however, is not about the making of subjectivity, but about the writing of theory.

[6] Different disciplinary starting points tend to produce somewhat different questions, and a different sense of what counts as relevant answers. On one level, the anthropologist Ruth Behar's account of her difficult relationship to 'scientific' writing has much in common with Jane Tompkins's frustrations with literary theory (see Behar, *Translated* 330–1). On another level, however, Behar's 'vulnerable writing', defined as writing in which she tries to 'make my emotions part of my ethnography' (*Vulnerable* 18) cannot be properly understood without paying attention to the fact that Behar starts from the discipline of anthropology, which she describes as 'this business of humans observing other humans in order to write about them' (*Vulnerable* 5). Literary criticism and theory work on texts, not other people. A literary critic is not a 'participant observer' and the question of 'how women are to make other women the subjects of their gaze without objectifying them and thus ultimately betraying them' does not arise in the same way for a literary critic as for an anthropologist (*Vulnerable* 28). For Jane Tompkins to include her emotions in literary criticism is not necessarily the same gesture as for Ruth Behar to do so in her book on the life of a Mexican street peddler (see ch. 17 of *Translated* 320–42). To me, the most striking difference is the fact that Behar does not worry about 'theory', but about 'science', 'neutral observation', and 'impersonality'. On the other hand, both Tompkins and Behar agree that to be personal is to be autobiographical and particularly to reveal one's own emotions. A more thorough comparison of Tompkins and Behar might yield interesting insights about the difference that disciplinarity makes. I am grateful to Kathy Rudy for bringing Behar's work to my attention.

however, without making any claims as to whether *Phenomenology of Spirit* and *A Doll's House* break disciplinary boundaries or established generic divisions.

My main example in this essay will be Simone de Beauvoir's *The Second Sex*, which in itself is a perfect example of interdisciplinarity, a text that breaks down a host of generic boundaries as it freely moves to and from literature, memoirs, sociology, psychoanalysis, medicine, biology, history, art, and philosophy. Yet at the same time it is a marvellous attempt to write philosophy in a new key, an attempt so revolutionary that in the fifty years since its publication it has only recently come to be accepted (and then only in some quarters) *as* philosophy. If we are to break boundaries and undermine the existing *doxa*, we will surely do so not by proclamation but, like Simone de Beauvoir, as a result of asking questions that turn out to have no traditional disciplinary answer.[7]

Finally, I should say that there is nothing intrinsically feminist about the question of how to write theory in an intellectual situation marked by various forms of postmodern scepticism about knowledge. But, as Simone de Beauvoir might have said, it is significant that I, who happen to be a feminist, raise it. In contemporary theory feminists brought the question of the relationship between subjectivity and knowledge to the forefront of intellectual debate well before it became a fashionable postmodern issue. In this essay I shall frequently be drawing on feminist examples, simply because they readily come to mind. I also hope that the questions I raise will inspire others to consider whether my analyses are relevant in their own fields of interest.[8]

This essay falls in two main sections. Section II reads the first few pages of *The Second Sex* as an example of writing that is both personal and philosophical. Section I takes a closer look at contemporary accounts of the personal and the theoretical. I

[7] See Ch. 4 below, for Bourdieu's definition of *doxa*.

[8] As I was reading a review of books on the pedagogy of mathematics, I discovered that a number of the questions I raise in this essay (When does it make sense to 'get personal'? When is it relevant to stress location or subject position? When does personal anecdote and narrative deepen our understanding of a subject and when does it not?) appear to be relevant to ongoing debates about the teaching of mathematics in the USA. Only a maths teacher could tell me whether this is a superficial impression (see Gardner, 'The New New Math').

shall start by returning to 'Me and My Shadow', to find out what Jane Tompkins thinks the personal is, and what it has to do with the theoretical.

I. CONTEMPORARY THEORY

'All Alone and Feeling Blue'

Picking up a volume by Félix Guattari, Tompkins quickly puts it down in disgust. To her, the text exemplifies male theory speech. 'I find this language incredibly alienating', she writes. 'What strikes me now is the incredibly distancing effect of this language. It is totally abstract and impersonal' (131). Tompkins is angry with men for belittling women, and with theorists for belittling emotion:

> The disdain for popular psychology and for words like 'love' and 'giving' is part of the police action that academic intellectuals wage ceaselessly against feeling, against women, against what is personal. The ridiculing of the 'touchy-feely', of the 'Mickey Mouse', of the sentimental . . . belongs to the tradition Alison Jaggar rightly characterized as founding knowledge in the denial of emotion. It is looking down on women, with whom feelings are associated, and on the activities with which women are identified: mother, nurse, teacher, social worker, volunteer. So for a while I can't talk about epistemology. I can't deal with the philosophical bases of feminist literary criticisms. . . . I have to deal with the trashing of emotion, and with my anger against it (138).

According to this view, to engage in academic intellectualizing is to trash emotions and reject the 'touchy-feely', the sentimental, and, by association, women.[9] For Tompkins, the personal means above all the emotional and the sentimental, but also the private. Splitting herself in two, the professional critic and the private person ('me and my shadow'), she describes the latter as someone who 'talks on the telephone a lot to her friends, has seen psychiatrists, likes cappuccino, worries about the state of her soul. Her father is ill right now, and one of her friends recently

---

[9] As examples of off-putting theoretical writing, Tompkins quotes two philosophers and one literary critic (Guattari, Foucault, and Harold Bloom).

committed suicide' (122). Tompkins's plea for a 'personal criticism' is a plea for a criticism that would allow her to talk about herself and to identify with the experience of others:

> I think readers want to know about each other. Sometimes, when a writer introduces some personal bit of story into an essay, I can hardly contain my pleasure. I love writers who write about their own experience. I feel I am being nourished by them, that I'm being allowed to enter into a personal relationship with them. That I can match my own experience up with theirs, feel cousin to them, and say, yes, that's how it is (123).[10]

So Tompkins includes information about 'herself as a person', sitting at her desk writing the essay we are reading:

> Most of all, I don't know how to enter the debate [about epistemology] without leaving everything else behind—the birds outside my window, my grief over Janice, just myself as a person sitting here in stockinged feet, a little bit chilly because the windows are open, and thinking about going to the bathroom. But not going yet (126).

> This is what I want you to see. A person sitting in stockinged feet looking out of her window—a floor to ceiling rectangle filled with green, with one red leaf. The season poised, sunny and chill, ready to rush down the incline into autumn. But perfect and still. Not going yet (128).

I first read 'Me and My Shadow' in a manuscript version given to me by Jane Tompkins in the autumn of 1987, when I was visiting Duke University for the first time and had just started to think about my book on Simone de Beauvoir. Jane had been very welcoming to me. She and I had gone to yoga classes together. We also shared an interest in meditation. But this essay confounded me. Suddenly it was as if we were living on different intellectual planets. I felt that Jane was telling me that what I wanted to do—to think clearly about questions considered theoretical—was patriarchal to the core, and that there was no way for a woman to think theoretically without excluding her body, her emotions, her experiences. I felt that Jane was telling me that

---

[10] Tompkins later abandoned criticism for autobiography. In her memoir *A Life in School* she explains why.

systematic thought is and always will be the enemy of emotion, that there is no way of writing theory without producing alienation in oneself and others, and, in particular, that women (let alone feminists) who love theory are alienated, male-identified, and necessarily oppressive of other women. And so, to my dismay, Jane's essay made me feel that there was an unbridgeable gulf between us, that just as I could not understand why she wanted to set up such an absolute divide between thought and feelings, she could never understand my passion for theory, or for Simone de Beauvoir for that matter.

Jane Tompkins's delight in reading about the experience of others is based on the assumption that she will recognize her own in it, to be able to exclaim: 'yes, that's how it is'. But could she really recognize herself in Simone de Beauvoir's experience of falling in love with philosophy at the age of 16? In *Memoirs of a Dutiful Daughter*, Beauvoir tells us that even the boring and unadventurous philosophy lessons dispensed by the abbé Trécourt at her very Catholic girls' school allowed her to catch a glimpse of a different world, to realize that philosophy had the power to challenge everything she had been taught in her pious childhood, and everything she thought she knew about herself:

> the world of the grown-ups was no longer self-evident; it had another side, an underside, doubt was creeping in: if one went even further, what would be left? We did not, of course, go very far, but it was already quite extraordinary, after twelve years of dogmatism, to find a discipline that asked questions, and asked them of *me*. For suddenly my own self, hitherto only spoken of in commonplaces, was being challenged [*mise en cause*]. My consciousness— where did it come from? Where did it get its powers? ... Henri Poincaré's speculations on the relativity of space and time and measurements plunged me into endless meditations. I was moved by the pages where he evoked man passing through a blind universe: only a flash, but a flash that is everything! For a long time I was haunted by the image of this great fire blazing in the dark.[11]

---

[11] This passage comes from *MJF* (219–20). I am providing my own translation (see *MDD* 157–8 for the highly inadequate published translation). Over and over again I discover that even otherwise acceptable English translations of Beauvoir's works fall apart as soon as she starts using a philosophical vocabulary.

The young Simone de Beauvoir was deeply moved by the power of philosophy. It stirred her imagination, and allowed her to hope for liberation from her stifling Catholic environment. It didn't occur to her to consider Poincaré's speculations alien or irrelevant to her own concerns. She *was* that flash blazing in the dark: to her, philosophy was poetry. Beauvoir never lost the sense that philosophy was magical and poetic, and had the power to help her understand her own life. 'In truth there is no divorce between philosophy and life', she noted in 1948, as she was busy writing *The Second Sex* (*L'existentialisme et la sagesse des nations*, 12). Throughout the 1930s and the 1940s Beauvoir wrote in cafés where she also met her friends and lovers and conducted her professional life. The way she organized her everyday life reinforced her sense that life and philosophy were interconnected. In Beauvoir's writing, her philosophical imagination is constantly at work on material from ordinary life, turning everyday life into philosophy in *The Second Sex*, and showing us the philosophical significance of lived experience in *Memoirs of a Dutiful Daughter*.[12]

The young Simone's experience of the power, poetry, and personal challenge of philosophy is at odds with Jane Tompkins's experience of theory as repressive, alienating, and misogynist. Tompkins recommends that women turn their backs on the very theory Beauvoir delights in. According to her analysis, Beauvoir's passion for philosophy does not count as a genuine feeling, but rather as a sign of her alienated identification with male values. Paradoxically, Tompkins's respect for her own personal experience prevents her from respecting that of her illustrious predecessor. Locked into their different experiences Jane and Simone are stuck: there is, apparently, no possibility of further communication. In *Getting Personal*, Nancy Miller writes: ' "Just me and my shadow, walkin' down the avenue." The next line of the song goes, "Me and my shadow, all alone and feeling blue." But is the personal critic necessarily alone, immured in isolation?' (23). This is an excellent question. As long as the advocates of

---

[12] Francis Jeanson's reading of *Memoirs of a Dutiful Daughter* remains a masterly elucidation of the way in which the text embodies philosophy. An important excerpt of Jeanson's book is now available in English, in Elizabeth Fallaize (ed.), *Simone de Beauvoir: A Critical Reader*.

personal criticism turn self-contained individual experience into the linchpin of truth and reality, the answer is yes.[13] Cut off from dialogue, immured in her own experience, the personal critic will indeed be 'all alone and feeling blue'. Finding herself, the personal critic loses her connectedness to others.

Tompkins longs for the concrete and the everyday. Yet her defence of the personal remains as general and abstract as the theory she is attacking. For does it really make sense to claim that theory—all theory—is inherently oppressive, male, alienating, and so on? Are not the effects of theory dependent on what the theory says, who reads it, and in what context? In the section of her essay where she discusses some examples of theoretical writing, namely texts by Guattari, Foucault, Harold Bloom, and Jessica Benjamin, Tompkins herself recognizes that the effects of theory are enormously varied. Jessica Benjamin's essay on erotic domination is the only one to catch her imagination. On closer inspection, however, it turns out to be a theoretical essay without any personal narrative or self-revealing glimpses of the author. So, Tompkins muses, perhaps Guattari just adores reading sentences containing the words machine, structure, and determination, excitedly muttering 'Great stuff. Juicy, terrific', to himself as he goes (134):

> I will concede the point. What is personal is completely a function of what is perceived as personal. And what is perceived as personal by men, or rather, what is gripping, significant, 'juicy', is different from what is felt to be that way by women. For what we are really talking about is not the personal as such, what we are talking about is what is important, answers one's needs, strikes one as immediately *interesting*. For women, the personal is such a category (134).

The right to define what is to count as interesting has always been fought over in the academy. Bourdieu would call it the struggle for distinction, and Tompkins is right to say that some

---

[13] Nancy Miller answers no: 'I would rather argue that this mode of criticism, far from being turned in on itself . . . is on the contrary, to bring back an old-fashioned word: engaged' (24). I agree that engagement is personal, but all personal writing is not necessarily *politically* engaged. Unfortunately, Miller chooses not to pursue her wonderful intuition about the loneliness of the personal critic any further.

people use their power to impose their own interests on others. That 'theory' has been used in this way in the American academy over the past two or three decades is clearly true. Yet there are two conflicting meanings of 'personal' at work here. If we use the word 'personal' to describe *whatever* we find interesting (so that if I am passionate about machines, or theory, then machines, or theory, are 'personal' to me), then the personal can't be of greater immediate interest and relevance for women than for men. In fact, on this definition the personal doesn't even have to be personal. Tompkins's argument, after all, is that the problem for women in academia is that men, precisely because they feel passionately interested in Guattari, or Foucault, or Harold Bloom, display a chilling disdain for women and the emotions associated with them. If, on the other hand, we stick to the definitions operative everywhere else in the essay, namely that in scholarly (literary and theoretical) texts, the personal means (1) emotion and sentiment, or (2) autobiographical information, or (3) any reference to actual persons, concrete situations, and everyday life, then the claim that the personal is always of particular interest to women is simply too sweeping to be true.

Tompkins's essay does seem to be thoroughly anti-intellectual. It casts me—and Simone de Beauvoir, and any other woman who loves theory and philosophy—as some kind of intellectual police force waging war against everything she passionately wishes to include in her own writing. Beauvoir and I become the twin incarnations of death-dealing, male-identified theoretical alienation. 'Me and My Shadow' is a very angry text: 'The rage I feel inside me now is the distillation of forty-six years. It has had a long time to simmer, to harden, to become adamantine, a black slab that glows in the dark', she writes (137). For a long time I simply could not deal with this essay. Although I felt deeply challenged by Tompkins's views, I had no idea how to respond to such anger. Back in 1987 I just put the essay aside, probably disappointing her by giving her no response at all.

Yet 'Me and My Shadow' stayed with me. For although I was truly upset at the way the essay seemed to want to block women from access to theory and philosophy, I actually agreed that Jane Tompkins had identified a major problem in contemporary theory, namely the tendency to produce alienating, obfuscating, and off-putting language. And I also *almost* agreed with her point about emotions. I would say that emotional responses to texts, whether literary or theoretical, are good starting points for further investigation, in which we go on to work hard to widen and deepen the emotional response through deeper understanding. By deepening our thought we can also deepen our feelings. To respond emotionally to a text is to care about it. If the response is boredom, that is also an emotion, and usually signals disengagement from the text. As such it is as analysable as rage or delight. Some texts deserve an enraged or a bored response, others do not: the intellectual challenge is to show why or why not. If a student feels enraged by Rousseau's treatment of Sophie, she can go on to find out what it is in the text that makes her react that way, what the alternatives might have been, how other people reacted at the time and how they react now, and so on.

Where I disagreed with Tompkins was in the assumption that serious and systematic thought somehow must block access to genuine emotions, so that the two become mortal enemies. The alienation I too detect in quite a lot of contemporary theory is not absent from certain kinds of autobiographical criticism. Instead of alienating oneself in a theoretical vocabulary, or in a picture of oneself as a Great Theorist, one alienates oneself in a picture of oneself as a Uniquely Interesting Human Being. (Simone de Beauvoir's analysis of narcissism in *The Second Sex* is pertinent here.) The two forms of alienation can be equally effective in making the reader wonder why she should bother to read another sentence of this kind of material.[14] Although Tompkins's solution

---

[14] The anthropologist Ruth Behar recommends 'vulnerable' writing, that is to say writing that reveals the anthropologist's own emotions, in ways that reminds me of Tompkins. Yet she also worries about the limits of the practice: 'Even I, a practitioner of vulnerable writing, am sometimes at a loss to say how much emotion is bearable within academic settings,' Behar writes (*Vulnerable* 17). Then she tells the story of a colleague's heart-rending paper which started out as ethnography but ended with the woman's own experience of being beaten by a former husband. Behar writes: 'When my colleague had finished speaking, a terrible silence, like a dark storm cloud, descended upon everyone. A part of me wished the cavern in the middle of the room would open up and swallow us all, so we wouldn't have to speak' (*Vulnerable* 17). This story is food for thought.

(to turn her back on theory) was wrong, I thought, her sense that there was a problem was right. There *is* something wrong with the way a lot of theory is written these days. An increasing number of intellectual women from different disciplines tell me that they have given up reading feminist theory because it seems obscure, abstruse, and removed from their interests and experiences. Such common experiences cannot all be due to the limitations of the readers.

Changing social conditions explain some aspects of the problem. Without a powerful women's movement, feminist intellectuals no longer have a strong sense of constituency. Writing for the narrower audience of the academy, the feminist intellectual is justified in using a more specialized language than she might have done in the 1970s. But this is not all there is to it. Nowadays even highly educated women who take a strong interest in feminism, tell me they can't bear to labour through another obscure and theory-laden book on the subject. Some such complaints may well be motivated by laziness or anti-intellectual prejudice, and have no claim to be taken seriously. Moreover, many books are justifiably written for specialists in narrow fields: it would be ridiculous to complain about obscurity just because I don't instantly understand the language in a book devoted to medieval theology, or to the finer points of the philosophy of Quine, or Deleuze for that matter. In any case, the problem of obscurity can't be reduced to a question of specialist vocabularies. Carefully defined terms used stringently are per definition not unclear, however difficult and specialized they may be. It is impossible to assess the effects of a theoretical style without asking who the theory is addressed to, and what it actually is about. There can be no question of setting up some general rule for *the* correct way to write theory.[15]

The problem of off-putting obscurity arises most urgently in the case of theory that wishes to make a political or cultural

---

What exactly went wrong in the seminar presentation? Why was silence—the wish not to engage in conversation—the dominant response? When (under what circumstances) is 'vulnerability'—in this case, heart-rending emotional openness—neither useful nor productive?

[15] Different subject matter usually gives rise to somewhat different style or tone, even in texts written by the same author at roughly the same time.

difference in the world beyond the academy, but which is written in such a way that it fails to reach more than a highly specialized and elite audience. Theory does not have to be ponderous to read. Some contemporary US feminists, such as Elaine Showalter, Camille Paglia, and Catharine MacKinnon are capable of writing with admirable wit and sharpness of style.[16] Historically, many of the most intellectually challenging thinkers in the Western tradition have displayed great mastery of style (just think of Plato, Rousseau, Thoreau, Nietzsche, and Freud) without ceasing to present serious problems of interpretation and understanding. An aspiration to clarity is not going to keep genuine difficulty out of a text. In his wonderful study of Mallarmé, Malcolm Bowie shows that difficulty and obscurity are two different things. This distinction is as useful for someone who wishes to defend difficult poetry or difficult theory against anti-intellectual attacks as it is for someone who wishes to make theory as readable as it can hope to be, given its subject matter.[17] In the higher reaches of academia

[16] These examples are symptomatically marginal to feminist theory. Some would say that Elaine Showalter is not a theorist at all, others would call Paglia an anti-feminist, and some fervently pray that MacKinnon would stop referring to herself as a feminist.

[17] Entitled *Mallarmé and the Art of Being Difficult*, Bowie's delicious epigraph comes from Mozart and Da Ponte's *Così fan tutte:* 'Cara semplicità, quanto mi piaci!' Bowie reminds us that there are many different ways of being difficult: 'Mallarmé's poems are difficult in different ways and at different levels of intensity. Certain of them are difficult to come at, to get meaning from, but yield to pressure. . . . [O]ther poems have difficulty at their centre, being concerned with open metaphysical questions. . . . Such poems are centred upon difficulties which are the product of an intended and scrupulous indecision on the poet's part' (ix–x).

In the same way, there are many different ways of producing theoretical obscurity: among the more common methods we find vagueness of thought and imprecision of language. In recent theoretical writing I have been struck by the obscurity produced by an excessive generality of reference to other theorists. A statement may be secured by a reference to 'Foucault's theory of discursivity', for instance. But Foucault's understanding of discourse and discursivity is not simple and straightforward, and has given rise to different interpretations. Given that different readers probably have quite different ideas of what Foucault actually means by discursivity, the theoretical point the author is trying to secure by the reference may either be dramatically misunderstood or perceived as a puzzling non sequitur by many readers. Another way of formulating this problem is to say that such writers of theory too readily assume that their readers will be exactly like themselves.

there is nevertheless a tendency to assume that the clearer (or the more elegant) the writing, the less intellectually challenging it must be.[18]

Asking for clarification of an obscure theoretical claim, I have quite often been told that I fail to appreciate the deliberate opacity of the text and, moreover, that my wish to understand what is and what is not being claimed amounts to a wish for 'transparent language'. This amounts to telling me that I am guilty of an epistemological sin. To want language to be transparent is to subscribe to a simplistic realist thesis about the relationship between language and the world, to turn language into a mere window on to the world so that the less it is noticed the better. To ask for 'transparent language', then, is to ask language to efface itself as a living, material structure. This is indeed a grievously problematic request, but luckily one that has nothing to do with a wish for clarity. Just as there is a difference between difficulty and obscurity, clarity and transparency are not synonymous. To put a difficult thought with some clarity and precision is not going to make it any simpler or less challenging than it actually is. Rather, it will make intellectual difficulties and problems more salient and more pressing than if they are masked by a mess of imprecision and approximations. Wittgenstein's *Philosophical Investigations*, to give a fairly extreme example, shows that writing

[18] In her influential essay 'The Race for Theory', first published in 1987, the same year as 'Me and My Shadow', Barbara Christian eloquently complains about the aridity of theoretical language in terms very similar to those of Jane Tompkins: 'as a student of literature', Christian writes, 'I am appalled by the sheer ugliness of the language, its lack of clarity, its unnecessarily complicated sentence constructions, its lack of pleasurableness, its alienating quality' (230). But Christian does not write in order to recommend a turn to the personal, but in order to defend her wish to reach an audience that differs from the standard academic audience. The connection between intended readership and theoretical style is obvious, and lends itself to a Bourdieuian analysis of the quest for symbolic capital. Bourdieu, however, is an implacable theorist: every attempt to write theory in a more simple way, he would surely say, is going to be taken more seriously if it comes from a writer who already has accumulated much theoretical capital than if it comes from someone who hasn't. The same is true for the turn to autobiographical writing among academics: graduate students usually do not have enough symbolic capital to attempt it. Interesting studies could be done on these matters.

striving for clarity of thought and simplicity of style is not synonymous with intellectual banality and lack of interpretative challenge. Freud's very different style demonstrates exactly the same
thing. As Einstein is supposed to have said: 'Everything should be
made as simple as possible, but not simpler.'

'Me and My Shadow' teaches us that there is a profound
connection between the question of the personal and the question of style. This is its most important, yet curiously undeveloped,
insight. Finding the right diagnosis, Tompkins proposes the
wrong cure. In this essay I shall try to show that we do not have to
give up on theory to avoid alienating obfuscation in academic
work, and that we do not have to choose between the personal
and the theoretical. The personal is not the enemy of serious
thought. To imply that it is, is to reinforce the very dichotomy that
Jane Tompkins experiences as a painful split in her own life. To
expand on Beauvoir: there is no necessary divorce between life
and philosophy, between the personal and the theoretical,
between feelings and thought.[19]

To the many contemporary critics who have acknowledged the
importance of the personal because they consider self-consciously
subjective expression to offer an escape from the twin horrors of
objectivity and universalism, Beauvoir's position must appear
unconvincing. Would she also say that there is no necessary
divorce between the first person and the third person, between
speaking *as* and speaking *for*? Isn't she herself a typical example
of the universalizing Enlightenment tradition that the turn to the
personal is trying to undermine? Such questions will be discussed
in Section II of this essay. In what remains of Section I, I shall
examine some further issues arising out of the contemporary
debates about the personal. Throughout I try to show that the
term 'the personal' has different meanings for different critics.

The discussions in Section I are intended to prepare the
ground for Section II, where I turn to my main task, namely to
show through a close study of Beauvoir's philosophical style

---

[19] In an essay written in 1988, that is to say shortly after reading 'Me and My
Shadow', I try to show, with the help of Freud, that the intellectual is shot
through with emotion and desire. See 'Patriarchal Thought and the Drive for
Knowledge' (Ch. 7 below).

exactly how she uses herself (her own subjectivity) in order to produce a philosophical analysis of women's condition. The purpose of this exercise is to show that Beauvoir has a profound contribution to make to contemporary debates about the relationship between the personal and the theoretical. Her philosophical style, I claim, can show us a way (not the way) to write theory without losing ourselves or our connectedness to others.[20]

Ad Feminam: *The Argument for Location and Its Excesses*

Painting a rosy picture of the personal, Jane Tompkins thinks of it as warm, emotional, loving, giving, autobiographical, embodied, and concrete. Unfortunately, however, there are less pleasant ways of 'getting personal', to quote Nancy Miller's delightfully ambiguous phrase. It would seem that many critics believe, much like Jane Tompkins, that because the personal has been undervalued in academia, it is now time to privilege it. Unlike Tompkins, however, some of these critics do not believe that we have to choose between the personal and the theoretical, declaring instead that the two always 'go together'. Although this sometimes leads to sympathetic analyses of the factors that contribute to the production of someone's beliefs, it is on the strength of this claim that some critics proceed to reduce an intellectual argument to its personal components, as if the personal circumstances of an intellectual claim were always more important than the claim itself. They are in fact making use of a classical rhetorical strategy, namely the *ad feminam* argument.

According to the OED, the phrase *ad hominem* means 'to the man' or 'to the person'; an *ad hominem* argument is 'directed to

---

[20] My wish to show the relevance of Beauvoir to problems in contemporary feminist theory makes my project similar to that of Nancy Bauer, who in her important work on Simone de Beauvoir also shows how Beauvoir teaches contemporary feminist theory a new method of philosophical appropriation. The difference is that Bauer shows what we can learn from Beauvoir's inventive and imaginative relationship to the works of other philosophers (particularly Hegel, but also Sartre and Descartes), whereas I want to show what her way of writing teaches us about how to use oneself in the writing of theory. In Bauer's discussion of Beauvoir's relationship to Descartes, our two projects intersect more closely than elsewhere.

the individual, personal; appealing to feeling not reason'. Developed to assist the male participants in Greek and Roman public and political life, classical rhetoric never coined the term *ad feminam* to describe arguments directed 'to the woman'. To argue *ad feminam* or *ad hominem* is to attack the person who makes the argument one detests, rather than the argument itself, usually in order to move the audience, to stir their passions against this abhorrent person. In a court of law or in political debate such arguments have their uses, but they are hardly philosophically or logically respectable. Traditionally the quintessentially sexist form of the *ad feminam* argument has been the dismissive 'you say that because you are a woman'. The point of the argument is to discredit the speaker, not to engage in debate with her. The effect is to make the person attacked feel as if nobody listened to what she actually said. The attacker, on the other hand, has to be suspected of having run out of better arguments: in intellectual circles the *ad feminam* attack is usually one of last resort and brings no credit to its user. In reviews it is always used negatively, as a point of criticism of the author who engages in it.[21] Thus the *ad feminam* argument usually backfires: instead of discrediting one's opponent, one manages only to discredit oneself.

In contemporary academia the recent emphasis on the personal has nevertheless led to some confusion about what exactly is to count as an *ad feminam* argument.[22] For if we are

[21] I have only ever seen the actual phrase *ad feminam* or *ad hominem* argument used with negative connotations, but I suppose one might imagine a positive version of the practice, if not of the phrase: 'I will support whatever *she* is saying because her subject position is one that I wish to support,' might be a form of *ad feminam* praise (but the formulation '*ad feminam* praise' sounds odd). Although humanly nicer, the argument is as intellectually vacuous as the *ad feminam* attack.

[22] Nancy Miller's use of the phrase *ad feminam* is representatively ambiguous. Referring to 'attacks on academic feminism', she writes: 'What should we make of this published violence against feminist ideology in general and individual critics in particular (ad feminam)?' (*Getting Personal* x). Here it is not clear from the context whether the attacks took the form of arguments against some named person's views ('Jane Smith's critique of essentialism is derivative, or insufficiently argued, for the following reasons'), or whether they took the form of saying something like 'Jane Smith's critique of essentialism is entirely due to her wish to remain on good terms with the feminist Mafia that currently runs our

justified in thinking that the speaker's subject position and social location affects his or her understanding of the world, surely it cannot be unjustified to point out that since so-and-so actually is a white, heterosexual, bourgeois male, his views exhibit traces of his male privilege? In the same way, wouldn't it be quite fair to tell me that I am criticizing Judith Butler's account of the sex/gender distinction (see Chapter 1, above) just because I am heterosexual and she is not? Or perhaps I am dissatisfied with Butler's account of sex and gender just because I am Norwegian and she is not? If our views are indeed influenced by our 'location', then such questions cannot be easily dismissed. In practice, I think most of us can tell the difference between an *ad feminam* argument and a serious investigation of 'location' or 'context' or 'speaking position', yet in the present intellectual climate it sometimes becomes difficult to justify one's sense that there is a difference. I shall nevertheless try to do so here.

I shall start by considering two examples of *ad feminam* argumentation and its effects. Hostile reductions of her philosophical and political positions to her personal circumstances have been extremely common in the critical reception of Simone de Beauvoir. Instead of discussing the meaning and implications of (say) her claim that the highest human value is freedom, or that the French war in Algeria was a deeply unjust and shameful colonialist venture, critics endlessly focus on her private, personal, and emotional motivations for saying so. Insisting that Beauvoir only says this or that because she was trying to please Sartre, because she was male-identified, because she was a sexually licentious woman living in sin, or because she hated her bourgeois parents, they try to dismiss her views without engaging with them. The strategy is deeply sexist: the point is to convey that whatever passes for thought in this woman is really only the symptoms of her frustrated sexuality, her neurotic emotional life, her desperate dependence on a man, or her hostility to other women. In my book on Beauvoir I described the effects of the strategy as follows:

---

universities/the influence of her lesbian lover/her vicious and unfeminine careerism'. According to the usual definition, the latter would certainly qualify as an *ad feminam* attack, the former not.

the hostile critics' favourite strategy is to personalize the issues, to reduce the book to the woman: their aim is clearly to discredit her as a speaker, not to enter into debate with her. These critics are out to cast doubts on Beauvoir's right to produce any kind of public discourse. By discrediting her status as a speaker, they intend to preclude any further discussion of what she actually says (75).

[P]olitically motivated critiques of Beauvoir contain surprisingly little discussion of politics and much apparently pointless dwelling on her personality and private life. . . . The intended effect is to depoliticize her by presenting her political choices not as the outcome of careful reflection on the issues at stake, but as the inexplicable *élans* of an overemotional or even hysterical woman. Having reduced their opponent to a neurotic woman, such hostile critics avoid having to reveal—and defend—their own politics, let alone their own personal problems (81).

In short, the main effects of the strategy are to discredit the woman as a speaker, to cast doubt on her right to participate in the conversation, to dispense the hostile critics from having to take the woman's thought seriously, and to protect the critics from inquiry into their own neuroses and blind spots.

Let me move on to the second example. If I permit myself to criticize, however mildly, a point in a visiting feminist speaker's talk I may be told that I have failed to be 'supportive'.[23] Insofar as this comment is based on the assumption that intellectual disagreement is always 'unsupportive' (unhelpful? unproductive? irrelevant?), it is in itself problematic. But let us take the worst case scenario. Let us assume that I am someone who generally goes around feeling vicious and spiteful, full of hostility towards every feminist theorist in the world except myself. Let us further assume that my public question after the talk was uttered in a provocatively hostile tone. In short, let us assume that I am a person sadly lacking in humanity, love, and forbearance. Let us then note that so far no mention has been made of the argument of the visiting feminist nor of the content of my response to her. The statement has been reduced to the speech act, or rather, to

[23] I am not implying that feminists engage in hostile uses of the personal more than other academics. Readers might want to consult their own experience for other examples.

one particular circumstance of the speech act, namely the personality of the speaker. Whatever was actually said has disappeared from view. Moreover, further discussion is now impossible. The diagnosis of my personality has taken the place of intellectual exchange.

Once I recognize that I have miserably failed to be 'supportive' (or 'sisterly' for that matter), all I can do is to find a therapist, turn to religion or whatever else it takes to turn myself into a better person. What I cannot do, is to come back to the theoretical point I originally made, for the accusation of 'unsupportiveness' has now thoroughly discredited me. The accusation turns out to be a version of the *ad feminam* attack. Branded as a hostile and unloving woman I have apparently lost my right to participate in feminist intellectual debate. (At this point it ought to be obvious that it does not matter in the least whether I actually did intervene in the discussion out of hostility. The point is to impute disreputable motivations, not to describe them accurately.) By speaking up for 'supportiveness', moreover, my interlocutors imply that their own psychiatric and sisterly credentials are above suspicion. The hostile reduction of the theoretical to the personal dissolves into anti-intellectualism and velvet-gloved censorship (if all critical statements will be taken as evidence of one's spiteful nature, one may be excused for thinking that it is better to say nothing at all). Blocking intellectual dialogue, this particular turn to the personal yet again leaves us 'all alone and feeling blue'. To stress the point: the main problem with *ad feminam* argumentation is that it locks us into our variously discredited subject positions and so makes productive intellectual exchange impossible.[24]

Whereas my first example, that of hostile uses of the personal against Simone de Beauvoir, seems clearly reprehensible, it is not at all clear what goes wrong in the second case. It is not even clear *that* anything goes wrong. Should I not be prepared to accept the accusation of 'unsupportiveness' as a fair interpretation of, say, the effect of my remarks? Let me stress that the remark 'That was unsupportive' does not have to be an *ad feminam* attack. It can be

---

[24] I realize that I have focused entirely on *ad feminam* argumentation of a diagnostic or clinical kind. There are others, but they will have to be left for another day.

offered as part of a discussion of when—under what circumstances—it is right for feminists to disagree in public, for instance.
I may say that in a sexist society, to take another intellectual
woman seriously enough to want to engage in discussion with her
is politically more valuable than to shut up for fear of producing
an 'unsupportive' effect.[25] My interlocutors may want to point out
that although there is some value in this, I forget that in the
specific situation at hand, there was a potential major donor to
the women's studies programme present, well known for her
dislike of disagreement. One possible outcome of such a discussion is that I acknowledge that I misjudged the situation.[26] This is
a fair enough debate to have, and it is not *ad feminam* to the extent
that it no longer necessarily tries to discredit me as a speaker, yet
it still counts as a derailing of any discussion concerned with the
visiting speaker's paper. The question my interlocutors have to
weigh is under what circumstances it is worth doing that.

Nothing is less contentious among US literary critics today
than the claim that someone's race, class, sex, sexuality, nationality, and individual experiences (of sexual abuse, rape, and racism,
but also other, more innocuous experiences) affect his or her
understanding of the world. As Linda Alcoff puts it in a frequently
quoted phrase, the general assumption is that 'a speaker's location is epistemically salient' (7). Yet, in the cases I just described,
this assumption—one that I share—appears to breed a disastrously reductive anti-intellectual stance. How do we prevent a
proper concern for speaking position from degenerating into *ad
feminam* argumentation? It may help to describe *ad feminam* arguments as *reductive* and *irrelevant* deployment of the argument for

[25] From a slightly different angle, namely the problems of speaking for
others, Linda Alcoff produces a thoughtful critique of the 'retreat response', the
decision to say nothing for fear of being ideologically incorrect: 'But surely it is
both morally and politically objectionable to structure one's actions around the
desire to avoid criticism . . . In some cases perhaps the motivation is not so much
to avoid criticism as to avoid errors, and the person believes that the only way to
avoid errors is to avoid all speaking for others. However, errors are unavoidable
in theoretical inquiry as well as political struggle, and moreover they often make
contributions' (22).
[26] This is one way to claim responsibility for one's words. See Alcoff for
further discussion of what it might mean to take responsibility for what one says.

'location' (by which I mean the claim that the location of the
speaker matters for the meaning of the speech act). Then the
question becomes more concrete: what do we need to do to avoid
reductionism and irrelevance?

Since every theory can be used reductively, no theory can be
rejected simply on the grounds that some of its practitioners are
reductionists. Ultimately, the only antidote against reductionism
is sound judgement. Reductionisms nevertheless do different
things to different theories. Linda Alcoff provides a fairly poststructuralist analysis of the reductionism that concerns us here:

> [It] involves a retrograde, metaphysically insupportable essential-
> ism that assumes one can read the truth and meaning of what one
> says straight from the discursive context. . . . Such a reductionist
> theory might, for example, reduce evaluation to a political assess-
> ment of the speaker's location, where that location is seen as an
> insurmountable essence that fixes one, as if one's feet are super-
> glued to a spot on the sidewalk (16).

What has gone wrong, in Alcoff's view, is that a general assumption of 'epistemic salience' has been essentialized and made
absolute: 'To say that location *bears* on meaning and truth is not
the same as saying that location *determines* meaning and truth,'
she writes (16). Location and positionality should be understood
as multiple and shifting, not as a given essence. Furthermore,
Alcoff argues, we should not claim that a given speaking position
always has the *same* effects: 'we need to analyse the probable or
actual effects of the words on the discursive and material context.
One cannot simply look at the location of the speaker or her
credentials to speak, nor can one look merely at the propositional
contents of the speech; one must also look at where the speech
goes and what it does there' (26).

Offered as a protection against reductionism, these are useful
reminders. But there is nothing here to guard against irrelevance.
Must we always look at 'where the speech goes'?[27] Do we really, as
Alcoff also puts it, in each and every case have to 'analyse the

---

[27] I think Alcoff underestimates the difficulty of knowing 'where the speech
goes'. Sartre's *What Is Literature?* contains thoughtful considerations on this
subject.

probable or actual effects of the words on the discursive and material context' (27)? In spite of her sensitive and thoughtful discussion of the problems attending her position, Alcoff wants to hang on to the claim that 'there is no possibility of rendering positionality, location, or context irrelevant to content' (14). Yet even the briefest of considerations of contemporary critical practice shows that we don't in fact always analyse the location and circumstances of the speaker we are concerned with, nor do we always engage in discussion of our own speaking position before saying something. Simone de Beauvoir reads Hegel in order to fashion her own, highly original understanding of women's oppression, and never lets the fact that Hegel was a bourgeois, sexist, white male stop her.[28] Luce Irigaray and Judith Butler both return to Plato in order to discuss sex and gender without even mentioning the effect of his speech acts in Greek fifth-century BC society, and without saying anything about their own 'location'.[29]

Ought these women to have spent lots of time uncovering the effects of Plato's or Hegel's interventions in their own time and society? Should they not, at the very least, have discussed the potential effects of rereading Plato in their own time and society? If one thinks that location is *always relevant*, the answer has to be yes. But then these theorists' freedom to use a text for their own creative purposes would be severely curtailed. Most of us became intellectuals because we felt challenged and inspired by writing and ideas. Because we read with an eye to what we can use and what we need in our own situation, there is no reason why we should always have to reconstruct the historical location of the original speech act, or indeed offer up our own autobiography as a preface to everything we say. The insistence that location and speaking position is *always* relevant, or that it is always incumbent on the speaker to guard against malignant consequences of her speech act, magnifies the speaker's powers, encourages her to take a paranoid stance towards her audience, and, however paradoxically, also casts the reader or

[28] See Bauer and Lundgren-Gothlin, *Sex and Existence* for divergent analyses of Beauvoir's appropriation of Hegel. The question of how successful Beauvoir's use of Hegel is remains a fascinating topic of discussion.

[29] I am thinking of the title essay in Butler's *Bodies that Matter* and the long last section devoted to Plato in Irigaray's *Speculum of the Other Woman*.

listener as nothing but a passive victim of the speaker's discursive violence.[30] On this model, the writer becomes too powerful and the reader too unfree. Thus the theory radically underestimates the fact that a speech act is also an *encounter* between a speaker and a listener or a writer and a reader.

This may sound too idealist, too oblivious of differences in power between speakers and listeners. Alcoff is right to stress that 'Certain contexts and locations are allied with structures of oppression, and certain others are allied with resistance to oppression. Therefore all are not politically equal, and, given that politics is connected to truth, all are not epistemically equal' (15). In cases where the powerful speak to the powerless, the picture of master speaker and victimized listener is more relevant than in cases where the powerful or the powerless speak among themselves. All speech acts do not take place in situations of unambiguous domination. The fact that some do is no reason to claim that we must *always* analyse the location and position of an utterance. Even when a speech act does take place in a situation of domination, this is not always the most important thing to say about it. One still needs to give some reasons for such claims, not simply postulate them as obviously true.

If we admit that there is such a thing as utterly irrelevant invocations of personal circumstances, we have invalidated the claim that analysis of 'location' and 'speaking position' is always relevant. It does not follow that knowledge is not situated, but neither does it follow that it is. If all knowledge is always situated, the statement cancels all the way through. It simply means that no statement is any less situated than any other. If this is so (and I am not here out to deny such claims), then it follows that the claim that all knowledge is situated tells us nothing at all about when—under what circumstances—we should *raise* the question of location. In my view, only

---

[30] Joyce Trebilcot, for example, thinks that any attempt to persuade anyone of anything at all is an act of violence. In an essay arguing against trying to persuade others to accept one's own beliefs, she writes: 'the term "persuasion" must be construed broadly so as to include not only argument and discussion but also other forms of deliberately influencing people's beliefs, such as various kinds of reward and punishment (e.g., bribery, blackmail), the inducement of conversion experiences, and so on' (5).

when there is something problematic about the speech act do we need to analyse it more fully. Problems may arise at any time in a statement's lifetime: the fact that so far nobody to my knowledge has found anything problematic about Judith Butler's lack of interest in ancient Greek society, doesn't mean that the question could not arise under future, as yet unforeseen, circumstances. But it is neither possible nor desirable to produce theoretical prescriptions intended to guard against all possible future eventualities. The demand that we *always* examine 'location' is one such prescription.

Once a problem of interpretation or evaluation has arisen, however, we do need to look to who is speaking, what was said, to whom it was said, under what circumstances it was said, and so on. This is where I feel inspired to draw on J. L Austin's remark that in order to solve questions about meaning we need to examine 'what we should say when, what words we should use in what situation' ('Plea' 182). It is incumbent on the person who wishes to raise the question of 'location' to show why it is relevant, that is, first to show what problem of evaluation or meaning has arisen, and then to show that her investigation of 'what we should say when' helps to resolve the issue. The fact that so many speech acts appear to be felicitous—that they do *not* go wrong, misfire, or backfire—is of great theoretical interest. We do not need a theory of language or speech acts geared only to emergencies, crises, and conflicts. Although such theories heighten literary critics' sense of excitement, it leaves us resourceless in front of the ordinary and the unremarkable, so that we will have nothing to say about the many felicitous speech acts we all engage in every day. The only way out—and one frequently taken—is to insist that these too are in fact *always* the sites of failure, crisis, and melodramatic intensities, and if we don't notice it, it is because we are enslaved to dominant ideology, blinded by false consciousness, or incapable of resisting the master discourse. I find this implausible.[31]

---

[31] The question I am raising here and in the previous paragraph is really one that goes to the core of the difference between a Wittgensteinian and a Derridean account of language, and this paper is not the place to discuss it further. I am much indebted to Martin Stone's lectures on Derrida and Wittgenstein at The School of Criticism and Theory at Cornell in the summer of 1997 for clarifying the issues at stake (see Stone, 'Wittgenstein').

I am now in a position to answer my own questions about the white heterosexual male or the reasons why I am dissatisfied with Butler's understanding of sex and gender. The idea that my reading of Butler could be adequately explained by the fact that I am Norwegian or heterosexual or whatever else, is utterly preposterous, a clear case of *ad feminam* argumentation. The same is true for the assumption that because someone is a heterosexual, white male his views can be discarded without further consideration. There is a world of difference between finding patterns of misogyny and racism in a text and using the author's personal characteristics to dispense oneself from the hard work of reading. If someone engages with Chapter 1 in this book and carefully establishes that there are patterns of heterosexism or Norwegian nationalism in it, then I cannot complain about unfair rhetorical strategies. Once this has been shown, however, the question of why I of all people have such attitudes no longer appears all that interesting or relevant.[32]

In short, any claim about motivations, intentions, or general bias based on subject position that appears to be unsupported by a fair-minded reading of the text in question is irrelevant to intellectual work. To me, the worst aspects of *ad feminam* argumentation remain its cavalier disinterest in serious thought and its attempt to discredit the speaker, and so to block further discussion.

Against Impersonality and Objectivity

As we have seen, in 'Me and My Shadow' the personal is pictured as concrete, embodied, emotional, warm, feeling, and autobiographical. Theory on the other hand is pictured as impersonal, and to Tompkins that means unfeeling, cool, objective, distanced, disembodied, and abstract. The personal, moreover, gets linked to concrete, sensuous, pleasurable language; the theoretical to an obscure, abstruse, and unpleasant aridity of style. In contemporary theory, the distinction between speaking for oneself—speaking *as*

---

[32] The writer's project largely determines what is relevant: if someone—God forbid!—had decided to write a biography of me, then the question of my motivations and intentions and how I came to have them might be highly relevant.

the person one is—and speaking *for* (in the place of, on behalf of) others often gets mapped on to this set of binary opposites. It is generally assumed that speaking for others is a bad thing. By the late 1990s the idea that some kind of turn to the personal will rescue us from arrogant impersonality, discriminatory objectivity, and imperialist universalization appears to have congealed into established academic *doxa* among literary critics.

In October 1996 the *PMLA*, the journal of the Modern Language Association of America, devoted a special issue to 'The Place of the Personal in Scholarship'. In this issue there is a general 'Forum' where twenty-six different letter-writers discuss the question of the personal. Reading through these letters is an illuminating exercise. Whatever their individual disagreements about what the personal is, the writers are overwhelmingly in agreement about what it is not. With striking consistency the contributions cast 'objectivity' and 'universality' as the twin drag-ons to be slain by the knights of the personal.

Some contributors focus exclusively on the opposition between a free, playful expression of self and a rigid search for objectivity. The wish to mask the personal or the self stems from a scientistic need to 'make literary studies respectable, objective, and scientific', one contributor writes (1147).[33] 'We are, willy-nilly, personal', he declares: 'Let's go with it, then. Let's enjoy it. Let's chuck the pretensions to infallibility customary to our profession and have some fun' (1147). Later on he also enjoins us to 'be creative' since in this postmodern age we cannot pretend to be objective. Aspirations to objectivity only reveal our pretensions to infallibility. Against such dour scientism is pitted an upbeat, free-wheeling spirit of creative personalities playfully expressing themselves. Many writers echo the idea that 'scholarly prose, like imaginative literature, is inevitably personal' (1147).

I imagine that anyone influenced by psychoanalysis (as I am) would agree that our desires and unconscious investment reveal themselves in all our speech acts, and often where we least expect it. Yet psychoanalysis is not the theoretical source of the recent

[33] All unattributed quotes come from the 'Forum' section of *PMLA* 111/5 (Oct. 1996), 1146–96.

turn to the personal, and for good reason. The psychoanalytic claim is that there is always someone who writes, and that the writer always leaves traces of her subjectivity in her work. Since this is equally true for *Critique of Pure Reason* and 'Me and My Shadow', we can conclude that whatever present-day postmodern academics want from the personal, it is not adequately explained by invoking the psychoanalytic understanding of subjectivity and desire. The idea expressed in many of the letters in the *PMLA* Forum is that because there is subjectivity in everything, then nothing is objective. This is a kind of 'pan-subjectivism', akin to the pan-sexualism that Freud always strenuously rejected. Such 'pan-subjectivism' overlooks the difference between claiming, as psychoanalysis does, that there is subjectivity in every belief, and claiming that every belief is purely subjective.

What is excluded from the *PMLA* Forum is any serious examination of the meaning of 'objectivity'. Imprisoned in a binary opposition with the personal, objectivity becomes the villain of the piece. It would seem that most contributors think the word is always used to mean something like the point of view of a pure clinical gaze situated outside every human context. On such a definition, clearly, nobody is objective, and to pretend that one is, is just to indulge in fantasy. But this is not the only possible meaning of the word. Even today, literary critics can be overheard saying things like 'The Dean gave a fairly objective account of the troubles in our department', or—more likely—hotly disputing the Dean's account on the grounds that it was *not* objective. In both cases, objectivity seems to have a potentially valuable and realizable meaning. This meaning is absent from every recent discussion of the personal that I have seen: in the *PMLA* Forum, for example, objectivity (and impersonality) is consistently reduced to being the repudiated and rejected Other of the personal. There is also a striking absence of nuanced views. Caught in a binary taxonomy of their own making, the *PMLA* Forum participants tend to believe that there are only two options: to admit to being subjective (good) or to pretend to be objective (bad). Underlying this binary grid, quite obviously, is the belief that objectivity does not exist, or rather, that the word objectivity can be given no useful meaning.

A frequent move is to tie the refusal of objectivity to a refusal to speak for others, on the grounds that the repudiated desire for universality is an ethically disreputable attempt to silence others: 'When we invoke objectivity and universality, we appeal to power and mystify our personal investments so as to speak for everyone. In doing so, we silence those who cannot make similar appeals' (1147). No contributor challenges the opposition produced here between the personal and the universal or objective, although some wish that the two could go together: 'Objectivity must be allowed as part of the personal', one person writes (1148). On the understanding of objectivity evident in the *PMLA* Forum, however, it is hard to see how this could happen.

Others attempt to deconstruct the opposition between the personal and the objective and/or universal by declaring that everything is personal, only to resurrect it as an opposition between knowledge and ignorance, between those who know they are speaking personally and proudly say so, and those who either don't know how personal they are or deliberately pass their subjective and situated utterances off as universal: 'What worries me is not scholarship that seems narrowly personal but rather scholarship where the personal does not recognize itself as such and thus passes for the universal' (1150). Objectivity, understood as impersonal, scientistic, and oppressive of difference, has no defenders: 'The writer who believes in the possibility of objectivity will not be on the lookout for bias and will do nothing to correct for it, thereby increasing the likelihood that the analysis will be compromised by it. . . . Scholars who don't reveal their participation in interactions they analyse risk the appearance of hiding it' (1152).

A somewhat different approach is taken by those who wish to align the personal with the literary, with the use of the first person singular, and with the everyday. Some think of narrative—either any narrative, or only narratives about real as opposed to fictional persons—as personal. Others are slightly more restrictive, and think of the personal much in the same terms as Nancy Miller who defines it as 'an explicitly autobiographical performance within the act of criticism' (*Getting Personal* 1). Such critics often see the turn to the personal as a way to escape the arrogance and authoritarianism that according to them invariably accompanies the deployment of theory. In the *PMLA* Forum, one writer feels that by adding some 'quasi-confessional' material to his work of criticism, he is escaping from the professional posturing that is rife within the discourse of theory today. He overcomes his fear of acknowledging that there are things he doesn't know, of not being up to scratch theoretically, by turning to the personal:

> The most valuable way we can personalize, hence humanize, the teacher–student relationship, I suspect, is not to make our lives an open book but something altogether more self-exposing: to offer up our thought processes as a kind of open text from which students can learn that it is all right to say: 'I don't know', 'I don't understand', 'Help me out' (1153).

For this writer, the personal is a pedagogical tool, opposed to forbidding theoretical arrogance and displays of mastery. In this he again sounds very similar to Nancy Miller, who in a happy phrase says that the unveiling of her own lack of mastery in class is a feminist strategy designed to undermine the 'standard peacock model of graduate teaching, designed to dazzle the hens' (*Getting Personal* 41). Countered by confession, theoretical arrogance and one-upmanship will crumble, or so the personal critic hopes.

The personal is also conceived of as closer to 'real life', and is often invoked as a means to bridge the gap between scholarship and the 'world beyond the page' (1158), yet strangely enough nobody explicitly claims that the personal is the political. Only one contributor bemoans the fact that the current adherents of the personal have forgotten the original meaning of the phrase. While we once used to claim that the personal is the political, meaning that personal experience was 'part of a larger system of (gender) ideology', nowadays the phrase 'has come to mean that the personal is all there is of the political', she writes (1166).

A few contributors do have some worries about personal criticism. Yet, although the Forum is divided into two sections, the first entitled 'The Inevitability of the Personal' (seventeen contributors) and the other 'Problems with Personal Criticism' (nine contributors), there isn't actually much of a difference between them. Most of the contributors to the second section also stress the virtues of the personal while offering up some reservations. One critic in the first section lists a number of dangers, but thinks they can be overcome. On his danger list are shameless self-indulgence, irrelevance, offering a personal reason for overlooking the obvious, being so entranced with the personal genesis of a theory that one forgets the obligation to mention contrary evidence. Finally, he warns against the potential arrogance of the personal: 'the foregrounding of personal testimony may turn out to be nothing more than an appeal to another kind of authority: my conclusions must be true because I believe them' (1160). Another contributor also stresses the potential authoritarianism and self-enclosure of the personal:

> Perhaps the most immediate concern with the personal in scholarship—or at least the one that seems most troublesome—is related to rebuttal, dialogue, and other interactions in knowledge production. While some may argue that scholarship is not an equal interaction but a genre of communication that intends to silence other voices, the collegial, collective, and communal process of producing, evaluating, and disseminating knowledge is necessary to intellectual activity. The personal seemingly stifles this process by silencing the judgments and critiques of others (1166).

Arrogance, in fact, appears to be the only quality which ends up on both sides of the divide between the personal and the impersonal. Theoretical arguments are taken to be arrogant because they intimidate and silence others, but the same thing is said about expressions of personal experience. The general wish not to silence others appears to express the most widely shared ideal among US literary critics, namely the wish to construct situations in which everyone is equally free to participate in the intellectual (or social or political) conversation. As we shall see, this is an ideal shared by Simone de Beauvoir.

One writer sees the current turn to the autobiographical as a symptom of the *loss* of meaningful individuality: 'Our critics speak personally not for a real self but for a self conceived as representative of an approved ideology, race, or sexual preference—self-stereotyped as subaltern postdeconstructionist, a black male lesbian, and so on' (1164). What emerges here is the difference between the personal understood as any aspect of subjectivity, including quite factual aspects, and the personal taken to mean something like a truly individual perspective on the world.

Finally, some contributors link the turn to the personal to the academic star system. Only a very established critic can permit herself to 'get personal'. 'Call it a matter of class', one critic writes: 'I'm reminded of a colleague who met her dissertation advisor at the convention. He said he was organizing a national conference on subalternity. I asked why he didn't offer her a place. "I'm too subaltern to be subaltern," she replied. She meant she doesn't teach at a distinguished university and hasn't published enough' (1168). In order to indulge in the luxury of the personal, one needs to have tenure, and preferably the power and prestige that may make people interested in one's experiences. In my experience (to get right down to it), the personal in the sense of the autobiographical is not (yet) an option for graduate students, whereas the personal in the sense of 'saying where one is coming from' and indulging in the obligatory denunciations of universality and objectivity has become more or less compulsory for them.

What conclusions can be drawn from the views of the twenty-six contributors to the *PMLA* Forum on the personal? There is a major difference between those who consider that nothing short of autobiographical narrative will do, and those who consider the personal to mean any trace of subjectivity in a text. For some, the statement 'I am a Chinese American woman' is personal, for others Jane Tompkins's descriptions of the weather and her liking for cappuccino are what is required. Others again wish for something like the expression of a person's uniquely individual outlook on the world. Some think that only the first person singular is personal, others see the self or subjectivity transfusing the scholar's text whether she knows it or not. If she doesn't know it, she is a universalizing dinosaur, if she does, she must explicitly signal the fact, or she will become a treacherous purveyor of the universal anyway. Among these critics there is no willingness to grant that even when she does not explicitly say so, a writer might still realize that she is writing as a person, and even as a writing subject situated in history.

When it comes to determining what is to count as 'personal' writing, Anne Fernald's interesting paper on Virginia Woolf and the essay adds some relevant points to the debate in the *PMLA*. Placing the contemporary turn to the personal in its historical context, Fernald reminds us that the tradition of essay-writing from Montaigne to Virginia Woolf embodies the best personal writing Western culture has ever produced. Compared to the works of such forebears, contemporary academics' struggles to get personal appear singularly unimpressive to Fernald. For her, the personal means that which bears the stamp of a unique individual's thought, and not just a generic expression of subject position. The point of writing personally is to convey serious thought in a better and more accessible form than one otherwise could have managed: 'when the personal is brought to the service of an idea, it becomes the most persuasive criticism there is' (187).

Persuasively showing that the mere use of the first person singular or autobiographical narrative is not enough to produce an impression of personal thought, Fernald argues that in contemporary academia the turn to the personal often amounts to a set of not so hidden appeals to the reader to like and admire the writer: 'The problem is [the writer's] desperate desire for us to care for and approve of her and to believe that her interest in her topic is heartfelt', she writes, before adding the *coup de grâce*: 'As to our liking her, no one, in person or in print, has ever come to be liked by pleading for us to like her' (183). For Fernald, Virginia Woolf's essays represent the antithesis to such posturing: 'Woolf tells us something about herself to help bring into focus the complexity of the idea, the seriousness with which she approaches the topic, not because she wants us to like her' (177).

As far as I can see, the *PMLA* Forum contributors tend to agree that the politics of the turn to the personal is to be found in its undermining of discourses of arrogance, mastery, impersonality, objectivity, and universality, in short discourses redolent of the vices usually attributed to theory and philosophy. In this way, the personal does become the political, but only because a certain theory declares that this is the theoretically correct way to undermine the authoritarian universalism of theory. This leaves us with the question of how to write theory at all, a question I will return to in Section II.

Impersonality and Objectivity: Take Two

What struck me most of all in the special issue of the *PMLA* was that nobody seemed to think that subjectivity can become a prison-house from which a few moments of impersonality could offer a delightful respite. Anne Fernald is the only recent critic I have read who makes the point: 'Woolf makes thinking seem personal in part by creating an argument passionately committed to securing "the greatest release of all . . . which is freedom to think of things in themselves" ' (172).[34] As we shall see, Simone de Beauvoir shares Virginia Woolf's sense that one of the major strategies of sexism is to imprison women in their subjectivity, thereby severely curtailing their freedom to transcend the narrow confines patriarchy has prepared for them. Creativity requires the freedom to escape the given, the familiar, and the known as well as the freedom to return to it. Psychoanalytic theory offers us the thought that insofar as we are shackled and bound by our neuroses, the impersonality of the analyst's voice will help us to relate more freely to the world and less compulsively to ourselves. Here, however, the impersonal does not mean the unfeeling or the unsympathetic, it means the fact that the analysand doesn't know anything about the analyst as a person. Contemporary literary critics, however, appear utterly impervious to such ideas: in the late 1990s the impersonal and the objective have overwhelmingly bad press, at least among American critics.

The philosophical ground for the turn to the personal and the rejection of objectivity is the idea that knowledge is 'situated'. A famous feminist version of the claim is that knowledge—all knowledge—is gendered, that 'women's ways of knowing' are different from men's or, in the full-blown version, that 'women's experiences constitute a different view of reality, an entirely different "ontology" or way of going about making sense of the

---

34 Fernald is quoting Woolf in *A Room of One's Own*. She also reminds us of T. S. Eliot's unfashionable plea for impersonality in 'Tradition and the Individual Talent'.

world' (Stanley and Wise 117). In her wonderful essay 'Knowing Tornadoes and Other Things', Cora Diamond distinguishes between strong versions and weak versions of this claim.[35] The strong version is the one just quoted. Weaker versions will claim, less dramatically, that in our patriarchal society child development, for instance, will produce

> men who in their mature thought separate subject and object, or mind and body, or who think in terms of what belongs to individuals as such rather than what belongs to them by virtue of webs of relationships, as so on. . . . The intellectual structures we find in the sciences and in our theorizing about knowledge are supposedly rooted in the way men shape their identity in the context of our child-rearing practices (Diamond 1003).

Diamond points out that both the weak and the strong argument proceed from 'theories about how a pervasive masculine bias can or must characterize knowledge in our society' (1004). The alternative, Diamond notes, is to start from what she calls 'epidemiological data', to begin by 'looking at different bodies of knowledge, bodies of knowledge with different characteristics, associated with different populations' (1003). 'Whether experience shows something about the world or about the experiencer depends, and we learn on what, in different contexts, it does depend', Diamond adds (1006).

Taking her own advice, Diamond goes on to analyse specific examples of knowledge. First there is the particular scientific model of knowledge exemplified by meteorology. I will quote Diamond's description of this at some length, since it seems to exemplify exactly what postmodern critics deplore the most, namely the scientific, objective, mode of knowledge:

> The person seeking scientific knowledge of tornadoes, the meteorologist, can properly ignore all the rich full experience that one might get by actual direct experience of a tornado. Science seeks the laws governing tornadoes; it does not seek to convey *what it is like* to be in a tornado. . . . [I]n the case of the tornado, if you the meteorologist want an accurate account of the changes in wind-speed and

---

35 I shall give a fairly detailed summary of Diamond's arguments because I have the impression that her essay is little known both among feminist theorists and among literary critics.

direction during the tornado, you do not if you can help it want to rely on the actual experience of people in the tornado's path, what it felt or looked like to them, but rather, if possible, on instruments, because people who have gone through the tornado will exaggerate in their accounts; their accounts will be affected by their emotions and will lack accuracy. The kind of experience relevant to scientific knowledge of tornadoes will be the experience of looking at the output of sophisticated and carefully designed measuring instruments (1006–7).

This model of knowledge, Diamond shows, is fine for tornadoes. Used to study phenomena such as pregnancy or sexuality, however, it leads to the assumption that 'just as you the scientist do not need to consider people's experience of tornadoes, you do not need to consider women's experience of pregnancy' (1007). She then shows that on the tornado model, it is not only women's experiences that fail to qualify as knowledge (their understanding of their lives is *mere* experience, that of their doctors is knowledge), but also the experience of animal trainers:

> when the trainers' experience with dogs or horses is treated by scientists as irrelevant to genuine knowledge, this is precisely because there is in that experience, and in their expression of it, their love of animals. The scientific view is not that sentimentality may distort one's experience . . . it is the far stronger and deeply questionable view that the experience of the person who loves animals reveals only that person's own emotional state (1008).

The fact that the animal trainers whose knowledge is discounted by scientists are often men working in the police force and the army, shows that the tornado model of knowledge is not necessarily gendered, at least not in any simple way.

The tornado model of knowledge is impersonal, Diamond writes, in the sense that the data obtained 'can be compared to the data of others; one's hypotheses can be evaluated by anyone. . . . The ways scientific knowledge is built up detach it from people's particular traits like their maleness' (1010). Diamond stresses that just as there are many different styles of knowledge, there are different sorts of impersonal knowledge. Think of the kind of knowledge one obtains when asking a 'travel agent for information about plane schedules to Detroit. One hopes for a correct answer, the answer one could get from *any* competent travel agent' (1010).

Diamond's point is at once simple and powerful:

> Techniques of impersonal knowledge may themselves be in the service of all sorts of good or bad individual or social projects. The availability, that is, of facts that bear no stamp on them of who, what sort of person, came to those facts, got them into the body of knowledge, serves all sorts of further ends (1011).

It follows that it is actually immensely useful for revolutionaries to have impersonal knowledge lying around. This is precisely the kind of knowledge that can be picked up and put into the service of projects quite different from those which originally motivated the development of that knowledge in the first place. Terry Eagleton once remarked that to discard objectivity is also to discard conflict.[36] Instead of the common terrain necessary to any struggle over different interests and claims, one gets bland consensualism, which works to gloss over conflict in the manner of the most naturalizing ideology.

Diamond finally shows that the kind of knowledge tourists regularly ask for (what is in the soup? where is the post office? is it handmade?) may well be impersonal and objective, but nevertheless 'serves some people's ends much more than those of others. . . . What the right answer is to "Where is the post office?" is independent of the particular person who answers, but there being practice in handling such questions is useful to tourists rather than natives' (1011). To Diamond, this means that 'Knowledge that is impersonal in the sense of being relatively abstract and detached from experience may not be at all impersonal, in the second sense, in that it is tied to the aims of some people rather than others' (1012). Some knowledge is actually gender-free, impersonal and neutral (Diamond's example is $7 + 5 = 12$). Once we recognize this, we can go on to ask whose projects this knowledge serves.

This is a question which will have different answers in different cases. One of the valuable insights emerging from a reading of Cora Diamond's unjustly neglected essay is that impersonal

---

[36] Private communication.

knowledge—the tornado model—may be put to feminist as well
as to non-feminist use. Simone de Beauvoir and Virginia Woolf
both thought that knowledge of our actual conditions of life
would make the struggle against injustice easier, not more difficult. Audre Lorde agreed. Quoting Simone de Beauvoir, Lorde
writes: 'It is in the knowledge of the genuine conditions of our
lives that we must draw our strength to live and our reasons for
acting' ('Master's Tools' 113). It is precisely because some kinds
of knowledge are impersonal in the sense of not bearing the
mark of the individual person(s) who first discovered them, that
they are available to anyone who needs them. On the other
hand, the knowledge of children in a good children's book is
personal, Diamond shows. The author's knowledge of children is
embodied in the book she wrote for them. It cannot just be
picked up and used by someone else without losing some or all
of its original features. To reject 'impersonal' or 'objective'
knowledge is to reject a mode of knowledge that potentially can
be made more democratically available to all than 'personal'
knowledge, which per definition remains tied to the person who
developed it.

Discussing the reception of *The Second Sex*, Beauvoir writes that
it was precisely the objectivity of her tone that irritated her sexist
opponents:

> A wild cry of rage, the revolt of a wounded soul—that they could
> have accepted with a moved and pitying condescension; since they
> could not pardon me my objectivity, they feigned a disbelief in it.
> For example I attacked a phrase of Claude Mauriac's because it
> illustrated the arrogance of the First Sex. 'What has she got against
> me?' he wanted to know. Nothing; I had nothing against anything
> except the words I was quoting. It is strange that so many intellec-
> tuals should refuse to believe in intellectual passions. (*FC* 200; *FCa*
> 264; TA)

Beauvoir's irritation at Claude Mauriac's personalizing (*ad
hominem*) interpretation of her critique of his writing, as well as
her defence of intellectual passions, are timely reminders of the
limitations of the personal. Even more important is the fact that
the contemporary tendency to bundle objectivity and impersonality together is not shared by Beauvoir. Although she thinks of

The Second Sex as an objective account of women's condition, she doesn't think of it as impersonal in the 'tornado model' sense. The kind of knowledge we find in it does bear the mark of its writer, but this is not enough to deny the text its claim to objectivity. Beauvoir, in short, makes an assumption similar to that of Cora Diamond, namely that the meaning of the word 'objective' is not going to be the same in a philosophical or feminist essay and in meteorology. In the introduction to *The Second Sex* Beauvoir writes:

> But it is doubtless impossible to approach any human problem with a mind free from bias. The way in which questions are put, the points of view assumed, presuppose a hierarchy of interests; all properties [*qualités*] cover [*enveloppe*] values, and there is no so-called objective description which does not imply an ethical background.[37] Rather than attempt to conceal principles more or less definitely implied, it is better to state them openly at the beginning. Then one will not have to specify on every page in just what sense one uses such words as *superior, inferior, better, worse, progress, reaction*, and the like (*SS* xxxiv; *DSa* 30; TA).

For Beauvoir, then, one achieves greater objectivity by stating one's general principles openly, and not by describing what one is wearing at the time of writing.

Instead of worrying about whether a certain insight is 'impersonal' because we assume that it therefore *must* be masculinist and falsely universalizing, we would be better off asking whether the mode of knowledge employed is suitable for the case at hand, and whose purposes the information thus gathered serves. It follows from Diamond's analysis, I think, that we need to ask the same questions of modes of knowledge considered to be 'personal'. Are we engaged in discussing a question where personal insights are relevant and useful? Whose interests does the deployment of the personal serve in the case at hand? Only in this way can we hope to account for the very different effects and purposes to which the personal is put by American TV talk show

---

[37] The French formulation is 'qui ne s'enlève sur un arrière-plan éthique' (30). In Sect. II below, I discuss Beauvoir's use of the expression *s'enlever sur* (*un fond*) at length.

hosts on the one hand and by Virginia Woolf in *A Room of One's Own* on the other.[38]

I shall end this discussion of the difficulties that arise from an uncritical embrace of the personal and the subjective and an equally uncritical dismissal of the impersonal and the objective by turning to Roland Barthes's classical analysis of ideological uses of personal information about writers. We have already seen that some critics find it highly desirable to include in their critical texts information about the writer's person, particularly in the form of autobiographical passages. We have also seen that one or two voices worry about the links between such autobiographical performances and the academic star system. There are in fact striking similarities between a certain form of 'autobiographical performance' in criticism and celebrity journalism.[39] The kind of details Jane Tompkins (and she is far from the only one) considers relevant and pleasurable to present for our consumption is that she is wearing stockings, that she has a famous husband who is into epistemology, that she likes cappuccino, is thinking about going to the bathroom, and that she lives in North Carolina. These are precisely the kind of details Roland Barthes picks up on in his acerbic and very funny piece on 'The Writer on Holiday' collected in that genuinely popular, political, and personal book of criticism called *Mythologies*.[40] This is how Barthes starts his short essay:

[38] To mention some examples of different uses of the personal: in his thoughtful essay on the academic star system David Shumway distinguishes between autobiograpy used 'to make an academic argument' and autobiography used by marginal or oppressed groups to 'establish communal identity' (97). Charles Altieri also stresses 'fostering community' as one function of the critics' turn to autobiography (58, 66).

[39] The connection between the recent turn to the personal and the culture of TV talk shows has been pointed out by many critics: 'the autobiographical move afoot in scholarly writing today is part of a larger trend that I call the Phil Donahue syndrome: the multiplication of talk shows, audience participation shows, call-in shows, and so on, featuring guests who bare it all, figuratively and sometimes literally, before a fascinated audience. Are academics suddenly admitting they have emotions and entrails and genitals, that they have hit their wives, or have to go to the bathroom, or prefer anal sex for the same reasons as the folks on TV, whatever those reasons?' Candace Lang writes (44).

[40] I am grateful to Richard Moran for reminding me to reread Barthes's text.

> Gide was reading Bossuet while going down the Congo. This
> posture sums up rather well the ideal of our writers 'on holiday', as
> photographed by *Le Figaro*: to add to mere leisure the prestige of a
> vocation which nothing can stop or degrade (29).

Barthes's errand is to show that bourgeois French culture in the
1950s represented writers as divine creatures, endowed with a
different essence from other workers. When a worker goes on
holiday he is nothing but a simple holidaymaker, whereas a writer
is always and everywhere a writer. Whenever the writer goes on
holiday, the newspaper marvels, he still reads and writes. 'And he
who does nothing confesses it as truly paradoxical behaviour, an
avant-garde exploit, which only someone of exceptional independence can afford to flaunt' (30). The result is to produce a mysti-
fied image of the writer as a deified, sacralized creature, eternally
in thrall to his Muse, his divine source of inspiration:

> Thus the function of the man of letters is to human labour rather
> as ambrosia is to bread: a miraculous, eternal substance, which
> condescends to take a social form so that its prestigious difference
> is better grasped. All this prepares one for the same idea of the
> writers as a superman, as a kind of intrinsically different being . . .
> (30).

The very representation of the writer's prosaic, everyday existence serves to reinforce this mythological and mystifying picture
of what a writer is:

> this myth of 'literary holidays' is seen to spread very far, much
> farther than summer: the techniques of contemporary journalism
> are devoted more and more to presenting the writer as a prosaic
> figure. But one would be very wrong to take this as an attempt to
> demystify. Quite the contrary. True, it may seem touching, and
> even flattering, that I, a mere reader, should participate, thanks to
> such confidences, in the daily life of a race selected by genius. I
> would no doubt feel that a world was blissfully fraternal, in which
> newspapers told me that a certain great writer wears blue pyjamas,
> and a certain young novelist has a liking for 'pretty girls, *reblochon*
> cheese and lavender-honey'. . . .
>   To endow the writer publicly with a good fleshly body, to reveal
> that he likes dry white wine and underdone steak is to make even
> more miraculous for me, and of a more divine essence, the prod-
> ucts of his art (31).

Barthes's analysis presupposes that someone else does the writing. Yet the writer who gives interviews while on holiday participates in the mystifying cult of his own divine essence. If we are to follow Barthes, the academics who indulge in the kind of 'autobiographical performances' where they tell us what they are wearing when they are writing, what kind of food they like, and so on are in fact mythologizing themselves. Since nothing is less unusual than the fact of having a human body that eats, drinks, has sex and wears clothes, such information can only be interesting on the assumption that although we all do these things, it is truly surprising that a *literary critic* should do so. A more narcissistic version would go: although we all know that *other* literary critics do these things, what is truly surprising is that this *particular* literary critic does it. The assumption is that there is something about this specific person, or about the class of people known as literary critics, that is so extraordinary, so godlike as to warrant such exhibitions. As Barthes puts it, 'By having holidays, he displays the sign of his being human; but the god remains, one is a writer as Louis XIV was king, even on the commode' (30).

Barthes's mythologies are intended as a critique of the kind of ideology that seeks to represent as natural that which in fact is socially produced. For Barthes, then, what is reprehensible here is the attempt to represent ordinary human activities as extraordinary simply because a certain social category of people carry them out. But this is not an argument against including ordinary actions and circumstances in theoretical texts. On the contrary, Barthes's scathing critique of more or less self-mythologizing pretentiousness gives us all the more reason to try to write about the ordinary and the everyday in non-mythologizing ways.

Some Preliminary Conclusions

Speaking in the first person about one's own experience easily blocks further discussion. Instead of acknowledging the presence of others, we isolate ourselves, ending up 'all alone and feeling blue'. The insertion of autobiographical performances in literary criticism does not always make the writer vulnerable, since it can just as easily turn into a narcissistic and self-mythologizing performance. As

Anne Fernald shows, only when the personal is in the service of original thought, as in the case of Virginia Woolf, do we experience it as illuminating rather than embarrassing. In my view, the claim that every speech act has something personal in it is true, but precisely for that reason it does not justify explicitly autobiographical writing any more or less than it justifies haughtily impersonal performances. In short, the effects of the personal will depend—on the context, on what the personal is taken to mean in any given case, and on the interests the personal performance is supposed to serve. I have also tried to show that the much maligned impersonality can be experienced as liberating. Just as there are different ways of being personal, there are different ways of being impersonal, and for different purposes. Poetic impersonality, accurate train tables or flight schedules and Diamond's tornado model of knowledge are a few examples of such different ways. The postmodern quest for the personal is a theory-generated attempt to escape from the bad effects of theory, and as such bears all the hallmarks of theoreticism: it is overgeneral, prescriptive, and impervious to experiences running counter to the theory.[41]

Here it must nevertheless be acknowledged that there are at least two routes to the personal. In the case of Jane Tompkins the motivation appears to be classically humanist. This is why she perceives *all* theory as alienating; for her, the goal is to reach her own true humanity, to let her own emotions and feelings shine forth unfettered by theoretical obstruction. Although the end result in many ways is quite similar to, say, the autobiographical performances of Nancy Miller and Jane Gallop, the motivation that drives their turn to the personal appears to be grounded in postmodern considerations concerning the subjectivity of knowledge.[42] This also seems to be the case for just about all the

[41] Insofar as the wish to write autobiographically is theory-driven, the 'person' or 'subject' produced is going to conform to whatever theory the critic prefers. Charles Altieri makes a similar point when he claims that Jane Tompkins's dwelling on her wish to go to the bathroom is 'driven by theoretical considerations about how to write personally, and motivated not by communication but by desires to stage the self for certain effects' (67 n. 3).

[42] I am thinking of Miller's *Getting Personal* and Gallop's *Thinking Through the Body* and *Feminist Accused of Sexual Harassment.*

contributors to the *PMLA* Forum. The true sign of this is the fact that such critics do not, like Jane Tompkins, reject *all* theory. They reject *bad* theory, usually conveniently generalized under the label 'Enlightenment theory'.

The rhetorical move which consists in declaring that what follows is said by a white male bourgeois heterosexual, or by a black lesbian working-class woman usually does not work. Unless there is something in the text that somehow exemplifies what it means to speak as this or that type of subject, one might just as well not bother. As Linda Alcoff puts it, 'Simple unanalyzed disclaimers do not improve on this familiar situation [of oppression] and may even make it worse to the extent that by offering such information the speaker may feel even more authorized to speak and be accorded more authority by his peers' (25).[43]

Attempts to produce autobiographical anecdotes as part of the theoretical text are often quite embarrassing to read. As Wendy Lesser remarks, 'We may at times be embarrassed *by* [the essay-writer], but we should never feel embarrassed *for* him' (quoted in Fernald 171). Autobiographical material can liven up a text, but only if the reader is convinced of the relevance and interest of the material. Even if the narrative included is relevant, there is another question that matters even more: what is the power of the story? Can it function as an example, as a specific case study? Does it challenge us to think further for ourselves? Or does it just invite us to like and admire the author? As I will discuss at length in relation to Simone de Beauvoir, the power of thought developed through careful examination of a particular case can be immense. But the more powerful the thought, the less it matters whether the case is autobiographical or biographical, personal or impersonal, true or fictional.

As for Jane Tompkins's claim that theory prevents us from expressing our emotions, there is some truth in that, at least if she means that one can't write theory and at the same time focus exclusively on one's own rage or elation. At some point there will have to be some widening of perspective, some attempt to universalize, or

43 Alcoff is referring to people in a privileged position. I think the criteria of relevance and power or interest applies to all attempts to 'get personal' or to invoke location.

the experiences described will not be theory. (Raw, courageous autobiography is a wonderful thing to write, but my question throughout this essay is not how to write a good autobiography but how to write good theory.) Although theorists from Darwin to Freud have taken emotions utterly seriously, and although every theoretical inquiry is fuelled by emotion, desire, sexuality, child-hood traumas, and so on, once we have pointed out that this is the case, we really shall have to get on with the theoretical inquiry our subjectivity has impelled us to undertake. Whether or not we tell our readers all about the personal motivations for undertaking the work they are reading is a matter of judgement: the criteria of power and relevance still apply.

Cora Diamond's analysis of different modes of knowledge is based on a fundamental methodological stance. To her, very general theoretical arguments purporting to demonstrate that masculine bias *must* exist are unconvincing (see 1004). It is not that she doubts that such bias exists, the question is rather how to demonstrate in a convincing way that it does. As we have seen, Diamond recommends that if we want to find out whether know-ledge—some specific kind of knowledge—is gender-biased, we should actually analyse different forms of knowledge. I share Diamond's distrust of arguments about bias and exclusion derived from highly general and abstract theoretical claims. They always take the form of assuming that if the claim is right, then such and such a phenomenon simply *must* be sexist, racist, or whatever. Once this conclusion has been established, no amount of experience to the contrary can prevail. No wonder that the number of musts and shoulds in contemporary theoretical prose is astonishingly high.[44]

Against such theoreticism I too would recommend analysis of the concrete phenomena that interest us. This is the only way to get away from the horrifying grid of binary oppositions that

[44] Nina Baym's 1987 essay entitled 'The Madwoman and her Languages: Why I Don't Do Feminist Theory' picks up on this linguistic symptom: ' "she must . . . she must . . . she must." If that *she* is *me*, somebody (once again) is telling me what I "*must*" do to be a true woman, and that somebody is asserting (not inci-dentally) her own monopoly on truth as she does so. I've been here before' (61 n. 32).

structure so much contemporary theoretical debate on the question of subjectivity and the personal. In this essay I am neither denying nor asserting that the impersonal must be masculinist or exclusionary, or whatever. Instead I am trying to show that there are all kinds of situations and contexts in which the simplistic assumption that the personal = good and impersonal = bad don't hold. At the same time, it is evident that the opposite and equally simplistic assumption (the impersonal = good, the personal = bad) doesn't hold either. Freed from this picture of how things *must* be, we can emerge from the straitjacket of binary oppositions and move into a world in which we might find more than two intellectual alternatives to choose from.

Now, finally, we are in a position to see that the problem with the postmodern turn to the personal is that it is derived from a highly general theory about knowledge (knowledge is always situated; to say so is always necessary and important; claims to objective knowledge are always just a way of imposing the interests of the dominant class or group; and so on). In their style and mode of writing, postmodern theories tend to be as generalizing and universalizing as the Enlightenment theory they oppose (as if there were such a thing as *one* monolithic Enlightenment theory, any more than there is *one* postmodern theory). This kind of theory generates the belief that if we always claim to be speaking *as* the singular individuals we are, then this *must* make our texts less arrogant, less universalizing, less domineering, more properly situated, and perhaps also more capable of reaching out to others.

I have tried to show through numerous examples that such assumptions are by no means generally true. In my discussion of *ad feminam* argumentation, I stress that the turn to the personal needs to be justified by showing what problem it solves. In the same way, I have tried to show that one cannot assume that any attempt to turn to the impersonal is a universalist, patriarchal plot. The analysis of the particular case—of the individual speech act—will tell us whether this is a likely explanation. What I am warning about here, is the tendency to let theoretical parameters block our openness to conflicting and contradictory evidence. If all I ever seek are cases that confirm my theory, the likelihood is that I will find them, but at what intellectual cost?[45]

So what are we left with? In my view, two closely related problems require further examination. The first is: how do I manage to undo the idea that the third person is always exclusionary, always oppressive, always opposed to the first person, or in other words, the belief that the only alternatives we have are either speaking *as* or speaking *for*? At this stage I suspect that such a very limiting way of looking at speech acts may be another one of those pictures that 'hold us captive', as Wittgenstein would say, but I have not shown that this is so. Linda Alcoff makes some very useful points about the difficulty of keeping the first and third person separate, but she does not propose any alternative ways of framing the question.[46] Are there any? The second, related, question is: how do I manage to write in a way that manages to make strong theoretical claims without falling into the trap of overgeneralizing? Theory cannot relinquish its wish to make claims that are valid for others without ceasing to be theory. What I need now

[45] Some readers will surely notice that I have said nothing about the 'subject' in this discussion of the turn to the personal. Some defenders of the personal think in terms of a traditional humanist subject, others don't. I find that the question of how the individual critic figures the subject is of very limited interest in this context. It certainly seems to make no difference to their recommendations as to when to 'get personal', for instance. Thus Pamela Caughie criticizes Linda Alcoff for not consistently deconstructing the 'I' (see 'Let It Pass'). Although Caughie declares that she herself knows that her subjectivity is an effect of her own discursive performance (and so on), as far as I can tell, Caughie uses the word 'I' in exactly the same way as Alcoff. It seems to me that what Caughie is asking for—and in this she is by no means alone—is some kind of preliminary metaphysical statement about the nature of 'the subject', after which we continue to use language in exactly the same way as before.

[46] I should add that Alcoff thinks that in some situations it is better to speak for (on behalf of) others than to remain silent. Her insistence on concrete analysis of specific speech acts is very similar to mine. The difference between our analyses is that I don't subscribe to the general idea that we *must* always investigate location, or that impersonal and objective knowledge *must* be sexist, racist, or otherwise oppressive in every case. Alcoff proposes specific analysis as a way to attenuate the consequences of her general theoretical stance, whereas I propose it as a starting point for further discussion. I imagine that in many cases we might reach exactly the same conclusions about the meaning and effects of a given speech act.

is to find a different model, some other path to insight. In short, I need a case study of sufficient power and relevance to advance my understanding of these questions. It is at this juncture that I turn to Simone de Beauvoir and *The Second Sex*.

II. THE SECOND SEX

Introduction

In order to try to answer some of the questions I have raised, I want to study Simone de Beauvoir's philosophical style by taking a close look at the beginning of *The Second Sex*. I shall focus on the first five pages, or the first three paragraphs of the text, starting from the beginning and continuing until Beauvoir reaches her justly famous conclusion that woman is the Other.[47] I should perhaps say, by way of warning, that what follows is an extremely long and detailed close reading of a short excerpt from a philosophical text. The inspiration and energy to undertake such a reading come from my overwhelming frustration that Simone de Beauvoir in general is still not being seriously read among feminist and other theorists.[48]

By philosophical style I mean the way Beauvoir thinks: how she constructs an argument, what kind of examples she uses, how she chooses to express an idea, what kind of vocabulary she draws on, what tone she uses. The word 'style', from the Greek *stulos* (column), is used to describe the difference between a Doric and an Ionic column, or 'the characteristic manner of literary expression of a particular writer, school, a period, etc.'. Style also designates 'a manner of speaking or conversing'. In such contexts, style is often opposed to content: style becomes the manner but not the substance, the clothing that dresses the man, but not the man himself. Style can also refer to a specific person's way of being in

[47] I am referring to the first three paragraphs in the two-volume French Folio edition of *Le deuxième sexe* (*DSa* 11–15). In the American 1989 Vintage edition this corresponds to the first *six* paragraphs, or the first four pages (*SS* xix–xxii).

[48] Obviously, I don't mean to include the increasing number of scholars specializing in Beauvoir studies among those who fail to read her works in sufficient detail.

the world: 'a mode or manner of living or behaving; a person's bearing or demeanour'. Taken in this sense, the form/content opposition is not necessarily in play; we have arrived at Buffon's 'Le style est l'homme même' ('the style is the person', to paraphrase a little).

The word 'method' has interesting affinities to style, and comes from the Greek *methodos*, a word produced by combining *meta* (with, after) with *hodos* (way). When I say that I want to study the *way* Beauvoir thinks, etymologically speaking this means that I want to consider her method. Unlike style, however, method can mean 'systematic arrangement, order', or 'order in thinking or expressing thoughts'. A method is often taken to be an underlying plan or grid that can be uncovered and abstracted from the finished work. In this sense, method comes to mean something like a set of general principles for how to go about things. But method can also mean a 'mode of procedure; a (defined or systematic) way of doing a thing in accordance with a particular theory or as associated with a particular theory or as associated with a particular person'. To speak of Beauvoir's method in this latter sense would simply be to speak of a way of thinking associated with her person, and with existentialist philosophy. When method is used in this sense, philosophical method and philosophical style become virtually interchangeable terms. The kind of inquiry I want to undertake here is situated precisely on the level where method shades into style, or in other words: when philosophy shades into literary criticism.

Insofar as the concept of style still tends to conjure up binaries such as style/substance, surface/depth, and form/content, I should say that these terms do not have to be seen as mutually exclusive. To read *for* style is not necessarily to read *against* content: these two terms do not always operate on different sides of a divide. To read for philosophical style is to ask *how* something is being said without in the least neglecting or ignoring *what* is being said. Fundamentally intertwined, form and content, style and substance (or whatever terms we prefer) collaborate in the production of meaning. It is confusing and unhelpful to pit them against each other. Style is therefore not well understood if one thinks of it as a surface which either conceals or conveys the real meaning lurking in the depths beneath the rhetorical effects. The *what* is not 'deeper' than the *how:* they are both right there, in our words.

One final introductory note: I do not mean to imply that Beauvoir's style is uniform and unvarying throughout *The Second Sex.* What I am claiming is that the pages I am about to analyse are characteristic of her thought at its best. I will show that Beauvoir arrives at the claim that woman is the Other not through metaphysical speculation but through analysis of expressions and anecdotes from everyday life. I will also show that her argument gains much of its impressive power from the way she uses herself as a philosophical case study, or in other words, from the way in which she makes the personal do philosophical work for her. It will also emerge from my reading that Beauvoir's way of writing philosophy has strong affinities with ordinary language philosophy, particularly with the work of Stanley Cavell. When these affinities are brought out, Beauvoir's work gains new dimensions, not least when it comes to the question that interests me here, namely what Beauvoir's philosophical style can teach us about the personal and the philosophical.

The Style is the Philosopher

To convey more concretely what I mean by 'philosophical style' and what difference style can make, I will start by briefly comparing the beginning of *The Second Sex* to the beginning of another influential feminist text, Luce Irigaray's *Speculum of the Other Woman.* Both books start by raising the question of femininity, yet the first few lines in each text immediately reveal interesting differences in philosophical style. This is how *The Second Sex* begins:

> I have hesitated for a long time to write a book on woman. The subject is irritating, especially to women; and it is not new. The quarrel over feminism has spilt enough ink, and now it is more or less over: let's talk no more about it. It is still talked about, however. It seems that all the voluminous nonsense uttered during the last century has done little to illuminate the problem. After all, is there a problem? And if so, what is it? Are there women, really? Most assuredly the theory of the eternal feminine still has its adherents

who will whisper in your ear: 'Even in Russia women still are *women*'; and other well informed persons—sometimes the very same—say with a sigh: 'Woman is losing her way, woman is lost.' We [*on*] no longer know if women still exist, if they will always exist, whether or not it is desirable that they should, what place they occupy in this world, what place they should occupy in it. 'Where are the women?' an ephemeral magazine recently asked. But first: what is a woman? (*SS* xix; *DSa* 12; TA).[49]

'I' is the first word of *The Second Sex*. 'J'ai longtemps hésité à écrire un livre sur la femme', Beauvoir writes.[50] In this way she introduces herself firmly yet unobtrusively as the author of her own text. To my ears, this does not sound like a phenomenological or metaphysical I, but like the everyday I of the person who is writing the philosophical text we are about to read.[51] A few pages later we will learn that there is nothing easy or self-evident about this woman's claim to philosophical authority and authorship, yet here, at the outset, Beauvoir chooses to write as if it goes without saying that she has the right to start her essay by saying I in such an unremarkable way.

In the passage quoted the dominant pronouns are I and we, but the French *on* also makes an appearance. The characteristic value of *on* is that it always includes the speaker: according to context it may be translated either as 'one' or 'we'. The text is also punctuated by a number of questions that appear to be addressing the

---

[49] The usual problems with the English translation of *The Second Sex* are everywhere apparent in the first few pages. I amend the translation as necessary. In English the last sentence of this quotation appears as the first sentence in the second paragraph of the text. In French, on the other hand, the first three pages constitute one long paragraph.

[50] In Parshley's translation the first sentence reads: 'For a long time I have hesitated to write a book on woman'. This loses the effect Beauvoir creates by starting her book with 'I'.

[51] Some readers may still want to challenge the idea that *The Second Sex is* a philosophical text. By now, however, the depth and intensity of Beauvoir's philosophical engagement has surely been established beyond doubt. Texts such as Le Dœuff, *Hipparchia's Choice*; Kruks, *Situation*; Lundgren-Gothlin, *Sex*; Bergoffen; Vintges; and Bauer all demonstrate the philosophical interest of Beauvoir's great essay. The question of what it may mean to take Beauvoir seriously as an original philosopher, however, is far from settled. Bauer in particular asks pertinent questions about how to read Beauvoir once we have agreed that she is to be read as a philosopher.

reader. These are not necessarily rhetorical questions, in the sense that they do not always take for granted that everyone knows what the right answer is.[52] By asking 'is there a problem?' Beauvoir encourages the reader to consider for herself whether she thinks there is a problem, what she thinks a woman is, and whether she thinks these are good questions. Initially, at least, Beauvoir's text presents itself as an invitation to the reader to make up her own mind about the questions it is exploring.

There is also a great deal of irony in the text. Beauvoir's dead-pan quotation of silly ideas about women is an attempt to send up the 'mythologies' of everyday life, to use Roland Barthes's expression. But her irony is not entirely dismissive: the fact that there are misguided believers in the eternal feminine helps Beauvoir to demonstrate that the question of what a woman is and what her role in the world should be, is far from settled. The initial 'let's talk no more about it' is countered by evidence that nonsensical ideas about women still prevail. By claiming that the very same connoisseurs declare both that the eternal feminine never disappears and that woman is lost, Beauvoir reveals the confusion of sexist thought. By being ironical about the confusion of others, Beauvoir justifies the writing of *The Second Sex* by presenting it as an exercise in lucidity. Towards the end of the introduction, she makes this point explicitly: 'It is striking', she writes, 'that everything women write [*l'ensemble de la littérature féminine*] these days is animated less by a wish to demand our rights than by an effort toward lucidity. As we emerge from an era of wild polemics, this book is offered as one attempt among others to analyse our position' (*SS* xxxiii–xxxiv; *DSa* 29-30; TA).[53] For Beauvoir, the lucidity

[52] The OED defines a 'rhetorical question' as one that is 'asked not for information but to produce effect'. The example given is *who cares?* for *nobody cares.* Much more could be said about rhetorical questions, but this is not the place to do so.

[53] Parshley's curiously biased translation of the phrase *l'ensemble de la littérature féminine* is 'books by women on women'. And in the last sentence quoted, Beauvoir writes: 'ce livre est une tentative parmi d'autres pour faire le point'. Parshley's translation here is even more bizarre: 'this book is offered as one attempt among others to confirm that statement [about the lucidity of women's writing]'. Admittedly, *faire le point* is difficult to translate well. The expression is nautical in origins, and originally meant to find one's bearings, to find out

and objectivity of philosophy permit her to overcome and undo sexist ideology.[54]

Irony is a matter of tone: either we hear it or we don't. The more subtle the irony, the more it tends to split the audience between those who get it and those who don't. Among the readers who do get it, moreover, there are usually some who don't particularly enjoy the experience. For irony is a rhetorical manœuvre which can make the very act of understanding the author's point feel invasive and contaminating. To get the irony of a text, the reader has to be able to imagine the author's point of view, if only for the briefest moment. Resisting readers hear the irony, but resent not only its ideological point, but the very fact that they have been made to see what the world looks like from a politically alien point of view. Feminists exposed to sexist irony have ample experience of what it feels like to be caught in this rhetorical trap. As the French reception of the book showed, sexist readers of *The Second Sex* reacted with fury to Beauvoir's unerring targeting of their cherished beliefs in the eternal feminine. Whatever its fate among actual readers, irony is an invitation to the reader to share the writer's critical attitude to the object of the irony. It is up to the reader to notice the invitation, to decide whether to accept or decline it, whether to smile in delighted recognition or groan in exasperated resentment. However we react, to listen for irony is to listen for the attitude of the speaking subject. Like Beauvoir's use of 'I' and 'we', her irony also signals her presence in the text.

Turning now to *Speculum of the Other Woman*, we notice that Irigaray starts her book not by asserting her own subjectivity, but by masking her voice:

---

where one is on the map. It is commonly used to mean 'produce an overview', 'produce an analysis', and could very well be translated as 'to take stock'. *Le point sur . . .* means something like 'an overview of the relevant issues concerning . . .'. This meaning is echoed in the title of the French political magazine *Le point.*

[54] This does not mean that she thinks one can be objective in the sense of producing value-free descriptions. See pp. 159–60, above for a brief discussion of her understanding of objectivity and impersonality. In *The Second Sex* this discussion follows directly after the passage about lucidity quoted here.

'Ladies and Gentlemen ... Throughout history people have knocked their heads against the riddle of the nature of femininity—... Nor will *you* have escaped worrying over this problem—those of you who are men; to those of you who are women this will not apply—you are yourselves the problem.'[55]

So it would be a case of you men speaking among yourselves about woman, who cannot be involved in hearing or producing a discourse that concerns the *riddle*, the logogriph she represents for you. The enigma that is woman will therefore constitute the *target*, the *object*, the *stake*, of a masculine discourse, of a debate among men, which would not consult her, would not concern her. Which, ultimately, she is not supposed to know anything about (*Speculum* 13).

In the first sentence, Irigaray ventriloquizes or mimics the voice of Freud. The dominant pronoun in Freud's original text is the plural you (*vous*), and so it is in the paragraph following the Freud quotation, in which Irigaray muses on Freud's text. While Freud's 'you' addresses first men and then women, Irigaray's 'you' is defined as male. Although it erases all explicit markings of the subject position of the speaker, the impassioned opening passage of *Speculum* leaves the reader in little doubt about where Irigaray is and what her views are. In fact, Irigaray's ironic use of quotations focuses attention on the attitude of the speaker. After reading Irigaray's first paragraph the reader is bound to ask whether she is expected to agree with Freud or challenge him. The next paragraph tells her exactly what to think. Just as Beauvoir quotes the believers in the eternal feminine, Irigaray quotes Freud. Simply by quoting him, she produces a certain distance between the reader and Freud; and by being ironical about the quote she invites the reader to share her attitude, to hear Freud's words in the same way as she does. To quote someone is a speech act like any other: the responsibility for the quotation lies with the speaker. To quote someone ironically, moreover, is certainly not to efface one's own voice; on the contrary, it is to lay bare one's trust in that voice.

[55] At this point a footnote in the text, in French as well as in English, signals that Irigaray is quoting Freud's fictive lecture on femininity from *New Lectures on Psycho-Analysis*.

Beauvoir and Irigaray both trust that their own tone will convey their point. Irigaray's constant use of ironic quotations—her famous mimicry—is an invitation to the reader to share the speaker's attitude and evaluations.[56] In *Speculum,* Irigaray's Plotinus chapter ('Une mère de glace') is a wonderful example of this.[57] Located near the middle of the book, the chapter is composed entirely of quotations, without a single word of commentary. Irigaray is gambling on the idea that having read so far, the reader will be so immersed in her arguments, so used to her tone, her way of quoting male thinkers ironically, that no more commentary is necessary. The gamble pays off, I think. By the time they reach the Plotinus chapter most readers of *Speculum of the Other Woman* are ready to read him in the way Irigaray herself would have done it, thus taking a chapter composed entirely of quotations to be a critique, not a simple report or summary.[58] Thus, in an act of astonishing rhetorical brilliance, Irigaray manages to convey her critique of Plotinus by relying almost entirely on tone.[59]

Beauvoir's and Irigaray's styles both emphasize the question of who is speaking, and more particularly, the question of whether women have the right to speak the language of philosophy. Clearly Beauvoir's existentialist and Irigaray's psychoanalytic approach lead them to raise similar questions about subjectivity. Yet, at the same time, the difference between Irigaray's emphatic 'you' and Beauvoir's unassuming 'I' indicates that the two women

[56] Naomi Schor defines Irigaray's mimesis (*mimétisme*) as follows: '[It has] been widely and correctly interpreted as describing a parodic mode of discourse designed to deconstruct the discourse of misogyny through effects of amplification and rearticulation that work, in Mary Ann Doane's words, to "enact a defamiliarized version of femininity" ' ('This Essentialism' 53).

[57] The Plotinus chapter has the same title both in the French and English. In French the title contains two puns, on *mère/ mer* (mother/ocean) and the double meaning of *glace* (ice/mirror). Irigaray signals by an initial footnote that Plotinus is being quoted (see *Speculum* 168–79; *Spéculum* 210–26).

[58] As with other uses of irony, Irigaray's irony will not only create a split between readers who read the chapter ironically and those who don't, but also between the readers who gladly join in the critique of Plotinus, and those who resist doing so, although they full well understand that they are intended to.

[59] 'Almost', because the selection of the quotations and their organization also helps to produce the desired effect.

will respond differently to the question of sexual difference. By placing her own everyday 'I' on the philosophical scene, Beauvoir indicates that she thinks of the ordinary and the everyday as integral to her philosophical project of analysing women's situation. Irigaray's masking of the speaking subject, on the other hand, seeks to foreground the thought that a woman under patriarchy is doomed to mimicry, not least when she wants to write philosophy. To my ears, however, there is a great deal of tension between Irigaray's evident trust in the power of her own tone of voice, and her belief that as a woman writing under patriarchy she will somehow never find her own words. In Irigaray the ordinary plays no philosophical role. Unlike Beauvoir, Irigaray doesn't quote gossip and hearsay or ephemeral student publications. In short, Beauvoir's and Irigaray's different attitudes towards the use of the first person singular and the ordinary and everyday are symptomatic of their different understanding of what philosophy is, how it should be written, and in what voice women can speak of or to the philosophical tradition.

What this brief comparison shows is that a writer's philosophical style reveals a great deal about her philosophical purpose and attitude. Whatever rhetorical strategies a writer uses, it is always possible to detect in them traces of her subjectivity.[60] Read in this way, philosophical style becomes a record of subjectivity.

'What Is a Woman?' Beauvoir's Rejection of Essentialism and Nominalism

On the first page of *The Second Sex* Beauvoir asks 'What is a woman?' Her answer is an ironic expression of exasperation with sexist replies to the question:

> All agree in recognizing the fact that females [*des femelles*] exist in the human species, today as always they make up about one half of humanity.[61] And yet we are told that 'femininity is in danger'; we are exhorted to 'be women, remain women, become women'.

[60] It does not follow, of course, that we always *have* to read for the writer's subjectivity. We still need to show why it is relevant and important to do so in a particular case.

[61] I discuss Beauvoir's distinction between *femelle* and *femme* in Ch. 1, above.

Therefore every female human being is not necessarily a woman;
to be so considered she must share in that mysterious and threatened reality known as femininity. Is this attribute something
secreted by the ovaries? Or is it fixed in a Platonic heaven?[62] Is a
rustling petticoat enough to bring it down to earth? (*SS* xix; *DSa*
11–12; TA).

What makes this passage ironic is Beauvoir's pretence of taking
absurd ideas seriously by bringing philosophical logic to bear on
them. The series of questions that closes the passage are intended
at once to make us laugh at the confusions of sexist common
sense and to show that philosophical reason will help us to break
the hold of such everyday mythologies. Like Descartes, Beauvoir
considers reason an instrument of liberation available to everyone.[63]

Precisely because she believes that she has as good a grasp on
reason as everyone else, Beauvoir refuses to accept uncritically
whatever philosophers have had to say about women. Essentialist
thinkers get short shrift: 'In the times of St. Thomas [femininity]
was considered an essence as certainly defined as the somniferous
virtue of the poppy', she writes. 'But conceptualism has lost
ground', she continues, so that today femininity is considered by
biologists and social scientists to be the effect of a *situation*. The
conclusion is clear: 'If today femininity no longer exists, then it
never existed' (*SS* xix; *DSa* 12).[64]

---

[62] '[Est-elle] figée au fond d'un ciel platonicien?', Beauvoir writes, obviously
assuming that her readers instantly will grasp the reference to Platonic essences.
Parshley's translation rewrites and expands the point, probably in the belief that
without explicit help, American readers might miss the reference: 'Or is it a
Platonic essence, a product of the philosophical imagination?'

[63] Nancy Bauer provides a thoughtful discussion of Beauvoir's philosophical
relationship to Descartes: 'the routine condemnations of Descartes in the feminist philosophical literature overlook what is productively radical about the
Cartesian method of doubt. In these aspects, this method [is]—not acciden-
tally—exactly that employed by Beauvoir in *The Second Sex*. This chapter in fact
attempts to make good the unusual claim that one of Simone de Beauvoir's
central aspirations in *The Second Sex* is to rewrite Descartes's *Meditations* from the
ground up (50).

[64] Beauvoir develops the notion of situation at great length in *The Second Sex*.
I discuss it in some detail in Ch. 1, above.

The next question follows logically: 'But does the word *woman*, then, have no content?' (*SS* xx; *DSa* 12; TA). Enlightenment thinkers, rationalists, and nominalists would say that it doesn't, Beauvoir writes. For them, women are 'merely the human beings arbitrarily designated by the name *woman*' (*SS* xx; *DSa* 12). At this point, Beauvoir chooses to give an example. American women are particularly inclined to agree with such mistaken views, she writes, producing Dorothy Parker as her evidence: 'I cannot be just to books which treat of woman as woman. . . . My idea is that all of us, men as well as women, should be regarded as human beings', Parker writes, at least according to Beauvoir (*SS* xx; *DSa* 12).[65] This kind of humanism is instantly dismissed: 'But nominalism is a rather inadequate doctrine', she continues, 'and the antifeminists have had no trouble in showing that women simply *are not* men:

> Surely woman is, like man, a human being; but such an assertion is abstract. The fact is that every concrete human being is always in a specific situation [*spécifiquement situé*].[66] To refuse to accept such notions as the eternal feminine, the black soul, the Jewish character, is not to deny that Jews, Negroes, women exist today—this denial does not represent a liberation for those concerned, but rather an inauthentic flight. Clearly, no woman can without bad faith pretend to be situated beyond her sex (*SS* xx; *DSa* 13; TA).[67]

[65] Here it becomes clear that Beauvoir does not imagine that she is writing for an audience of American readers.

[66] This passage reminds me of Sartre's 1946 text *Réflexions sur la question juive* (translated as *Anti-Semite and Jew*) where he criticizes 'the tendency that we have noted in many democrats who wish purely and simply to suppress the Jew in favour of the *man*. But *man* does not exist: there are Jews, Protestants, Catholics; there are Frenchmen, Englishmen, Germans; there are white, black, and yellow people' (175; my translation).

[67] Disastrously, the last sentence is omitted in Parshley's translation. This omission is particularly galling since it deprives the English-language reader of evidence that Beauvoir does not at all think of sexual difference as something to be avoided or denied. The rest of his translation of this passage is also full of philosophical howlers. When Beauvoir declares that every human being is always in a specific situation, Parshley has her say that 'every concrete human being is always a singular, separate individual'. When she claims that to deny that women, Jews, and blacks exist is not a liberation, but an 'inauthentic flight', Parshley has her say that it is a 'flight from reality', thus losing the reference to bad faith that is implied in the adjective *inauthentique*.

What Beauvoir attacks here is both the post-Enlightenment humanism which hopes to make all differences disappear by insisting on our common humanity ('we are all human beings'), and the nominalist idea that sex and/or gender are nothing but the effects of discourse, an arbitrarily applied signifier. Both types of argument lose sight of the fact that women exist in the world. To pretend to be beyond one's sex or race is to be in bad faith. At this point, Beauvoir produces three examples supplementing the quote from Dorothy Parker. The first concerns a woman writer who didn't want her photograph in a series of pictures devoted to women writers, but wanted it to be included among the pictures of famous male writers. In order to achieve this, she used the influence of her husband. The second is about a young, frail Trotskyite woman who wanted to get into a fist fight at a political meeting because she was in love with a young activist and wanted to be his equal. Finally, there is a quick reference to the 'attitude of defiance' that American women are stuck in. According to Beauvoir, American women refuse to accept the fact that they are women, and in so doing show that they are obsessed by that very fact.

The most significant thing about these examples is that they are there at all. That the inclusion of three everyday examples and a quote from a book review by a middlebrow woman writer is a significant stylistic feature in a book of philosophy is obvious. In comparison, there are no such examples in Irigaray's *Speculum of the Other Woman*, and only two in Judith Butler's *Gender Trouble*.[68] Taken from

---

[68] If I have overlooked examples in *Speculum*, I hope someone will correct me. In *Gender Trouble* I may also have missed some cases. The two I have in mind are, first, the example concerning the scientists who decided to classify a person with XX chromosomes and anatomically ambiguous genitalia as male (see *Gender Trouble* 106–11), and, second, the various references to male drag shows, used as examples of the destabilizing and subversive effects of playing gender against sex.

My point is not that one approach is intrinsically preferable to another, but rather that a theorists' use or non-use of examples is revealing of her philosophical stance. Different kinds of theory tend to generate different attitudes to examples. The highly abstract and generalizing nature of much poststructuralist theory is bound to produce the feeling that examples are irrelevant to the argument at hand. The paucity of examples then reinforces the impression that the text is overgeneralizing. Beauvoir's existentialism, on the other hand, cannot proceed without analysis of concrete cases. I shall return to the question of the value and effect of examples, particularly anecdotes.

her own observations, from stories her friends have told her, from the literary gossip in Paris, and from a book review that Beauvoir probably read on her trip to America in 1947, Beauvoir's examples are strikingly ordinary and unpretentious. This fact alone has surely contributed to the belief that a book based on such evidence cannot possibly be taken seriously as philosophy.

Since Beauvoir's use of examples in this passage is such a significant aspect of her philosophical style, I shall study them in some detail. First of all, I suspect that the quote attributed to Dorothy Parker is made up from memory, and misattributed to boot. Here is the context of Beauvoir's reference to Parker:

> American women, in particular, are prepared to think that there is no longer any place for woman as such; if a backward individual still takes herself for a woman, her friends advise her to be psychoanalyzed and thus get rid of this obsession. In regard to a work, *Modern Woman: The Lost Sex*, which, incidentally, is highly irritating, Dorothy Parker has written: 'I cannot be just to books which treat of woman as woman. . . . My idea is that all of us, men as well as women, should be regarded as human beings'. But nominalism is a rather inadequate doctrine, and the antifeminists have had no trouble in showing that women simply *are not* men (*SS* xx; *DSa* 12 13; TA).

Beauvoir is notoriously inaccurate in her references, and she has a particularly infuriating tendency to get names and titles wrong.[69] I was not entirely surprised, therefore, to discover that in spite of considerable effort, I could not trace the quote attributed to Dorothy Parker. The book Parker is supposed to have reviewed, and which Beauvoir seems to have read, since she says it is 'highly irritating', is Ferdinand Lundberg and Marynia Farnham's controversial, sexist, and deeply essentialist *Modern Woman: The Lost Sex*, which was published in New York in January 1947.[70] The

---

[69] In the French text, the title of the book is given as *Modern Woman: A Lost Sex*.

[70] The major point of *Modern Woman* is that women in 1947 fail to have orgasms because they do not devote themselves entirely to husband and children. To work outside the home is to give in to masculine strivings. The ideal woman is totally feminine; to try to combine femininity and masculinity is impossible: 'The plain fact is that increasingly we are observing the masculinization of women and with it enormously dangerous consequences to the home, the children (if any) dependent on it, and to the ability of the woman, as well as her

standard bibliography of Dorothy Parker's work shows that Parker did not write book reviews in 1947. Nor does she seem to have written anything else of relevance to the theme.[71]

Beauvoir arrived in New York on 25 January and left for Paris on 17 May 1947. *America Day by Day* shows that she read American newspapers, magazines, and literary and political journals avidly throughout her stay.[72] There were a number of prominent reviews of *Modern Woman: The Lost Sex* in the spring of 1947, some of which Beauvoir is bound to have seen. In fact, it probably was one of the first American books to come to her attention during her trip to the United States. *Modern Woman* was negatively reviewed by Margaret Mead in the *New York Times* on 26 January, the day after Beauvoir's arrival in New York. I can't imagine that Beauvoir failed to run out to buy the leading American newspaper on the first day of her stay, a day which she spent walking around Manhattan, according to the account of it in *America Day by Day*. Nor can I imagine that she skipped a review of a book so relevant to her own work on *The Second Sex*, which she was in the middle of writing when she left for the United States. *Modern Woman* instantly became highly controversial, not least among American intellectuals. Mary McCarthy, whom Beauvoir met several times that spring, published the most brilliant and by far the funniest review of the book ('Tyranny of the Orgasm') in the *New Leader* on 5 April. But neither Mead nor McCarthy make the point that Beauvoir attributes to Parker.

---

husband, to obtain sexual gratification' (235). This kind of thing goes on for 500 pages. The book may well be one of the examples Beauvoir has in mind when she criticizes the tendency to think in terms of 'femininity' and 'masculinity'.

[71] My source here is Randall Calhoun, *Dorothy Parker: A Bio-Bibliography*. This book is not totally reliable. (Parker's story 'Song of the Shirt, 1941' is listed as appearing in the *New Yorker* in 1947, in spite of the fact that it appeared, as the title indicates, in 1941.) I nevertheless find it hard to believe that Calhoun would have overlooked a review of a widely noticed and much debated book.

[72] Already on 5 Feb. she writes: 'During this first week I had been too enchanted by my discovery of New York to be depressed by my reading of the daily and weekly papers, but this morning all the anger and fear I had suppressed make my heart heavy' (*L'Amérique* 61, my translation; see *America* 41 for the English translation). As this book was going to press, Carol Cosman's excellent new translation was published. Page references are to this edition, far superior to the old 1953 translation.

Although I couldn't find anything by Dorothy Parker that even remotely connected her to *Modern Woman: The Lost Sex*, there is a connection of sorts between Parker and the book. On 22 February 1947 Marynia Farnham, New York psychoanalyst and co-author of *Modern Woman*, wrote an article on women's writing in *The Saturday Review of Literature* entitled 'The Pen and the Distaff'. This was the lead article of the week, and prominently featured three photographs of women writers on the first page. The first of these was of Dorothy Parker, with the caption 'Dorothy Parker, defying attempts at pigeon-holing, has something of a corner on unrelieved hostility toward both sexes' (7). This sentence is repeated in the text. Farnham sees Parker as an exception to her general rule, which is that most women writers display an 'intense hostility to men' (29). It is of course more than possible that Beauvoir read something by Parker that I haven't been able to find.[73] In the absence of more relevant evidence, however, Farnham's article does establish a connection between *Modern Woman* and Parker that might explain Beauvoir's misattribution.

Farnham's article would have struck Beauvoir, an *agrégée* in philosophy, with particular force, since the photograph under that of Dorothy Parker is of Ayn Rand, with the caption 'Ayn Rand, of "The Fountainhead", and another non-categorite, shows a rare preoccupation with a philosophical problem'.[74] The text running next to this picture confidently states that history, politics, and economics are a man's world, and then continues: 'Philosophy finds us in like case. There is no woman's name in the philosophical roster. The indication would appear that women have little interest in the problems of man's relation to the moral world' (7). This is Farnham's conclusion:

> [Women] leave aside with barely a nod the broad abstractions, the great struggles of man's spirit with the material or moral world. They do not strive with logic. Theirs is the immediate, the sensed and intuitively known, the deeply felt, the life of the heart. These

[73] All credit for the laborious research that went into the question of what Parker did or did not write in 1947 goes to my research assistant, Virginia Tuma.

[74] For the sake of completion, the third photograph is of Lillian Smith, with the caption 'Lillian Smith consistently displays an equally rare concern with a social disaster' (Farnham 7).

things fit neatly into what is known and observed about the essentially feminine which remains much unchanged—the intimate, personal, immediate, and intuitive (30).

Other reviews of *Modern Woman* do make the point that Beauvoir attributes to Parker, but not in exactly the same words. Thus Dorothy Van Doren, reviewing in the *New York Herald Tribune Weekly Book Review* on 9 February, writes that she found the book 'deeply disturbing' because she cannot accept that 'man, including woman . . . should be categorized, reproached and stigmatized solely on the performance of his or her reproductive system', and then concludes that the book misses out on the 'most exquisite and complex [organ in man], the one which cannot be seen by mortal eye. It is what makes man a man' (16). Van Doren's insistence on the invisible but essential humanity that makes 'man, including woman' a man, is a strong candidate for Beauvoir's criticism of humanist nominalism. The fact that her first name is Dorothy is one reason why Beauvoir might have thought of Dorothy Parker in this context.[75]

Beauvoir's analysis does not depend on the historical accuracy of her reference. Even if Dorothy Parker never said what Beauvoir thinks she said, there is plenty of evidence that this kind of nominalism was common in America at the time. As I have shown, there is also evidence that it was a common reaction to Lundberg and Farnham's book. What Beauvoir requires to make her argument stick is an example, whether made-up or not, that the reader will accept as illuminating of the problem at stake. (I shall return to the question of why Beauvoir's examples do not need to be empirically true.)

Beauvoir's next three examples are intended to exemplify and expand on her rejection of nominalism. They follow the claim that 'no woman can without bad faith pretend to be situated beyond her sex'. The first case is that of the well-known woman writer:

[75] Reviewing in the *New Republic* on 10 Feb. 1947, Frederic Wertham rejects *Modern Woman* on similar grounds: 'After all, most of what we know about women and their share of the suffering in the world is universally human and not specifically female. This book dehumanizes the whole question and treats women in a way that is belittling, unfair and fundamentally untrue' (38).

Some years ago a well-known woman writer refused to permit her portrait to appear in a series of photographs especially devoted to women writers; she wished to be counted among the men, but in order to gain this privilege she made use of her husband's influence. Women who assert that they are men lay claim none the less to consideration and respect from men (*SS* xx; *DSa* 13; TA).

I have an idea that Beauvoir has Colette in mind. But I can't prove it, since I haven't been able to find the 'series of photographs' in question.[76] This story seems to me to be typical of a certain French kind of intellectual gossip, and as such it is not necessarily more accurate than the Dorothy Parker reference. Again, the point is not whether we believe that Colette or any other well-known woman writer in France did this, but whether we believe that some woman in such a position might have done something like this.

The next example concerns the young Trotskyite: 'I recall also a young Trotskyite standing on a platform at a boisterous meeting and getting ready to use her fists, in spite of her evident fragility', Beauvoir writes. 'She was denying her feminine weakness; but it was for love of a militant male whose equal she wished to be' (*SS* xx; *DSa* 13). Here Beauvoir presents the example as a personal recollection. And in this case, she remembers accurately. The young Trotskyite alluded to here is the French writer and lifelong socialist activist Colette Audry (1906–90), who was Beauvoir's colleague at the *lycée* Jeanne d'Arc in Rouen from 1932 to 1936, and who remained a lifelong friend and supporter of Beauvoir and Sartre. Audry's book of memoirs, *La statue* (1983), shows that Beauvoir became a good friend to her in 1932, precisely at a time when Audry was struggling with an impossible and contradictory passion for another young Trotskyite.

[In 1936] I already had four years of politics behind me, all burdened, illuminated, shaken by a happy and unhappy love affair, which I could not finish, and which I don't want to write about. . . . My friend was only two years older than me, but he had entered into politics seven or eight years before me, and mathematics had prepared him to move easily among economic facts. Thus I found myself yet again in the situation of a student, a situation I no longer

[76] Perhaps a Colette scholar can put me right.

wanted. . . . Above all, I obscurely felt that to be in such a situation
with a man placed me in great danger. I rejected it furiously. This
was deep-rooted weakness of character or plain stupidity. Because I
was a woman I despaired of my strength, I despaired of ever control-
ling the situation, and I would not admit it. . . . To put an end to the
story: I did have the love, but I lost the man. It is enough to say that
thirty years later neither of the two had forgotten—what one calls
forgetting. That matters in a life, after all.

    As I was going through this difficult time, I was not reduced to
my own resources. One morning in October 1932, a young woman
with blue eyes came up to me in the teachers' room and wanted to
get acquainted. It was the recently arrived Mlle de Beauvoir (*Statue*
206–7).

Finally, there is the reference to the American women: 'The
clenched attitude of defiance of American women proves that
they are haunted by a sense of their femininity' (*SS* xx; *DSa* 13;
TA).[77] This is Beauvoir's own assessment of women's condition in
America. Her thought is that although American women insist
that they are 'men', their endless defiance and bitter recrimina-
tions reveal their sense of being at a disadvantage because they
are women. This is a theme Beauvoir had recently developed in
America Day by Day:

That American women are not really on a tranquil equal footing
with men is proved by their attitude of protest [*revendication*] and
defiance. They despise, and often rightly so, the servility of
Frenchwomen, always ready to smile at their men and to put up
with their moods, but the clenched tension they display on the
pedestal masks the same amount of weakness. Whether they are
docile or demanding, the man remains king: he is the essential,
woman the inessential; the praying mantis is the antithesis of the
submissive servant girl in the harem, but both depend on the
male. The Hegelian dialectic of master and slave is confirmed in
this domain, too: the woman who wants to be an idol is really
subject to her worshippers. Her whole life is consumed in ensnar-
ing the man and keeping him subject to her law (*L'Amérique* 453–4;
my translation).[78]

---

[77] 'L'attitude de défi dans laquelle se crispent les Américaines . . .'. The difficulty is to render *se crisper* adequately. The verb represents a clenching or
contraction of muscles, but is also linked to nervous tension and irritation.

[78] The new published English translation may be consulted in *America* 330–1.

In this example, then, Beauvoir's Hegelian analysis of the power relation between the sexes that was to become one of the main themes of *The Second Sex* is explicitly linked to a comparison between France and the United States. This example shows how important Beauvoir's American experiences were to the writing of *The Second Sex*. It is also striking to note that the page devoted to a denunciation of humanist nominalism is framed by references to American women who refuse to believe they are women.

In the first paragraph of *The Second Sex*, then, essentialism is linked to the canonical fathers of philosophy, exemplified by Thomas Aquinas and Plato, whereas nominalism is represented as a contemporary American phenomenon. The examples make it resplendently clear that Beauvoir has no intention of following either line of thought. After reading Beauvoir's account of America in 1947, contemporary postmodern nominalism in America starts to look like the historical heir to the discredited humanist nominalism of the postwar period. Both types of nominalism claim—for different reasons, to be sure—that it is a mistake to believe that one is a woman. It would be interesting to know more about the social and historical conditions that make such views appear particularly plausible to important groups of American intellectuals. Beauvoir's much underrated *America Day by Day* would be a good place to start looking for an answer.

I have already said that Beauvoir's examples are ordinary and unpretentious. What strikes me now, after investigating them more closely, is how steeped they are in women's writing and women's experiences. In my more or less frustrating search for the sources of Beauvoir's examples, I found myself reading Colette, Mary McCarthy, Margaret Mead, Colette Audry, Dorothy Van Doren, Marynia Farnham, Dorothy Parker, and many others. The depth of Beauvoir's engagement with women's lives and writing is evident in these examples. The fact that she includes them in the introduction to a philosophical essay is brave, and already tells us that what we are about to read is not philosophy as it always was practised, but philosophy in a new key, one in which women are included right from the start. The common accusation that Beauvoir is a 'male-identified' philosopher in *The Second Sex* could not be more unfair.

By the end of the first paragraph of her text, Beauvoir has dismissed essentialism and nominalism, that is to say, the two most common answers to the question 'What is a woman?' The fact that she so easily rejects positions that contemporary feminist theorists still feel deeply engaged by should make us wonder what her alternative is. Does she know something we don't?[79] The passage that closes the paragraph and also functions as the conclusion drawn from the examples concerning women who believe they can situate themselves beyond their sex, already indicates what direction she is heading in:

> In truth, to go for a walk with one's eyes open is enough to demonstrate that humanity is divided into two categories of individuals whose clothes, faces, bodies, smiles, gaits, interests, and occupations are manifestly different. Perhaps these differences are superficial, perhaps they are destined to disappear. What is certain is that at the moment it is stunningly evident that they exist (*SS* xx–xxi; *DSa* 13; TA).

There is a powerful reference to Descartes in the last sentence. Beauvoir's search for the one thing that is beyond doubt, the one thing that she can take for granted, the one thing on which she can ground her philosophical inquiry, has led her to the claim that what is *certain* is that for the moment women exist *avec une éclatante évidence*, as she puts it.[80] What she takes to be incontrovertibly true about women is the fact of their existence.[81]

Beauvoir, like other existentialists, believed that 'existence precedes essence'. This means that each concrete human being is involved in an open-ended process in which she constantly makes something of what the world makes of her (I discuss this further

[79] In Chapter 1, above, I attempt to explain why Beauvoir's understanding of the body as a situation is neither essentialist nor nominalist.

[80] My attempt at a literal translation is not wonderful. *Une éclatante évidence* can also be used to indicate that something is a blatant fact; *se rendre à l'évidence* means 'to yield to the facts; to acknowledge that one is in the wrong'.

[81] Nancy Bauer traces Beauvoir's rewriting of Descartes, focusing on Beauvoir's 'I am a woman' as a commentary to and rewriting of Descartes's 'I think therefore I am'. Bauer brilliantly establishes that Beauvoir's 'What is a woman?' is to be 'read as an attempt to displace Descartes' "What is a man?"' (50).

in Chapter 1, above). 'It is enough to go for a walk with one's eyes open', she writes. Perhaps she lifted her head from her café table to look out at the Boulevard Saint Germain as she wrote those words. A busy street in Paris will more or less instantly yield up examples of every one of the sexual differences listed by Beauvoir. What one discovers when one wanders down the Boulevard Saint Germain keeping one's eyes open are not eternal essences or historical constants, but the fact that in Paris in 1949 there are two kinds of human beings who mark their differences by their 'clothes, faces, bodies, smiles, gaits, interests, and occupations'. The idea is not that the meaning of these differences is self-evident, but that whatever they mean—and this is going to be the subject of Beauvoir's inquiry—nobody in their right mind will deny that they exist in Paris at that moment in history.

What Beauvoir is saying here is that she wants to take the fact of women's concrete existence as the starting point for her philosophizing. In so doing she shows herself as a true existentialist. Existentialism was born in 1932 when Raymond Aron told Sartre that if he started reading phenomenology he would be able to make philosophy out of an apricot cocktail. As Beauvoir tells it, the three of them were drinking apricot cocktails at the Bec de Gaz in the Rue Montparnasse when Aron said, pointing to his glass: ' "You see, my dear school friend, if you are a phenomenologist, you can talk about this cocktail and make philosophy out of it!" Sartre almost turned pale with emotion. Here was just the thing he had been longing to achieve for years—to describe objects just as he saw and touched them, and to make philosophy out of it' (*PL* 135; *FA* 156; TA).

The concrete sexual differences that surround her in everyday life are to Beauvoir in 1949 what the apricot cocktail was to Sartre in 1932. Beginning with sexual differences as she finds them, Beauvoir's project is to uncover the significance of these differences for the human beings shaped by them. Thus the thought that Beauvoir denies sexual difference, or has no philosophy of sexual difference, ubiquitous in recent feminist theory, finds no support in her text. Luce Irigaray is often mentioned as an example of a feminist who theorizes sexual difference, in contrast to

Beauvoir who dismally fails to do so. I now believe that this
mistaken contrast is best understood as the result of the critics'
failure to grasp *The Second Sex as* theory or *as* philosophy (as the
case may be). By this I mean that the critics' understanding of
what theory is, or what 'theorizing' should look like, prevents
them from seeing that Beauvoir is 'doing theory' on every page of
her book.

In the French text, the first five pages of *The Second Sex*
consist of only three paragraphs: the first runs for almost three
pages and the third for about two pages. The two long paragraphs are symmetrically distributed around a brief transitional
paragraph that ends by repeating the question 'What is a
woman?'. By its very brevity this paragraph stands out from the
rest of the text and marks a self-conscious transition from
Beauvoir's ironic critique of second rate philosophy and sexist
common sense to her own, original thought. It is significant
that the transitional paragraph, which I shall quote in full, takes
the form of a highly logical 'if . . . then' sentence. Again
Beauvoir shows that philosophical reason—impersonal logic
and objectivity—can be a powerful resource for those who wish
to emerge from ideological confusion and get back to fundamental questions:

> If her functioning as a female [*femelle*] is not enough to define
> woman, if we refuse also to explain her through the 'eternal femi-
> nine', and if nevertheless we admit, even if it is only provisionally,
> that there are women on earth, then we must ask ourselves: what is
> a woman? (*SS* xx–xxi; *DSa* 13; TA)

'I Am a Woman': The Body as Background

We have now reached the crucial third paragraph of *The Second
Sex*. Covering only two pages in the French text, this paragraph is
a landmark in feminist thought. At the beginning Beauvoir starts
by declaring 'I am a woman', at the end she affirms for the first
time that woman is the Other. How does she get from a declaration about herself to a general claim about all women? And in
what way do these claims answer the question about what a
woman is? This is how she begins:

The very act of stating the problem at once suggests to me a first answer.[82] It is significant that I raise it. A man would never think of writing a book on the specific [*singulière*] situation of males in the human race.[83] But if I want to define myself, I must first of all declare: 'I am a woman'; this truth is the background from which all further claims will stand out [*cette vérité constitue le fond sur lequel s'enlèvera toute autre affirmation*].[84] A man never begins by affirming that he is [*par se poser comme*] an individual of a certain sex: that he is a man goes without saying (*SS* xxi; *DSa* 14; TA).

Some feminist theorists would probably feel that Beauvoir here turns her back on the real problem. Perhaps, they might say, she unconsciously realizes that the very fact of uttering the question 'What is a woman?' is to condemn oneself to metaphysical essentialism. Since she doesn't wish to take up an essentialist position, the argument might go, she abandons the terrain of theory for that of autobiography: confession takes the place of analysis. This is why, they might say, Beauvoir never succeeds in *theorizing* sexual difference, as opposed to simply gathering more or less positivist information about it. Needless to say, I think this is to leap to conclusions, and fairly predictable conclusions at that. I want to suggest instead that if we allow ourselves to be patient with this passage, it will emerge as the cornerstone of a truly original effort to think beyond the narrow choice between theory and autobiography, beyond the

[82] 'L'énoncé même du problème me suggère aussitôt une première réponse'. There are several translation problems here. The first and most common meaning of *énoncé* is *énonciation* or *déclaration*. Yet the expression *l'énoncé du problème* usually means the terms, or the exact formulation, of a problem. Linguistically, after Benveniste, *l'énoncé* has come to mean the statement as opposed to *l'énonciation*, the utterance, the act of making the statement. Given that Benveniste only published this distinction after 1949, it is probably not relevant here. For once I agree with Parshley, and opt for the most common meaning, namely 'the act of saying or declaring something'.

Parshley translates *une première réponse* as 'a preliminary answer'. I don't think the answer given here is preliminary in the sense of being a preface or a preamble to a more substantial answer to come. Rather, I think it is the first of two answers of equal weight. (The second answer given in this paragraph to 'What is a woman?' is 'Woman is the Other'.)

[83] Beauvoir writes: 'la situation singulière qu'occupent dans l'humanité les mâles'. At this point she inserts a footnote stating that the Kinsey report only deals with male sexual behaviour, which is something else entirely.

[84] I will return to the translation of this significant phrase.

dichotomy between the first and the third person that irks so many contemporary critics, and, not least, beyond the opposition between essentialism and nominalism.

This passage is offered as a response to the question 'What is a woman?' The first thing Beauvoir does is to investigate the speech act of the original question. Who is likely to ask what a woman is? In what situation would they ask such a question? Her first discovery is that sexual difference manifests itself in her very interest in the question. (She has, after all, just declared that it is enough to go for a walk with one's eyes open to discover that men and women have different interests.) The composition of the passage is strikingly symmetrical. Twice a statement about herself is countered by a sentence about what a man would do or say (*I* raise the question; *a man* would never ask; *I* must declare; *a man* never begins). The structure produces a strong contrast: not, as one might have expected, between 'woman' and 'man', but between 'I' and 'man'.

Beauvoir here realizes that she is writing in a situation where, unlike male writers, she is forced to define herself as a sexed being; where she has no choice but to fill the empty shifter 'I' with her sexual difference. The first 'I' in the book ('I have hesitated for a long time to write a book on woman') was casual. It took itself for granted, without any philosophical ado. This 'I' ('I am a woman'; 'I must define myself', etc.) is showing signs of political and philosophical tension. In this sentence the idea that woman is the Other is already close. 'But if I want to define myself, I must first of all declare: "I am a woman"; this truth is the background from which all further claims will stand out [*cette vérité constitue le fond sur lequel s'enlèvera toute autre affirmation*]'.

The language here is crucial. In French *s'enlever sur un fond* is a somewhat unusual turn of phrase, particularly in this context. *Se détacher* would have been the more obvious choice, since *Le Petit Robert* defines it as 'to appear clearly as if standing out against a background'. In general, *détacher* always has connotations of visual separation, clarity, clear-cut contours, and so is often used about a colour or shape set off against a different background colour of some sort. If Beauvoir chooses to write *s'enlever* and not *se détacher*, it is presumably because she wishes to bring out a different nuance. Many of the most common meanings of *enlever* are obviously unsuitable for the context: Beauvoir does not appear to be thinking of kidnapping and ravishing, of stain-removing, or of something being taken away. One of the primary meanings of *enlever*, however, is 'to lift upwards' (*en + lever*), and so *enlevure* has come to be a technical term for sculptural relief. In English 'relief' may be used about visual as well as tactile effects (relief maps use colours and shading to indicate elevations and depressions); in French, however, *enlevure* is always tactile; an *enlevure* is something I should be able to feel in the dark. I don't mean to exaggerate the differences between these words: sculptural relief is visible too, and if I am in a landscape I could touch the church in the foreground as well as the trees in the background, yet the different sensory emphasis of these two words is obvious.

The image Beauvoir has in mind is now available. The fact that she is a woman is the truth which constitutes the background from which all further claims will stand out in relief, she writes. There are two facts here: first, it is a fact that she is a woman, second, it is a fact that whenever she wants to define herself, she is obliged to draw attention to the first fact. Beauvoir considers the fact of being a woman as the background against which the woman's speech acts stand out. The word 'claim' or 'assertion' (*affirmation*) indicates that she is speaking about her own intellectual undertaking: to write a book about women. Like all other acts, my speech acts define me, an existentialist would say. If I am a woman, my claims are inevitably going to be taken to stand out from the background of my sex. This means that, however hard I try to define myself through what I am saying and doing (through my self-assertions), my interlocutors will try to reduce my assertions to my sex. My struggle for existence will be met by their insistence on essence. I take Beauvoir to experience a sense of consternation at this discovery, to strongly wish for things to be otherwise.

There is a further complication in the sentence. In French, the verb is in the simple future tense (*s'enlèvera*). The published English translation uses the word *must*: 'on this truth must be based all further discussion', Parshley writes. This could give the impression that Beauvoir thinks that this is a desirable state of affairs, perhaps even that she thinks that the fact of being a woman always *ought* or *should* be taken into account. But Parshley here overlooks some common nuances of the French future tense. 'Tu ne sortiras pas' usually carries connotations such as 'you are not allowed to go out', or 'I predict that you will not manage to get yourself out of the house'. There is often a nuance of command, i.e. of being subjected to someone else's power, or of inescapable destiny ('under no circumstances will you be able to escape this fate'). Beauvoir is not in fact saying that the background of sex *must* be kept in mind whenever a woman speaks, nor is she saying that it *ought* to be or *should* be kept in mind: she is saying that it *will* be kept in mind whether the woman likes it or not, and whether it is relevant or irrelevant to whatever she is asserting. In other words, the meaning of the sentence is that whenever a woman speaks, there is no way the fact of her sex is *not* going to be taken into account.

This is contrasted to the situation of human males, who will not automatically be taken to speak against the background of a sexed—male—body whenever they open their mouths. As Nancy Bauer has shown, just by saying that she is a woman, Beauvoir indicates that she rejects the Cartesian body/mind split:

> In identifying sex difference as a starting point for a philosophical investigation, Beauvoir is implicitly denying that, as a woman, she can think within the confines of [the mind–body] split (75). Furthermore, since her inquiry is rooted in a sense of herself as being an instance of the generic concept 'woman' a certain Cartesian threat of solipsism is avoided from the start: to call herself a woman is to start with the idea that other beings like her exist—that is, other beings who are called, or call themselves, women (51).

Beauvoir writes: 'A man never begins by affirming that he is an individual of a certain sex; that he is a man goes without saying'. What is being begun here is a piece of writing, most probably a philosophical essay. Beauvoir is claiming that because she is a woman and not a man everything she says ('asserts' or 'claims') in *The Second Sex* is going to be related to the fact that she has a female body. The reception of her book in France certainly proved her point.[85]

But there is more. For Beauvoir's sentence 'But if I wish to define myself, I must first of all say: "I am a woman"; this truth is the background from which all further claims will stand out', sets up a strong intertextual link to a passage in the preface to Merleau-Ponty's *Phenomenology of Perception*:

> Perception is not the science of the world, it is not even an act, a deliberate taking up of a position; it is the background [*fond*] from which all acts stand out [*se détachent*], and is presupposed by them. The world is not an object such that I have in my possession the law of its making; it is the natural setting of, and field for, all my thoughts and all my explicit perception (x–xi).

Merleau-Ponty writes this in a context where he wants to explain that the body gives us our perceptions, and that without perceptions there is no world. The body is at once what we are and the medium through which we are able to have a world. Speaking of bodily perception Merleau-Ponty uses the same imagery of foreground and background as Beauvoir when she speaks of the fact of having a female body. For Merleau-Ponty the body is the necessary background for everything I do, and everything I do has the perceiving body as its obvious presupposition. This background is something like a general (not particular or individualized) condition enabling human agency and subjectivity to come into being. By speaking of background and foreground Merleau-Ponty means to warn against scientistic or positivist reductionism. A background is not the meaning or essence of whatever takes place in the foreground: the natural processes of the body cannot in themselves explain the acts and thoughts of human beings. On the other hand, the specific background that the body is cannot be thought away or denied, or presumed to have no effects on the foreground. Against Kantian idealism and scientistic positivism,

---

[85] Summarizing the reception of *The Second Sex* in *Force of Circumstance*, Beauvoir writes: 'Unsatisfied, frigid, priapic, nymphomaniac, lesbian, a hundred times aborted, I was everything, even a clandestine mother . . . But that even [François] Mauriac joined in! He wrote to one of the contributors to *Les Temps Modernes*: "Your boss's vagina no longer has any secrets for me" ' (197; *FCa* 260–1; TA).

Merleau-Ponty sets phenomenological materialism, one might say.[86]

To consider the body as a background is to allow that its importance for our projects and sense of identity is variable. Merleau-Ponty's visual metaphor (*se détacher*) makes me think of theatre and of landscapes. In a play, the background—the backdrop—is sometimes crucial to the understanding of the actors' words and gestures, whereas at other times a relentless focus on the background would be quite misplaced. Let us imagine a building placed against a dramatic landscape. If it is the building I wish to study, the landscape is a simple background to which I need pay no attention at all. If it is the landscape, however, the building may either be considered as a part of it, or be disregarded. The background is always there, but its meaning is far from given.

Beauvoir's tactile metaphor has slightly different connotations. The relief on a sculpture may be admired for its own sake, but it is usually quite difficult to focus on the relief without paying any attention to the sculpture it is a part of. The case of the sculpture produces a more integral unity between foreground and background than the case of the backdrop on a stage or the landscape behind an Italian church. The difference in metaphors signals a difference in emphasis. Choosing *s'enlever* rather than *se détacher*, Beauvoir deliberately uses an image that makes it somewhat more difficult to focus on the foreground without taking the background into account than Merleau-Ponty's *se détacher*. Her metaphor takes sexism into account; Merleau-Ponty's does not. By seeing the sexed body as a background which the woman is *obliged* to foreground whenever she is asked to define herself, Beauvoir indicates that for a woman living under patriarchy, the body is a far more inescapable fact than it is for a man. Whatever the woman says, she will have her body—her female sex—taken into account. We should note that this may or may not be what the woman wants. By thinking in terms of foreground and background Beauvoir avoids implying that women's words can be reduced to their bodies.

---

[86] For further discussion of Merleau-Ponty's and Beauvoir's critique of scientism and positivism, see Ch. 1, above.

In Chapter 1 I spent some time discussing Beauvoir's understanding of the body as a situation, as a fundamental part of lived experience. What is the difference between the body understood as a situation and the body understood as background? In Beauvoir's sentence, the body considered as a background is represented as a body perceived by the Other. The presence of the Other is implied in the attempt to define oneself (one rarely finds it necessary to declare 'I am a woman' to oneself), and it is explicitly there in the claim that this act of definition is the result of submission to an external obligation. The concept of situation also presupposes that there are others in the world and that we interact with them. But it is not a concept that applies exclusively to the body. The body is a situation, but so is the fact of going to high school, or being married. The body as a situation is the body as experienced by the human subject, the body as interwoven with the projects of that subject. Perceived as a general background for my existence, on the other hand, the body precedes and enables perception and experience. While the body as situation presupposes agency in the subject, the body as background enables such agency to come into being. At least this is the impression I get from reading Merleau-Ponty. It seems to me that Beauvoir in this sentence uses the idea of the body as a background a little differently, that she quite consciously chooses to imagine the acting and situated body as a background. This becomes quite clear when she goes on to discuss the 'assertions' coming from the woman involved in an abstract discussion with a man. The actual, physical female body sitting there at the café table discussing philosophy is both a situation for the woman who is talking, and a background to her words for the man who is talking to her.

The same expression—to stand out in relief from a background—also turns up in the introduction to the second volume of *The Second Sex*, entitled 'L'expérience vécue' ('Lived Experience'). In this brief text Beauvoir writes that women are starting to assert their independence. This doesn't happen without difficulty, however, for 'virile prestige' is far from extinct. In order to understand what it means to modern women to assert their independence, it is important to study 'women's traditional destiny'. Then she finishes the introduction as follows:

> I shall seek to describe how woman learns her condition, how she experiences it, in what kind of universe she is confined, what forms of escape she is allowed to have. Only then will we understand what problems arise for women who, inheriting a heavy past, strive to forge a new future. When I use the words 'woman', 'feminine' or 'female',[87] I evidently refer to no archetype, no changeless essence; after most of my claims [*mes affirmations*] the reader should understand 'in the present state of education and custom'. The point here is not to proclaim eternal truths, but rather to describe the common background [*fond*] from which every particular female existence stands out [*sur lequel s'enlève toute existence féminine singulière*] (*SS* xxxvi; *DSb* 9; TA).[88]

The second volume of *The Second Sex* is divided into four main sections entitled 'Formation', 'Situation', 'Justifications', and 'Towards Liberation'. This volume has given rise to much criticism, usually on the grounds that Beauvoir generalizes from an unrepresentative sample, that she takes the French experiences of her mother's generation and those of her own to be representative of women everywhere. It is also often assumed that she thinks that the situations she describes are such that no woman can transcend them. Thus her critique of motherhood or bourgeois marriage is often taken to mean that no individual woman could ever realize herself as an authentically free person within these institutions. If this were the case, Beauvoir would be an extreme determinist. On the other hand it has also been assumed that Beauvoir is a radical voluntarist, an idealist who thinks that women, just by an act of will, can throw off the sexist yoke and realize themselves, that they have only themselves to blame if they fail to rid themselves of their bad faith. If this were the case,

---

[87] Beauvoir writes: *les mots 'femme' ou 'féminin'*. In order to stress that the French *féminin* can refer to sex as well as to gender, I have chosen to translate it as 'feminine or female'. See Ch. 1, above, for a thorough discussion of sex, gender, and *The Second Sex*.

[88] Compare H. M. Parshley's translation: 'It is not our concern here to proclaim eternal verities, but rather to describe the common basis that underlies every individual feminine existence.'

Beauvoir would have no reason to claim that institutions and ideology ('myths') oppress women.

The play between foreground and background proposed by Beauvoir avoids reductionism and essentialism (the individual woman in the foreground cannot be reduced to the general historical situation which is her background) while still enabling us to grasp the historical factors that influence and shape the choices of individual women. In *The Second Sex* Beauvoir tries to produce a historical analysis of women's condition. A historical analysis cannot be all-inclusive or universal in the sense of reaching a level of abstraction that might hold for all women in all countries at all times. In order to have any analytic and historical power at all it needs to be specific and particular. Even if we think that Beauvoir is wrong to deal with women 'in the present state of education and custom [in France]', all we could do to correct her would be to propose that she deal with some other group instead. Since no such group is going to be more or less universal than any other, this would not make the analysis more or less representative of women's condition than the one Beauvoir proposes.[89]

Beauvoir does not attempt to describe or predict what any individual woman will make of the conditions in which she is brought up. Her own life was extremely unusual for a woman in mid-century France, yet she fully believed that it was informed and shaped by the traditional background she describes in *The Second Sex*. Describing her discovery of patriarchal mythology, she writes: 'it was a revelation to me: this world was a masculine world, my childhood had been nourished by myths forged by men, and I hadn't reacted to them in at all the same way I should have done if I had been a boy' (*FC* 103, *FCa* 136; TA). Beauvoir's fundamental understanding of subjectivity is based on the assumption that we continuously make something of what the world makes of us. The 'background' she is describing and analysing in the second volume of *The Second Sex* tells us what the world wants to make of women. She also includes many case studies and innumerable examples in which she shows what women, responding to this

---

[89] I return to the question of exemplarity and representation in the next section, 'My Spade is Turned', below.

situation, make of what the world makes of them. The very fact that Beauvoir quite often dwells on exceptional women demonstrates that she does not take her description of the general historical and social background to be invalidated when she moves the focus to a specific case in the foreground, however exceptional it might be.

Finally, Beauvoir's sentence—'this truth is the background . . .'— allows for two different political interpretations. On the one hand, she may be taken to mean that in a sexist society (such as Paris in 1949) a woman's claims will always be heard with reference to her body, but that in a non-sexist society this will no longer be the case. On the other hand, however, she may be saying that although sexism insists on reading a woman's books against the background of her sex, in a non-sexist society the same thing will happen to men as well. Here, in a nutshell, we find encapsulated the feminist conflict between a certain understanding of equality and a certain understanding of difference.[90] Is Beauvoir saying that the aim of feminism is to make sexual difference irrelevant, that we should all be treated just as the human beings we are? Or is she saying that the aim of feminism is to show that sexual difference is relevant at all times and in every social and personal situation?[91]

First, it is crucial to note that Beauvoir's sentence refuses to embrace either interpretation. There is no sign that what she *really* means is one or the other. Second, it appears that neither interpretation corresponds to the logic of Beauvoir's text. For the first interpretation (that sexual difference is irrelevant) sounds like an echo of the humanist nominalism she explicitly rejected just one page earlier: 'Clearly, no woman can without bad faith pretend to be situated beyond her sex'. The second interpretation (that

[90] See my discussion of the unsatisfactory opposition between a feminism of equality and a feminism of difference in 'Is Anatomy Destiny?' (Ch. 8, below).

[91] There are strong parallels between this claim and the idea, discussed in Sect. I of this essay, that 'location' is always relevant for the understanding of every speech act. I want to stress that I am not trying to *deny* that sex or location are always relevant: I am, rather, trying to shift the argument towards a different question, namely the question of when (under what circumstances) it is worth while *saying something* about sex or location.

sexual difference is always of fundamental importance) is no more convincing, for it makes sexual difference appear absolute (or essential) by assuming that there can be no situation in which it is *not* a significant factor, and this is a view that clashes with the existentialist belief that existence precedes essence.

By thinking of the body as a background, Beauvoir avoids both interpretations. To say that the sexed body is the inevitable background for all our acts, is at once to claim that it is always a *potential* source of meaning, and to *deny* that it always holds the key to the meaning of a woman's acts. Sculptural relief cannot always be understood by referring it back to the surface from which it stands out. Sometimes we need to understand the relief itself; at other times we want to consider how the relief affects the sculpture as a whole, and vice versa. In yet other cases, we want to see the whole sculpture as part of some larger context. In short, the sex of a body is always there, but it is not always the most important fact about that body. The dying body or the body in pain is not necessarily grasped primarily in terms of sexual difference. If I am trying to learn Chinese, this is evidently an act that I undertake on the background of my sexed body, but the relevance of saying so is not always obvious. If, on the other hand, I am trying to get pregnant, this is a project that certainly foregrounds my sexed body. More complex cases will arise from women's participation in different sports, or in other physical activities.

It follows from Beauvoir's analysis that in some situations the fact of sex will be less important than the fact of class or race; in other situations it will not. There can be no question of giving *one* of these factors general, overarching priority. The old debates about whether class-based exploitation or sex-based oppression are 'primary', never yielded a convincing answer. They were in fact doomed to failure precisely because they sought a general answer, one that would establish the correct hierarchy of oppressions once and for all. One does not get out of this problem, incidentally, by denying that there are hierarchies of oppression. In Spain in 1936, for example, it was more important for Republicans of both sexes to fight against fascism than against sexism (this is not to say that the Spanish Republicans were not sexist). In other cases there may be no hierarchy: fighting for women's right to education may be as useful for socialism as it is for feminism. In yet other cases, sex will be the dominant form of oppression, hierarchically more important than class-based oppression. This is surely the case in Afghanistan, where women without male family members die because the Taliban will not allow them to see a doctor without a brother or a husband present.

I take Beauvoir to be saying that women's oppression consists in the compulsory foregrounding of the female body at all times, whether it is relevant or irrelevant to the task at hand. But sexism also consists in preventing women from foregrounding the female body when they want it to be significant. (A Beauvoirean feminist would be critical of anti-sex and anti-pornography feminism.) In a scene of flirtation or seduction, for example, a woman may want to foreground her body. Thus Françoise in *L'invitée* (*She Came to Stay*) intensely wants Gerbert to notice her sexed body, to notice her as a woman. On the other hand, it can be annoying and painful to be interpellated as a sexed body when one is immersed in a project that has nothing to do with one's sex. The same logic holds for the raced body. To be cast as a representative of one's race when one is immersed in a project in which this is an entirely irrelevant element, can be painful and humiliating. A cartoon that appeared in the *New Yorker* is a perfect illustration of the point:

Frantz Fanon brilliantly captures the sense of fragmentation and dislocation that arises from the experience of being reduced to one's raced body against one's will. In a passage in *Black Skin, White Masks* he describes walking down the street in a French city, passing a white woman and her little daughter on his way. I quote the scene at length because it so perfectly conveys Fanon's pain and alienation, his sense that the gaze of the white man imprisons him in his subjectivity, a subjectivity that is reduced to the fact of his black skin:

> 'Look, a Negro!' It was an external stimulus that flicked over me as I passed by. I made a tight smile.
> 'Look, a Negro!' It was true. It amused me.
> 'Look, a Negro!' The circle was drawing a bit tighter. I made no secret of my amusement.
> 'Mama, see the Negro! I'm frightened!' Frightened! Frightened! Now they were beginning to be afraid of me. I made up my mind to laugh myself to tears, but laughter had become impossible (112).

> I was responsible at the same time for my body, for my race, for my ancestors. I subjected myself to an objective examination, I discovered my blackness, my ethnic characteristics; and I was battered down by tom-toms, cannibalism, intellectual deficiency, fetishism, racial defects, slave-ships, and above all else, above all: 'Sho' good eatin'.
> On that day, completely dislocated, unable to be abroad with the other, the white man, who unmercifully imprisoned me, I took myself far off from my own presence, far indeed, and made myself an object. What else could it be for me but an amputation, an excision, a hemorrhage that spattered my whole body with black blood? But I did not want this revision, this thematization. All I wanted was to be a man among other men. I wanted to come lithe and young into a world that was ours and to help to build it together (112–13).

There are situations in which we freely choose to be recognized as sexed or raced bodies, where that recognition is exactly what we need and want. Identity politics starts with such identity-affirming situations, but unfortunately goes on to base a general politics on them, thus forgetting that there are other situations in which we do not want to be defined by our sexed and raced bodies, situations in which we wish that body to be no more than the insignificant background to our main activity. As we are about to see, Beauvoir herself gives a marvellous example of just such a situation when she discusses the case of an abstract conversation where a man says to her: 'you say that because you are a woman'. Although this experience may be far less painful for the intellectual woman than the experience of racism was for Fanon, the juxtaposition of the two situations reveal that similar mechanisms of oppression are at work in the encounter between the raced and the sexed body and the Other.[92]

I am tempted to say: in certain situations I want to be considered as an intellectual, and not as an intellectual woman. Yet I do not say it. For this statement is not exactly right. I now realize that there is something in our language that makes it exceptionally hard to express what I do wish to say. It is far too easy to take my original impulse (to call myself an intellectual, rather than an intellectual woman) to mean that in some situations I wish to *deny* that I am a woman, and so to accuse me of being one of the humanist nominalists pretending to be situated beyond my sex. But I do not wish to claim that my body does not exist, or that I am not a woman. Beauvoir helps me to put it more clearly: In certain situations I wish my female body to be considered as the insignificant background of my claims or acts. This is not the same thing as to say that I wish my body to disappear or to be transformed into a male body. My wish does not represent an attempt to escape my particularity, to be considered as a neuter, or as some kind of universalized human being. It represents, rather, a wish to deny that the fact of being a woman is of any particular relevance to my understanding of trigonometry or my capacity to compose symphonies or think ethically.

Ever since feminism became part of public life, some women writers and painters (and so on) have felt that feminism is an ideology that locks women up in their particularized female subjectivity. Opposing such versions of feminism, they have

---

[92] I am not claiming that Fanon and Beauvoir understand racism and sexism in exactly parallel terms. For a brief comparison of the two writers, see ch. 8 of my *Simone de Beauvoir*.

refused to be called 'women writers' and 'women painters'.
Feminists have usually agreed that there is something anti-feminist
about such a refusal to call oneself a woman, often responding by
accusing such women of being male-identified and sadly lacking in
solidarity with their sex. But the fact is that women are right to
refuse attempts to make their subjectivity out to be coextensive
with their femininity. We have no reason to accept attempts to
imprison us in our 'femininity', whether such attempts originate in
sexist or in feminist thought. The problem arises when some
women assume that the only way to escape imprisonment in one's
sex is to deny that sex altogether, and so actually give in to temptation to say: 'I am a writer, not a woman writer.' In this way they
only manage to foreground their claim to universality at the cost
of sacrificing their femininity (here the word simply means their
'femaleness'). They forget, a Beauvoirean might say, that the sexed
body is both a background and a situation, and as such not a
phenomenon that can simply be disavowed.

For I also wish to acknowledge that I probably do read Kant or
Kierkegaard in ways I would not have done had I been a man. Yet
the fact that I read as the woman I am is no reason to deprive me
of my right to be considered an intellectual. *Must* I always refer to
myself as an 'intellectual woman'? Men who read Kant and
Kierkegaard in ways they would not have done had they been
women, usually refer to themselves as intellectuals or philosophers, not as 'intellectual men' or 'male philosophers'. This fact
does not lead people to accuse them of denying or repressing
their masculinity, or to consider them 'female-identified'. In
sexist ideology, men can be self-evidently male and self-evidently
intellectual at the same time. This is why the phrase 'an intellectual man' sounds quite odd whereas 'an intellectual woman'
sounds quite normal. Beauvoir's feminist goal is to produce a society in which women will gain access to the universal *as women*, not
as fake men nor as some impossibly neutered beings.

In a sexist society women often find themselves in situations
where they are obliged to make a 'choice' between being imprisoned in their femininity or having to disavow it altogether. That
sexist ideologies and practices produce this alienating split in
women's subjectivity is Beauvoir's most fundamental point in *The*

Second Sex. For her, both alternatives are equally sexist and equally alienating.[93] Because male subjectivity is not 'hailed' ('interpellated') in this way, this alienating 'choice' in fact defines women's situation under patriarchy. So insidious is this ideology that much feminist theory, whether willingly or not, has ended up espousing one alternative or the other. The amount of time feminists have spent worrying about women's 'equality' or 'difference' is a symptom of the success of this ideological trap. A genuinely feminist position would refuse either option, and insist, rather, that women should not have to choose between calling themselves women and calling themselves writers (or intellectuals, or painters, or composers). It remains an important feminist task to show that this way of thinking of female subjectivity produces an impossible ideological dilemma for women. By now I hope it is obvious that when I refuse to accept the terms of this 'choice', then it does not follow that I really wish to be a man.

To put this differently: it does not go without saying that what a woman does or says is always expressive of 'the woman in her'. Yet at the same time, it is undoubtedly true that whatever a woman does or says is done by a woman. It is because both claims are true that we get so confused about what 'femininity' actually means. What is admirable about Beauvoir's understanding of what a woman is, is precisely her capacity to convey this doubleness without reducing it to one or the other of its components, without acquiescing in it, and also without choosing one of the two equally unsatisfactory theories of what a woman is ('a woman is just a human being' *versus* 'a woman is always just a woman').

By considering the body as a background Beauvoir at once affirms that sexual difference is a fact of fundamental philosophical and social importance *and* that it is not necessarily the most important fact about a human being. Because she pictures the sexed body as the phenomenological background (not the content, essence, or meaning) against which a woman's choices and acts will be foregrounded, these are not contradictory claims. As I will now go on to show, Beauvoir's formulation also reveals

[93] I discuss Beauvoir's analysis of this dilemma below, in my reading of the intellectual conversation where the man says to the woman 'You think that because you are a woman'.

that her fundamental feminist project is to find a way of thinking about sexual difference which steers clear of the Scylla of having to eliminate her sexed subjectivity and the Charybdis of finding herself imprisoned in it.

'You Say That Because You Are a Woman'

I shall now continue reading the third paragraph of *The Second Sex*. In this section I will show that Beauvoir's philosophical style in *The Second Sex* has much in common with that of ordinary language philosophy. This in itself is an interesting observation with implications that ought to be studied in far greater depth than I can do here. My goal here is to show that when Beauvoir's analysis of women and sexism is read in the light of ordinary language philosophy, it gains new and important dimensions.

The text gathers pace after Beauvoir's self-definition. It is as if the realization that whenever she wants to define herself she *has* to say 'I am a woman' precipitates a host of path-breaking insights. In the next sentence she produces another reflection on 'what we should say when'. 'A man never begins', she writes, 'by affirming that he is an individual of a certain sex; that he is a man goes without saying' (*SS* xxi; *DSa* 14; TA). Beauvoir's first insight after her self-definition, then, is that there are situations in which a woman would say something, and a man would say nothing, and that one such situation is the situation of a woman about to undertake a philosophical investigation. A woman who wants to do philosophy, she realizes, has to make painfully explicit that which ordinarily goes without saying. This is also what philosophers who proceed from everyday language take the task of philosophy to be. What is striking in Beauvoir's text, however, is that she is led to this insight by thinking about what it means to her to have to define herself as a woman. Her insight arises both because she has had to place her own subjectivity in the text, and because she has had the intellectual resourcefulness to make that very fact a subject for philosophical reflection. Coming to an explicit awareness of the way her own subjectivity is bound up with her thinking, Beauvoir discovers a way of doing philosophy in which the personal and the philosophical are intrinsically linked.

It is because Beauvoir has to say 'I am a woman' at the beginning of *The Second Sex* that she ends up extending and expanding
her philosophical method in the direction of the autobiographical and the linguistic (I mean in the direction of asking what we
should say when). This is where *The Second Sex* differs most
dramatically from *Being and Nothingness*. By using such strategies
Beauvoir becomes a different kind of philosopher to Sartre, who
never starts by declaring that he is a man, because he doesn't have
to. Without signalling the fact as such, Beauvoir makes a decisive
shift in her philosophical style, both in relation to previous
philosophers and in relation to her own earlier essays.[94] Stanley
Cavell writes: 'One requirement of new philosophical answers is
that they elicit a new source of philosophical interest, or elicit this
old interest in a new way. Which is perhaps only a way of affirming that a change of *style* in philosophy is a profound change, and
itself a subject of philosophical investigation' ('Austin at
Criticism' 102).

In her considerations of what she would say as opposed to what
a man would say, Beauvoir shows that the question of 'what we
should say when' does not have to presuppose the invocation of a
falsely universalized 'we', a 'we' arrogantly pretending to know
the ways of language much better than anyone else. To 'examine
what we should say when' is to imagine 'what words we should use
in what situations', Austin writes ('Plea' 182). To take for granted
that a given situation must have a male speaker (or a white
speaker, or a bourgeois speaker) is as philosophically flawed as to
imagine that any other aspect of the speech act necessarily goes
without saying.

In order to prevent some common misunderstandings, I will
explain briefly what I take the appeal to ordinary language, to
'what we should say when', to imply and not to imply. For Cavell,
an appeal to 'what we should say when' is not an appeal to expertise or superior knowledge. On the contrary, if I want to take issue
with your understanding of a certain situation, I must first be able

---

[94] My sense is that Beauvoir's philosophical style in *The Second Sex* is different
from her style in *Pyrrhus et Cinéas* and *An Ethics of Ambiguity*. But this is not
certain: more work would be required to show whether or how far this intuition
is right.

to understand the way the world looks to you. My critique cannot come from the outside, and certainly not from above:

> Understanding from inside a view you are undertaking to criticize is sound enough practice whatever the issue. But in the philosophy which proceeds from ordinary language, understanding from inside is methodologically fundamental. Because the way you must rely upon yourself as a source of what is said when, demands that you grant full title to others as sources of that data—not out of politeness, but because the nature of the claim you make for yourself is repudiated without that acknowledgment: it is a claim that no one knows better than you whether and when a thing is said, and if this is not to be taken as a claim to expertise (a way of taking it which repudiates it) then it must be understood to mean that you know no better than others what you claim to know (Cavell, 'Knowing and Acknowledging' 239–40).

The ordinary language philosopher has no monopoly on meaning. No speaker of the language can meaningfully be thought of as more or less a speaker of it than anyone else.[95] Wittgenstein's 'the meaning of a word is its use' means that to be a speaker of the language is to contribute to its meanings. By the act of using words, we necessarily contribute to their meaning. 'What is normative is exactly ordinary use itself', Cavell writes ('Must' 21).[96] The idea that certain concepts wield a social power

[95] Nancy Bauer thinks in very similar terms when she writes: 'In answering "I am" to the question "What is a woman?" [Beauvoir] means not to distinguish herself but, to the contrary, to *count herself* as a woman (47).

[96] This sentence has been much misunderstood. Let me quote Cavell's own comment on it in 'The Politics of Interpretation': 'When in the title essay of *Must We Mean What We Say?* I come out with the assertion that "what is normative is exactly ordinary use itself," it is with a certain air of triumph, and what I felt (still feel) I was triumphing in was not the affirmation of a distinction between ordinary and some other kind of language; on the contrary, I felt I was winning freedom from such distinctions between the normative and the ordinary' (38). This explanation is offered in the context of a discussion of Stanley Fish's reading of Austin, where Fish claims that for Austin literary language is opposed to ordinary language. Fish believes that 'ordinary language' is a term that 'designates a kind of language that "merely" presents or mirrors facts independently of any consideration of value, interest, perspective, purpose, and so on' ('How Ordinary is Ordinary Language?' 97). As far as I can see, nothing could be further from Austin and Cavell's understanding of what ordinary

denied to others is not incompatible with this thought. The existence of evil and exploitative social systems does not invalidate Wittgenstein's recognition that all speakers of the language participate in the production of meaning. If anything, Wittgenstein's thought gives us a justification for resisting attempts to silence some speakers and impose the voices of others. To say that the meaning of a word is its use is not, either, to imply that there is only one use of any given word. The very fact that there is continuous struggle over meaning (think of words such as *queer, woman, democracy, equality, freedom*) shows that different uses not only exist but sometimes give rise to violently conflicting meanings. If the meaning of a word is its use, such conflicts are part of the meaning of the word.

An appeal to ordinary usage, then, is not an appeal to dominant ideology or a passive submission to 'regulatory discourses'. Let me quote Cavell again:

> An appeal to what we should ordinarily say does not constitute a defense of ordinary beliefs or common sense. . . . Proceeding from what is ordinarily said puts a philosopher no closer to ordinary 'beliefs' than to the 'beliefs' or theses of any opposing philosophy,

---

language is (see also Fish, 'How to Do Things with Austin and Searle'). On my reading of Wittgenstein and Cavell, the only thing ordinary or everyday uses of language are opposed to, are metaphysical uses of language, which Wittgenstein sees as cases when 'language goes on holiday' (*PI* §38), i.e. cases when language is doing no useful work at all.

The other reason why Cavell's statement about the normativity of ordinary language is so often misunderstood, has to do with the question of what 'normative' means. In our postmodern intellectual climate it is often taken to mean *ideologically* normative. But that is not Cavell's point. He means normative in the sense of having meaning at all. The word 'glass' is normative in the sense that in most cases when I say 'Could you give me a glass, please?' you will—most astonishingly—hand one to me. Nevertheless, there is always the possibility that in some particular case you will think that I mean something else. As Wittgenstein reminds us: '[Even] an ostensive definition can be variously interpreted in *every* case' (*PI* §28). But the existence of difficult cases does not make the easy ones go away. Cavell is not trying to say that a word only has one, normative use. Ordinary language philosophy is precisely engaged in analysis of what makes some speech acts felicitous and others not. This is not the place to go into these questions. The purpose of this footnote is simply to indicate that some common objections to the words 'ordinary language' and 'normative' are not well founded.

e.g., skepticism. In all cases his problem is to discover the specific plight of mind and circumstance within which a human being gives voice to his condition ('Knowing and Acknowledging' 240).[97]

On Cavell's understanding of the ordinary and the everyday, the ordinary is the arena where human struggle takes place. Murder and mayhem, revolution and resistance are as much part of the ordinary as successful communication and felicitous speech acts. The fact that we all experience misunderstandings or conflicts with distressing regularity surely makes that clear. Feminist analysis of sexism and the oppression of women is usually located within the sphere of the ordinary. The point made by Cavell and others is that we cannot even have struggle and disagreement unless we speak to each other on the basis of some common understanding (a shared practice) of what counts as political conflict or disagreement. If there is no such shared practice, we would not understand each other sufficiently to disagree: 'If a lion could talk, we could not understand him', Wittgenstein writes (*PI*, p. 223).

By examining two different situations—one in which a man begins a work of philosophy and one in which a woman does so—Beauvoir demonstrates that there are cases where the sex of the speaker has decisive influence on what 'we' would say, so that there cannot be any question of what 'we' would say' in general, if 'in general means 'without regard to sex'. This insight immediately leads to the realization that the two sexes do not, in fact, stand in a symmetrical relation to each other. The way we do or do not use the expressions 'I am a man' and 'I am a woman' shows that when it comes to philosophical writing, there is no

[97] Some critics believe that Wittgenstein or ordinary language philosophy *must* be conservative. This obviously deserves further discussion. Here I can just say that I would not be interested in this way of thinking about meaning if I thought such critics were right. In *Sexual/Textual Politics* I quote Vološinov who writes 'differently oriented accents intersect in every ideological sign. Sign becomes an arena of class struggle' (157). I still agree with this. It is important to note that Vološinov writes 'every *ideological* sign', not '*every* sign'. I take Vološinov to mean that we have to be able to *show* that a sign is ideological and also be able to analyse the different social interests that struggle over its use in a particular case. To me, this is compatible with Wittgenstein's fundamental understanding of meaning.

reciprocity between 'man' and 'woman'. A man, in other words, cannot stake his subjectivity in philosophy by saying 'I am a man', since this is a statement that has not been considered *subjective* by male philosophers.[98]

Beauvoir goes on to develop this insight. It is only on bureaucratic forms, she writes (her examples are marriage certificates and identity papers), that the terms male and female appear to have equal weight.[99] The two sexes cannot be compared to two electrical poles:

> the man represents both the positive and the neutral, so much so that one says 'man' [*les hommes*] in French to designate human beings; here the specific meaning of the word *vir* has been assimilated to the general meaning of the word *homo*.[100] Woman appears as the negative, with the result that every determination is ascribed to her as a limitation, without reciprocity (*SS* xxi; *DSa* 14, TA).

It follows that under patriarchy it does not really matter *how* one defines woman, for whatever qualities one ascribes to her, they will appear as negative in relation to the qualities of men. This is the fundamental reason why Beauvoir consistently refuses to engage in definitions of femininity.

At this point, Beauvoir packs the text with examples. Falsely symmetrical bureaucratic papers, genuinely symmetrical electric poles, and examples of what one would say in French and Latin follow on the heels of the analysis of her own speech act. The

[98] It was only after the feminist analysis pioneered by Beauvoir had become widely accepted that some men started to think of male subjectivity as sexed and particular.

[99] Beauvoir writes *masculin* and *féminin*. I think she means the fact of being a man or of being a woman, and translate 'male' and 'female'.

[100] Parshley omits the reference to what one says in French, which is philosophically unfortunate, but understandable since one says the same thing in English. He also omits the last part of the sentence (from 'here the specific meaning of *vir*' to the end) altogether. In his translation this sentence reads: 'man represents both the positive and the neutral, as is indicated by the common use of man to designate human beings in general . . .'. The effect is to conceal Beauvoir's use of linguistic examples to make her case, and to transform her reference to the French language into a falsely universalizing claim implicitly based on French and English, but not necessarily on other languages (in Norwegian, for example, the word for a human being (*menneske*) is not the same as the word for man (*mann*)).

result is an analysis of sexism (it turns woman into a relative being, the negative of man) which was to be shared by just about every feminist in the second half of this century. At this point, with no further transition, she goes on to tell an apparently auto-biographical story which the reader initially takes to be one more example of the tendency to cast women as relative beings. That the story does more work than that starts to become apparent when we read the comments that Beauvoir attaches to it:

> I have sometimes been annoyed, in the middle of an abstract discussion, at hearing men say to me: 'You think this or that because you are a woman'; but I knew that my only defence would be to reply: 'I think it because it is true,' thereby removing [*éliminant*] my subjectivity.[101] It would be out of the question to retort: 'And you think the contrary because you are a man', for it is understood that the fact of being a man is no peculiarity.[102] A man is in

[101] Parshley translates *éliminant par là ma subjectivité* as 'thereby removing my subjective self from the argument'. But he also translates Beauvoir's 'je savais que ma seule défense, c'était de répondre' as a straightforward present tense sentence: 'but I *know* that my only defence *is* to reply' (my emphases). My under-standing of the French is that Beauvoir tells us about a comment she has heard several times in the past, specifically in a past which still has effects in the present moment (this is the effect of the perfect tense: *je me suis agacée parfois*). Parshley is right to expect a present tense continuation. But that doesn't come. Instead we get a slightly odd imperfect tense. The imperfect has strong descriptive and evocative powers, it presents the past action from the inside, telling us 'this is what it used to feel like'. It can also indicate something that would (habitually) happen over an indefinite period in the past. It is as if Beauvoir first remembers that she has often been annoyed at the sentence 'you think that because you are a woman'. Then she continues by evoking fully what she felt and thought on those repeated occasions: 'je savais que ma seule défense c'était de répondre'. The next phrase continues in the same way: 'il n'était pas question de répliquer'.

The next phrase has to be translated 'it would be out of the question to retort'. To write 'it *was* out of the question' would make it sound as if Beauvoir were talking of one, specific occasion. In the same way, and for the same reason, I translate the first sentence as 'I knew that my only defence would be to reply'. The French, to my ear, is ambiguous as to whether Beauvoir ever actually used this defence. She could have said it, or she could simply be reporting the analy-sis that would go through her head at these occasions, namely that if she were to say something to this idiot, then this is what the situation would oblige her to say. I shall return to the possibility of remaining silent in the face of the man's claim.

[102] In this and the previous sentence the French text sets up a nice opposition between *répondre* (reply) and *répliquer* (retort), which indicates the difference in tone that Beauvoir has in mind here. Parshley translates both verbs as 'reply'.

the right in being a man; it is the woman who is in the wrong. In fact, just as for the ancients there was an absolute vertical with reference to which the oblique was defined, there is an absolute human type, namely the male.[103] Woman has ovaries, a uterus; there we have [*voilà*] the particular circumstances that imprison her [*l'enferment*] in her subjectivity; one often says that she thinks with her glands. In his grandiosity man forgets that his anatomy also includes hormones, and testicles. He thinks of his body as a direct and normal connection [*relation*] with the world which he believes that he apprehends objectively, while he considers the woman's body to be weighed down by everything specific to it: an obstacle, a prison (*SS* xxi–xxii; *DSa* 14–15, TA).[104]

Why does Beauvoir think that her only option is to reply 'I say it because it is true'? Let me stress that she thinks of this as her only option *for a reply*. To know that this is the only option is not necessarily to choose to take it up. She may decide to turn on her heel and walk off, or in some other way signify that she chooses to remain silent. What such a silence might mean, will be discussed later.[105] This passage tells us that if she were to reply to the man, then this is what she would say, not with a sense of pleasure or jubilation, but with a heavy sense of being forced to choose what might possibly be (in her eyes) the lesser of two distinct evils. Because she is a woman, the man's 'You think that because you are a woman', places her in an impossible situation. She can't very well deny that she is a woman, since that truth is the 'background from which all further claims will stand out', but she cannot, either, accept the man's claim, for instance by saying that 'of course I think this because I am a woman'. There are two reasons

[103] Parshley translates *le type masculin* as 'the masculine [type]', even in a context where it is a question of the male body with its testicles and hormones.

[104] This passage contains a number of terms emphasizing the fact that the woman is being turned into the particular as opposed to the man, who is perceived as universal. Since it is difficult to translate these without losing some of the philosophical overtones, I signal the original French in square brackets here:

being a man is no peculiarity [*n'est pas une singularité*];

Woman has ovaries, a uterus; there we have the particular circumstances [*voilà des conditions singulières*];

weighed down by everything specific to it [*tout ce qui le spécifie*].

[105] I am deeply grateful to Stanley Cavell for suggesting this example.

for this. First, it is not possible for her to relativize the man in the same way that he relativizes her: he doesn't think of himself as engaging his subjectivity in the discussion, or even if he does, he doesn't think of that subjectivity as having anything to do with his male body, and doesn't realize, therefore, that he is a *man* engaging in an intellectual conversation.[106] For this reason he would not understand what the retort 'and you think the contrary because you are a man' would imply: he would simply see it as a sign that the woman had given up trying to come up with 'proper' intellectual arguments to support her views. In this situation it does not help the woman to be as well or better educated as her interlocutor, or to have a superior or equally prestigious social position: it is the specific fact of her being a woman that is mobilized to undercut her arguments.

In other words, in a situation where the woman is defined as deviant in relation to an absolute, any reminders that his interlocutor actually is female will make the man experience what she says as relative, insignificant, and untrue. It is to save her intellectual integrity that Beauvoir has to 'remove her subjectivity', and it is precisely the fact of having to do that, that makes the situation unfair, unequal, and ultimately oppressive to her. To make her 'remove her subjectivity' is to choke her voice.[107] This is why the question of choosing silence as an alternative to this reply becomes so complicated. The man's comment is already an aggressive attempt to silence her. Were she to choose to remain silent, she would have to find some way of showing that *this* silence is *her own* silence. This is not exactly an easy task. (So perhaps turning on her heels?) In this context it is deeply significant that Beauvoir's 'I am a woman' *precedes* the anecdote: if she hadn't

[106] As mentioned before: this was surely a very likely scenario in France in 1949. In the 1990s some men will think differently. To explore such a different situation is precisely to follow up Beauvoir's invitation to consider her example in the light of our own lives. See also my discussion of disagreement on the following pages.

[107] For Beauvoir this is an act of oppression. In *Pyrrhus et Cinéas* (1944) she writes that the primary condition of freedom is to 'be allowed to appeal. I shall therefore fight against those who want to choke my voice, prevent me from expressing myself, prevent me from being' (113; my translation). I shall return to this quotation at the end of this essay.

established her subjectivity in the text precisely by placing that utterance before all the others, before telling us the story, she might not have been able to see that the man's arrogant 'You think that because you are a woman' amounts to an attempt to exclude her from philosophy.

Beauvoir complains that the man forces her to *eliminate* her subjectivity. But she also complains that the man's belief that the woman's body is somehow more limiting, more particular than his own, *imprisons* the woman in her subjectivity. In 1949, Beauvoir states, proudly and with much philosophical energy: 'I am a woman'. In 1931, however, she thought differently: 'I did not think of myself as a "woman": I was *me*', she writes in *The Prime of Life* (*PL* 62; *FA* 73). There is no reason to believe that she had stopped thinking 'I am me' in 1949. The difference is that she no longer believes that the statement 'I am a woman' is incompatible with the statement 'I am me'. Beauvoir, then, wants neither to eliminate her subjectivity, nor to be imprisoned in it; she wants to understand herself as a woman, without losing her sense of freedom (transcendence).[108] This is why she dismisses both essentialism and nominalism at the beginning of *The Second Sex*: we might say that while the former seeks to imprison women in their specific subjectivity, the latter seeks to divest them of it entirely. Beauvoir's feminist project is a sustained attempt to define a different perspective, one that firmly distances itself from both alternatives.

From a Beauvoirean perspective the problem with being imprisoned in one's subjectivity is that it implies that one *is* a woman in an essentialist sense. If one wholeheartedly believes that one *is* a woman in this sense, one is alienated and in bad faith. (This would be true whether the person in question had a female body, was a male-to-female transsexual, or someone with a male body living, dressing, and loving like a woman. To be alienated is to identify with the Other's image of what a woman is by attempting to freeze one's subjectivity into the desired picture,

---

[108] Kate Soper writes that Beauvoir attempts to encompass 'two contrary but equally compelling assertions of identity: "I am a woman" and "I simply am" '. Beauvoir's whole work, Soper adds, is 'the sustained expression . . . of this "woman–person" doublet' (*Troubled Pleasures* 176).

thus denying freedom by turning existence into essence.[109]) The person who takes herself to *be* a woman in this sense, loses her claim to universality—to be someone capable of speaking the truth—because her thought is now imagined to be pervaded by her femininity. This is why Beauvoir has to refuse to be imprisoned in her subjectivity.

To have to eliminate her subjectivity is no better, however. For then the woman is also alienated, this time either into an absurd picture of a general human being without sex, or into the picture of a man. (This is the option she would in effect be resigning herself to take up were she to say 'I say it because it is true'.) Losing touch with her subjectivity, she has to cut herself off from her own lived experience in the very act of philosophizing. Beauvoir is not about to accept an invitation to turn herself into a travesty in this way. Yet she can't just accept the man's alternative, accept that she says what she says because she is a woman, because the situation here described is one in which the man has just demonstrated his intellectual bankruptcy by having recourse to an *ad feminam* argument. One cannot win a debate with an opponent who sinks to such levels by responding in kind. So Beauvoir chooses to assert the truth of her claims instead. (She

---

[109] Rather than insisting that they are a man or a woman, some transgendered people insist that they are *neither* one or the other sex. Alice Myers, a woman—I mean woman in the usual physical sense—portrayed in Melanie Thernstrom's 1998 article 'Sexuality 101' is a case in point. An undergraduate at Harvard, Alice has changed her name to Alex, lives in the male dorm, has a girlfriend, but has had no hormone treatment or surgery. Alex accepts that he is female, and declares not that he is a man, but that he is *not* a woman. Alex doesn't want to call himself a woman because he does not want to do what women are conventionally supposed to do: 'You have to be constantly fighting society: I'm still a woman even though I'm sleeping with women. I'm still a woman even though I don't know how to cook and I hate wearing dresses. . . . It's so much easier for me to say "Screw it, I'm not a woman" and try to do what I want to do' (100). On this evidence it looks as if Alex's image of what a woman is, is alienated (fixed, other-imposed) in Beauvoir's sense of the word. Instead of identifying with a certain cultural image of femininity, however, Alex appears to build his identity on the denial of the same image.

In a presentation at the 1998 Chicago Humanities Festival, the well-known transgender activist Kate Bornstein stressed, in a very different way, that she considers herself neither male nor female.

does not, however, *deny* that her views have anything to do with the fact of being a woman.) Her response is a subtle hint—probably altogether missed by the man—that she wishes to claim her own particularity *without* abdicating her claim to speak with the ambition of the universal (i.e. to claim that what she is saying is true).

To spell out the implications: if the philosophical institution seeks to eliminate women's subjectivity, women (and that includes Beauvoir) simply cannot be philosophers. Or to be more precise: if a woman is barred from including her subjectivity in philosophy (in 'abstract conversations'), she cannot become the kind of philosopher who has to stake her subjectivity in her judgements. If, under such conditions, a woman *still* insists on becoming a philosopher, her only options would be to do mathematical logic, or various forms of positivist philosophy (i.e. to choose forms of work that do not draw on the thinker's subjectivity to any great extent), or, alternatively, to masquerade as a man, to persuade herself that she is 'just a human being', just like all her male colleagues. But since her male colleagues' maleness is not philosophically problematic to them, the woman philosopher who thinks she is 'just a human being' will from the outset be prevented from having recourse in her thought to the full range of her own experiences, whereas her male colleagues will not be prevented from doing so by their sex.[110] This means that although she may well produce serious work, she risks missing out on those exhilarating moments when one's thought truly seems to illuminate one's experience and vice versa, the moments when one finally recognizes that '*this* is how it is with me'. Without such moments, many of us surely would not feel much satisfaction in intellectual work at all. (I take the longing for such moments of human and intellectual satisfaction to be what gives Jane Tompkins's 'Me and My Shadow' its energy and interest.) For Beauvoir to say that there is no divorce between philosophy and

[110] The male philosopher's social class or race may interfere with his thought in somewhat similar ways. The question of sexuality or sexual desire, however, appears to be somewhat different. The tradition of male homosexuals claiming philosophy as their own stretches from Socrates to Foucault and beyond. There is work to be done on the reasons for this.

life, then, is to say that philosophy has to be a place where women's subjectivity is considered just as universal as men's. It is not least in *this* sense that Beauvoir's defiant 'I am a woman' becomes the truth which provides the background for everything she goes on to say in *The Second Sex*.

If we now move from the philosophical claims developed in Beauvoir's anecdote to its methodological and stylistic implications, the first thing to note is that she chooses to make her point through the telling of a story. This procedure is remarkably consonant with that of ordinary language philosophers: 'The appeal to "what we should say if . . ." requires that we imagine an example or story, sometimes one more or less similar to events which may happen any day, sometimes one unlike anything we have known', Stanley Cavell writes ('Aesthetic Problems' 95). In fact, Beauvoir is not only telling us a story, she is telling us a story about a conversation, consisting entirely of considerations of what a man and what a woman might say in a certain situation. The dialogue is the form or the genre closest to the heart of the kind of philosophy that proceeds from ordinary language.

According to Austin, the point of telling stories is to imagine concrete situations where it becomes possible to see whether we agree or disagree about what we should say in such a situation:

> no situation . . . is ever 'completely' described. The more we imagine the situation in detail, with a background of story—and it is worth employing the most idiosyncratic or, sometimes, boring means to stimulate and to discipline our wretched imaginations—the less we find we disagree about what we should say. Nevertheless, *sometimes* we do ultimately disagree . . . ('Plea' 184).

For Austin, then, disagreement is essential to the procedures of ordinary language philosophy: 'A disagreement as to what we should say is not to be shied off, but to be pounced upon: for the explanation of it can hardly fail to be illuminating' ('Plea' 184). Cavell expands the point:

> if we find we disagree about what we should say, it would make no obvious sense to attempt to confirm or disconfirm one or other of our responses by collecting data to show which of us is in fact

right.[111] What we should do is either (*a*) try to determine why we disagree (perhaps we are imagining the story differently)—just as, if we agree in response we will, when we start philosophizing about this fact, want to know why we agree, what it shows about our concepts; or (*b*) we will, if the disagreement cannot be explained, either find some explanation for *that*, or else discard the example. Disagreement is not disconfirming: it is as much a datum for philosophizing as agreement is ('Aesthetic Problems' 95).

Beauvoir's anecdote is an exceptionally good invitation to the dialogic process both Austin and Cavell see as constitutive of philosophy. 'I knew that my only defence would be to reply: "I think it because it is true" ', she writes. Many feminists in the 1990s would strongly disagree, insisting that they would *never* say, let alone be tempted to say, 'I think it because it is true' in the situation Beauvoir describes. Many of my students report that they would want to say: 'Of course I think this because I am a woman', adding 'and you think the contrary because you are a man', for good measure. I imagine that theorists as different as Luce Irigaray and Carol Gilligan might be inclined to agree with my students. Yet further discussion usually reveals that my students have made a number of presuppositions about the situation that Beauvoir most likely did not make. When I ask for some concrete examples of situations in which they would say 'of course I think so because I am a woman', it turns out that most of them overlook Beauvoir's reference to the 'abstract conversation'. Some take the man's reply to be an appeal to expertise. This is not a bad idea: in some situations, surely, the fact of being a woman (of having been brought up as a woman) bestows special insight. One student once suggested the following example: 'Of course I made wonderful suggestions about the table decorations. I think so well about these things because I am a woman.' Or in a different version: perhaps it makes sense to say that 'you say that the

---

[111] This is another reason why appeals to 'what we should say' are not appeals to expertise in the sense of knowledge of facts about language (see above, 208–9). Elsewhere Cavell writes: 'When the philosopher who proceeds from ordinary language tells us, "You can't say such-and-such", what he means is that you cannot say that *here* and communicate *this* situation to others, or understand it for yourself' ('Must' 21).

department will vote against this proposal because you are a woman', meaning 'because you have been trained as a woman in this culture, you have a unique insight into the emotional dynamics of faculty meetings'.

But this raises the question of the tone in which 'you say this because you are a woman' is spoken. As Cavell puts it, 'saying something is never *merely* saying something, but is saying something with a certain tune and a proper cue and while executing the appropriate business' ('Must' 33). If the man's phrase is to be interpreted as an invitation to the woman to admit expertise, the assumption is that the man is quite admiring in his tone. 'You say that because you are a woman' then becomes similar to something like 'You say that because you are a plumber', spoken on a tone of admiration or pleasure at the insight the other person has just produced. Beauvoir's story, not least the word 'retort', indicates that she felt irritation. Here we may suspect that she is excessively sensitive, a shrinking intellectual violet, or overly paranoid ('all men are out to get me'), but for the sake of the argument I will assume that her experience of irritation is a reasonable response to something in the man's remark. If so, it is likely to be a response to aggression or condescension. It is, of course, still possible to retort 'Indeed I say it because I am a woman', but now the tone of the reply is likely to be hostile, not proud or satisfied. At this point, in fact, both interlocutors would be angrily trading *ad feminam* and *ad hominem* arguments. The price one pays for this is to lose sight of the original 'abstract conversation' for ever. This is why Beauvoir replies 'I say it because it is true', but it is also why she doesn't say it without noting the loss of her subjectivity.

This discussion only opens the questions produced by Beauvoir's anecdote. In my teaching I have found that encouragements to imagine different situations and different examples, to imagine what Irigaray or Gilligan or Spivak might say, or to consider what we should say if the man in question was Frantz Fanon and not just any white Frenchman with philosophical ambitions, are immensely helpful in bringing out differences in different theorists' understanding of what a woman is and how sexism works. Different situations will produce different responses. What I have tried to do here is to indicate what motivates Beauvoir's temptation to reply 'I say it because it is true'.

But, someone might want to say, you have basically just told us that nothing can count as a counterargument to Beauvoir: every disagreement just confirms the brilliance of her method. This is what Cavell says about the best way of arguing against a claim based on ordinary language:

> I take it to be a phenomenological fact about philosophizing from everyday language that one feels empirical evidence about one's language to be irrelevant to one's claims.[112] If such philosophizing is to be understood, then that fact about it must be understood. I am not saying that evidence about how (other) people speak can never make an ordinary language philosopher withdraw his typical claims; but I find it important that the most characteristic pressure against him is applied by producing or deepening an example which shows him that *he* would not say what he says 'we' say ('Aesthetic Problems' 95).

The most telling argument against Beauvoir's anecdote, then, would be one that showed that given her own understanding of the social relations between men and women, *she* would not feel 'I say it because it is true' to be the best available response. I have not been able to produce such an argument. It certainly doesn't follow that nobody else could, but the fact that I can't is one reason why I think this anecdote is such a brilliant invitation to consider what it means to be a woman in a sexist world.

It follows from Cavell's analysis that even if we found evidence conclusively proving that every other woman in France in 1949 would say something different from Beauvoir in this situation, then this would neither prove nor disprove her claim about what *she* would say. Rather, such evidence would be important because it would give rise to analysis of the reasons for the differences. Since each woman's response is as valid as every other woman's (this is one implication of what it means to say that we are all speakers of the language), the point is to understand what motivates different

---

[112] This is yet another version of the fundamental idea that philosophy based on ordinary language is not a positivist science, that the point is not to gather statistics, or to appeal to one's own supreme expertise. The point, rather, is to invite the reader to think about what *she* would say.

responses, not to make Beauvoir toe the majority line (or vice versa). As Cavell puts it, 'one sample does not refute or disconfirm another; if two are in disagreement they vie with one another for the same confirmation' (*Claim* 19).

This is why it doesn't make sense to claim that Beauvoir's anecdote is 'exclusionary', for example because it doesn't stage a conversation between a black woman and a white man, doesn't represent an Indian woman or an American woman, and so on. No anecdote or story can represent a universal subject. All one can do is to place a concrete, particular subject on the linguistic stage. Beauvoir's anecdote succeeds if it helps its readers to reach a description of sexism that not only makes sense to those who read it, but invites them to think up new examples or new responses for themselves. If a woman in India or in South Africa or in Norway can show that there are presuppositions in the anecdote that Beauvoir has not noticed, presuppositions that would make one see that other ways of responding would make more sense, this is precisely to participate in the process of building a better analysis of what it means to be a woman, and of sexism. This is why Austin is right to say that disagreements are reasons for rejoicing. We should not forget, however, that some disagreements are so profound that all further conversation comes to a halt. There are cases where even after exhaustive effort we simply do not understand each other at all. These are the situations, as Wittgenstein puts it, when 'I have exhausted the justifications [and] have reached bedrock, and my spade is turned' (*PI* §217). The question is whether the man's 'You say that because you are a woman' produces such a situation. I shall return to this.

There is another sense in which empirical evidence is irrelevant to the procedures of the ordinary language philosopher. The example or story produced does not need to be empirically true. Even when I tell a story in the first person singular ('I have sometimes become annoyed in the middle of an abstract discussion . . .'), it doesn't matter whether I tell the truth. There is actually good reason to doubt the veracity of Beauvoir's anecdote. In *Force of Circumstance* she writes, with specific reference to the genesis of *The Second Sex*:

> I realized that the first question to come up was: What has it meant
> to me to be a woman? At first I thought I could dispose of that
> pretty quickly. I had never had any feeling of inferiority, no one
> had ever said to me: 'You think that way because you're a woman';
> my femaleness had never been irksome to me in any way (*FC* 103;
> *FCa* 136; TA).

Obviously, when it comes to the question of whether anyone
actually ever said to her 'you think that because you are a
woman', Beauvoir flatly contradicts herself. In her essay she
claims it sometimes happens, in her memoirs she claims it never
happened. Empirical research might establish the truth of the
matter. My guess is that Beauvoir told the truth in *The Second Sex*
and lied in her autobiography, but this is of no importance here,
since it makes no difference to the force of her argument
whether her story is empirically true or not. If an entirely fictive
story is found to be powerful when it comes to producing a careful analysis of some question, then it is philosophically useful and
valuable. It is in this sense that 'one feels empirical evidence
about one's language to be irrelevant to one's claims', as Cavell
puts it.[113]

The passage I have quoted here is followed by half a page of
quotations from Aristotle, Aquinas, Genesis, Bossuet, Michelet,
and Benda which all confirm Beauvoir's claim that for traditional
male philosophers 'Humanity is male [*mâle*] and man defines
woman not in herself but as relative to him; she is not regarded as
an autonomous being' (*SS* xxii; *DSa* 15). It is at the end of this
page—which is also the end of the third paragraph of *The Second
Sex*—that Beauvoir sums up her findings, and for the first time
uses the word 'Other' about women:

[113] Beauvoir's use of anecdote seems to be different from the use of anecdote
among new historicists. According to Joel Fineman's influential essay 'The
History of the Anecdote', the anecdote is the 'narration of a singular event', and
as such it is 'the literary form or genre that uniquely refers to the real' (67). For
a philosopher such as Beauvoir, the 'reality effect' of the anecdote does not seem
to be all that crucial. Fineman has historical anecdotes, such as those used by
Stephen Greenblatt, in mind. Beauvoir's and Greenblatt's apparently different
uses of anecdote are precisely an example of philosophical disagreement which
could give rise to new insights (about the nature of anecdotes, or existentialism
and New Historicism) if pursued further.

[Woman] is nothing but what the man decrees; thus she is called 'the sex', which means that she appears essentially to the male [*mâle*] as a sexed [*sexué*] being: since she is sex to him, she must be sex absolutely. She is defined and differentiated in relation to man and not he in relation to her; she is the inessential confronting [*en face de*] the essential. He is the Subject, he is the Absolute: she is the Other (*SS* xxii; *DSa* 15; TA).

What got Beauvoir to this point? What evidence has she produced for the claim that woman is the Other? In the first two paragraphs she refers to everyday life (her own and that of her friends), casual reading, literary gossip, common sense, and some mistaken philosophical beliefs. In the third paragraph, she adds extensive analysis of speech acts and linguistic examples (the final paragraph contains another one, namely the reference to the fact that women are called 'the sex [*le sexe*]'). Equally important is her reliance on evidence from her own experience of being a woman, including the feeling of irritation that the encounter with sexist attitudes sometimes produces. Finally, the importance given to the conversation with the man embodies Beauvoir's ambition to produce a world in which a woman's subjectivity is not taken to be either more or less particular or more or less subjective than anyone else's.

There is one striking difference between the preceding text and this rousing finale, which starts with the reference to Aristotle and goes on to invoke a whole list of other philosophers. So far Beauvoir has hardly named any philosophers at all, except extremely briefly in the first paragraph where she dismisses essentialism and nominalism. In that context the only philosophers mentioned by name are Plato and Aquinas, and even there Plato is referred to only by the adjective 'Platonic'. Here, however, she suddenly produces a long list of philosophical names, and then ends the paragraph with a long footnote challenging the views of one of her contemporary philosophical colleagues in France, namely Emmanuel Lévinas. It is as if the analysis of the anecdote of the woman in an intellectual conversation has made her feel free to engage with the philosophical tradition, to use it for her own purposes, and so finally express her distaste for sexist philosophy, however important and influential the philosopher in question may be. (Her first quote comes from Aristotle, who claims that woman is woman in virtue of a certain lack of qualities.) After this paragraph Beauvoir continues with a fairly scholarly discussion of the category of the Other in religion, anthropology, history, and philosophy, which I shall not go into here. It is as if the work carried out in these first pages of *The Second Sex* has enabled her to find her own voice even in relation to traditional philosophical material.

The footnote attached to the last sentence in the text ('she is the Other') is interesting. Here Beauvoir quotes Lévinas's essay *Le temps et l'autre* and says that like all the other philosophers she has just mentioned, Lévinas too writes from the point of view of a man: 'It is striking that he deliberately adopts a man's point of view without signalling the reciprocity of subject and object. When he writes that woman is mystery, he implies that she is mystery for man. Thus a description that presents itself as objective is in fact an affirmation of male [*masculin*] privilege' (*SS* xxii; *DSa* 16; TA).[114] The fact that she ends by launching into a debate with a contemporary French colleague shows that she now has found a voice that she thinks will hold, even in 'abstract discussion'. I read the footnote in which she engages in discussion with Lévinas as an embodiment of Beauvoir's hope that she will no longer need either to eliminate her subjectivity or to imprison herself in it during philosophical conversations. The fact that in this footnote she makes a perfectly clear, perfectly philosophical, but also perfectly feminist point tells us something about what voice Beauvoir's use of herself as a philosophical case study has enabled her to find.

'My Spade is Turned': Exemplarity, Failure, and Freedom

I have reached the end of the first three paragraphs of *The Second Sex*, and I have almost finished my analysis of Beauvoir's philosophical style. In the previous section I showed that Beauvoir

[114] My Lévinasian friends think that Beauvoir is unfair to Lévinas here. All they need to do to substantiate this is to show that Lévinas in fact does not write as if it goes without saying that the subject is male, and, more particularly, that he never implies that woman is more of a mystery for man than he is to her.

stakes her subjectivity in her philosophy by using herself—her own experience—as an example, and that her method is dialogical, so that the anecdote about the abstract conversation can be read as an invitation to try to find ourselves in Beauvoir's words. If we can't do that, our disagreement is as philosophically valuable as our agreement. Beauvoir, then, is neither simply speaking as herself without pretensions to represent anyone else (as if that were possible), nor simply speaking for (in the place of, on behalf of) others. She is, rather, staking her own subjectivity in an attempt to speak *to* the other.

Two sets of questions arise from this analysis. First, there is the question of exemplarity. Isn't there something arrogant about using oneself as an example? Isn't this another way of saying that Beauvoir is generalizing from the particular case? And doesn't this resurrect all the problems attached to the attempt to speak for others? Then there is the question of disagreement. So far I have taken it to be entirely productive. But isn't my analysis of Beauvoir's dialogic method far too sanguine, far too confident in something like the fundamental good will of human nature? What happens when the dialogue breaks down? When we have nothing more to say to each other? These are the problems I shall discuss in this last section, which will be followed by a brief conclusion in which I say something about what my reading of the first pages of *The Second Sex* has taught me about the contemporary turn to the personal.

Exemplarity

What does it mean to turn one's own experience into a philosophical example? I have said that the ordinary language philosopher does not claim to know better than anyone else what we should say when. To speak is to participate in the production of meaning. What I mean by my words will be taken as partly constitutive of what the words mean in the language. Fundamentally, it follows from this that my usage exemplifies the meaning of a word as well as anyone else's usage. To put this in another register: because I am a human being I am as good an example of a human being as you are. By making myself exemplary I am assuming that I am no better and no worse than anyone else. To put myself forward as exemplary, then, I do not need to place myself above anyone else. It is in this sense that *any one of us* can pretend to be representative of us all, put ourselves forward as representative or exemplary of what *we* might say.

I just put this argument in Wittgensteinian or Cavellian terms, a language which Beauvoir does not use. In *Pyrrhus and Cinéas*, an essay on the ethics of freedom first published in 1944, she herself formulates very similar thoughts in existentialist terms.[115] In this text, Beauvoir stresses that language and writing (among other acts in the world) are *appeals* to the other. 'Language is an appeal to the freedom of the other, because the sign only becomes sign when it is grasped [*ressaisit*] by a consciousness', she writes (*PC* 104).[116] What the writer wants, is the other's free and unconstrained response: 'I can only appeal to the other's freedom, not force it [*non la contraindre*]' (*PC* 112). The other remains free to respond or not respond to my appeals, however pressing, charming, or enticing they may be. If Beauvoir were to take the view that she knows better than anyone else what a woman is, she would, in her own vocabulary, be imagining that her knowledge and her experiences enable her to 'transcend the other'. If I imagine that my freedom transcends the other's freedom I cast her as limited and finite, as a thing, not as a transcendence. In short, I imagine the other as a lesser being than myself. A narcissist or a vain person might be satisfied with the adulation of such objectified others, Beauvoir writes, but such satisfaction is worthless, for as soon as I imagine that the other is not free, her response loses its value: 'The moment the other appears limited or finite to me, the place he creates for me on earth is as contingent and vain as he is' (*PC* 99). For Beauvoir, then, to write philosophy is to appeal to an other imagined to be

---

[115] I do not think of *Pyrrhus et Cinéas* as an unproblematic work. But I do think that Beauvoir's analysis of freedom, generosity, and the appeal to the other in this text was deeply influential on Sartre's *What Is Literature?* (1947) and that these views always remained fundamental to Beauvoir's understanding of writing. In *The Philosophy of Simone de Beauvoir* Debra Bergoffen has a useful chapter on *Pyrrhus et Cinéas* (45–71). All translations of *Pyrrhus et Cinéas* are mine.

[116] See also *PC* 95 for an example concerning books.

as free and responsible as she is.[117] The man in the abstract conversation has failed to see the woman as free in this sense. He draws the boundaries of the woman's consciousness, or to put it in ultra-existentialist terms, he imagines that he transcends her transcendence.

At this point someone will surely say that since it is obvious that all human beings are not equally free, Beauvoir's philosophy is pure idealism, and conservative or apolitical idealism at that. Beauvoir's concept of freedom deserves much more detailed discussion, but that will have to be the subject of another paper. Let me just briefly say that in *Pyrrhus et Cinéas* she distinguishes between two types of freedom, namely freedom as transcendence (as the existential condition of human beings, this is in principle the same for everyone) and concrete freedom (the social, political, material conditions in which each human being finds herself, and which clearly vary immensely). This is how Beauvoir summarizes the distinction in *The Prime of Life*:

> [In *Pyrrhus et Cinéas*] I distinguished two separate aspects of freedom. It is first the very modality of existence, which willy-nilly, in one way or another, takes up [*reprend à son compte*] all that comes to it from the outside; this internal movement is indivisible, and thus a totality for each individual. On the other hand, the concrete possibilities open to people are unequal. Some have access only to a small part of all those that are available to mankind as a whole, and all their efforts only bring them closer to the platform from which the most privileged are departing. Their transcendence thus loses itself in the collective and takes on the appearance of immanence. In more favourable situations, however, the project becomes a genuine going beyond the given [*dépassement*]; it builds a new future. An activity is good when it aims to conquer for oneself and for others such privileged positions: when it aims to free freedom (*PL* 459; *FA* 628; TA).

Precisely because my acts require the response of free beings, Beauvoir writes, I need to want (and work for) 'health, knowledge,

[117] Eva Lundgren-Gothlin has done fundamental work on the concept of the appeal (*l'appel*) in Beauvoir's texts. She is the first to have developed an analysis of what it means when Beauvoir calls female sexual desire an 'appeal to the other' in *The Second Sex*. Having changed her name to Eva Gothlin, she published an article on the appeal in English in 1999.

well-being and leisure for all human beings, so that their freedom
is not consumed in the effort to fight illness, ignorance and
poverty' (*PC* 115).[118] When it comes to the concrete situation of
writing philosophy or theory, then, Beauvoir would consider it
unethical to write in ways that revealed that she did not take the
other's existential freedom (to respond in whatever way he or she
pleases to her text, including not reading it at all) as seriously as
her own. Contemporary critics who unanimously agree that it is
unethical to write in ways that silence others, appear to agree.
Furthermore, on the existential and ethical level, nobody is more
or less free than anyone else. To imagine otherwise is to objectify
and diminish the other, to imply that some human beings are less
exemplary than others. For this reason, it is a cause for outrage
for Beauvoir that some people have far greater concrete freedom,
far more extensive opportunities, than others.

Beauvoir formulates an answer to the question of what a
woman is by putting forward her own experience as 'exemplary'
or 'representative' of the experience of women. Although the
terms 'exemplary' and 'representative' are not synonymous,
there is an intimate connection between them. To represent can
mean to stand for or speak for others. To exemplify is to be a
particular instance of the general. If I find the courage to make
an example of myself, I am doing so in the hope that it will be
recognized that my experience is an illuminating instance of a
more general state of affairs. But as soon as I make any claim at
all about any state of affairs, I am saying something about what
the world looks like to me. However much I stake my subjectivity
in them, such claims are in their very nature going to be general.
Whether I say 'it is raining' or 'woman is the Other', I am speaking for others, inviting them to see if they can find themselves—
their own experiences, their own world-view—in such claims,
hoping that they will be able to do so, but also knowing that they
may not. This is what happens when Beauvoir attempts to find out
what a woman is.

The difference I want to get at here is the difference between

---

[118] Beauvoir's distinction, in 1944, between existential and concrete freedom
represents a clear departure from Sartre's *Being and Nothingness* (1943), in which
there is no concept of concrete freedom.

speaking for others in a way which leaves no space for them to respond, or in a way that attempts to coerce a specific response: such ways of speaking would not be good faith appeals to the freedom of the other; they would be monologic and not dialogic. The other is not imagined to be as free as the speaker is. (The man in the abstract conversation provides a good example of this attitude.) This contrasts with attempts to speak for others by addressing them (appealing to them) in the hope of a response. This difference is erased by the simplistic insistence that to speak *for* is always to silence the other. If I speak out on behalf of someone else, I am usually not preventing them from speaking too. The difference turns on two elements: the presence or absence of a stance of superiority in the speaker, and the presence or absence of a dialogic attitude. If the other to whom I am speaking is imagined to be someone who knows less than I do about the meaning of words or the question of being human, or someone whose existential freedom is less extensive or less important than mine, I am not asking for the other's free response, but for adulation and thoughtless admiration. Contemporary critics are right to see such condescension as a form of discursive violence, as an attempt to silence or belittle the other. To determine whether such a stance is at work in a text, careful analysis is required. It is simply not enough to pick a 'we' or a 'they' out of context and claim that a text containing such rhetorical features must be 'exclusionary' or otherwise belittling of others.[119]

[119] This sounds a little abstract. To give an example: Elizabeth Spelman's discussion of 'exclusionism' in feminist theory has a tendency to do this. Spelman writes: ' "We need to hear the many voices of women." . . . Who are "we" here, what is the need, and what will the hearing involve? "We" are of course those who have been heard from, who have been calling the shots in feminism, who now recognize a need that can only be satisfied by hearing from other women' (163). I would have thought that there are many cases in which the 'we' in a sentence such as 'We need to hear the many voices of women' could refer to the writer *and* anyone who reads the text, or to anyone at all with an interest in feminist theory.

In *Sexual/Textual Politics* I deliberately wrote: 'recent work on Third World Women has much to teach us' (86). Some critics took the bait and upbraided me for excluding Third World women from my arguments. But 'us' in this sentence can refer to anyone at all with an interest in feminist theory, including women from the so-called Third World. It is not enough simply to be Nigerian or

To see one's own experience as exemplary, as an instance of a more general case, is not the same as to generalize from a particular case. While it is possible to do the latter without putting one's own subjectivity on the line, it is quite impossible to do the former without staking oneself in one's claims.[120] 'The problem of the critic, as of the artist', Cavell writes, 'is not to discount his subjectivity, but to include it; not to overcome it in agreement, but to master it in exemplary ways' ('Aesthetic Problems' 94). If my subjectivity—my experience—is to be of any use in my criticism or my philosophy, Cavell seems to say, I have to be able to make it exemplary. Otherwise it will remain staunchly particular, and so of no interest to anybody but myself. To make it exemplary is to show what light it can shed on a general question, not to claim that it is itself general, that it in some mysterious way already subsumes that of others.

By turning myself into an example in a way which does not assume that I know better than anyone else what the meaning of my experience is, I deprive myself of the feeling of invulnerability that an inner conviction of narcissistic superiority could provide. Such speech makes me vulnerable, regardless of what it is about. Unlike Ruth Behar, I don't think that 'vulnerable' speech needs to be about emotions or feelings or even about concrete autobiographical experiences. The sense of vulnerability, or risking one's whole being in one's writing, can be just as overwhelming for someone who puts forward an intellectual analysis in which she

---

Norwegian to understand one's own condition. Recent work on Nigerian or Norwegian women will have much to teach women who live in those countries, just as recent work on women in the US ought to be illuminating to women born and bred in the US. None of this implies that the 'recent work' in question should be listened to in a particularly subservient way: it will be a starting point for response, discussion, and criticism just like any other work. Nor does the statement imply that all women in all situations will learn the same things from the 'recent work' in question. To leap to such assumptions is precisely to produce the false generalizations the critics in question usually wish to avoid.

[120] In my book on Beauvoir, I approach the question of the personal in philosophy towards the end of ch. 5. But there I fail to understand the difference between using oneself as an example and generalizing from the particular case (see 146–7 for a discussion which in some ways now appears as an early attempt to write the present essay).

has drawn on her whole experience, and used all her intellectual and emotional powers, as for someone who publishes the rawest of autobiographies. Because my writing is an appeal to the other's freedom, I cannot coerce or control the other's response. Writing done in good faith (this means writing for which the writer is ready to take responsibility) is therefore intrinsically risky, whether or not I reveal autobiographical details about myself in the text. As Cavell puts it in a different context, 'To speak for yourself . . . means risking the rebuff . . . of those for whom you claimed to be speaking; and it means risking having to rebuff . . . those who claimed to be speaking for you' (*Claim* 27).

In whatever mode it occurs, it takes courage to turn oneself into an example. This is, I think, what Cavell means when he speaks of the difficulties of *finding one's voice*. Since we all are equally representative of humanity, why should I take it upon myself to say something? Surely there is an unbearable arrogance here. Why speak if you are no better than anyone else? (This kind of question comes right out of my non-bourgeois Norwegian childhood, where the first cultural commandment was 'don't believe there's anything special about you'.[121]) What is liberating about Cavell's view is that he makes it clear that one really doesn't need to be special in any way to have the right to speak: 'Who beside myself could give me the authority to speak for us? . . . [W]e are each in a position to give ourselves the right, take it from ourselves, as it were', he writes (*Pitch* 9). To speak is the birthright of any human being. Yet, even when this realization sinks in, I still need to find the courage to go ahead and make a spectacle (an example) of myself, my values, my judgements, my skills.

The moment Beauvoir writes the first word of *The Second Sex*, she enacts what Cavell in *A Pitch of Philosophy* has called the 'systematic arrogation of voice, or the arrogant assumption of the right to speak for others' (viii). Cavell's *arrogation* deliberately mixes 'arrogance' with 'arrogate' (to claim unduly, to attribute unjustly). In so far as I am speaking when others are not, there is

---

[121] Norwegians and Danes will recognize a very free translation of *Janteloven*'s first commandment: 'Du skal ikke tro at du *er* noe'.

always something undue, unfair, and unjust about it. By arrogating the voice of philosophy to herself, Beauvoir is taking, as Cavell says about Austin and Wittgenstein, 'what [she does and says] to be representative or exemplary of the human condition as such. In this way [she] interpret[s] philosophy's arrogance as the arrogation of the right to speak for us' (*Pitch* 8). For Cavell, the writing of theory or philosophy necessarily passes through such a moment of arrogation. In contrast, contemporary critics who worry about 'speaking *for*', sometimes appear to believe that it is possible to speak *without* such a moment of arrogation. But there is always someone who is not speaking. Even the most well-intentioned attack on 'exclusionary' writing is written in the presence of someone else's silence.

The moment she says 'I am a woman' Beauvoir makes her pitch to the reader. Arrogating voice to herself, she challenges the reader to think about the experiences she puts forward. The arrogance in her claim lies in the fact that she dares to speak at all, that she arrogates to herself the right to speak. But there is another form of arrogance here too, an ambitious wish to make us all agree with her, regardless of our own specific positions in the world. In 1949, for a woman to stake her right to philosophy— her right to be taken seriously as a philosopher—on the statement 'I am a woman' was wildly ambitious. No wonder, perhaps, that Beauvoir spent so much time later on trying to divert attention from her immodest claim, by insisting that *The Second Sex* should not be given the name of philosophy.[122]

To 'arrogate voice' to oneself as a thinker or critic, then, has nothing to do with dictating to others what they should think. It means, rather, to claim for oneself the right to appeal to the judgement of others: 'All the philosopher, this kind of philosopher, can do is to express, as fully as he can, his world, and attract our undivided attention to our own,' Cavell writes ('Aesthetic Problems' 96). The first epigraph to this essay is taken from the introduction to the second volume of Beauvoir's autobiography,

---

[122] Michèle Le Dœuff has called Beauvoir a 'tremendously well-hidden philosopher' (*Hipparchia's Choice* 139). Beauvoir herself kept giving interviews insisting that Sartre was the original philosopher, not she (see ch. 1 'Second Only to Sartre' in my *Simone de Beauvoir* for further discussion of this theme).

where she wonders how to defend her wish to write about herself at considerable length. Her justification is that if a person reveals herself with sincerity, it doesn't matter whether that person is remarkable or unremarkable. If there is honest self-examination, just about everyone will have something at stake in the text: 'It is impossible to shed light on one's own life without at some point illuminating the life of others', Beauvoir notes (*PL* 10; *FA* 1; TA). When Beauvoir writes about herself, then, it is not out of a sense of superiority to others. Any life can be as exemplary as any other life. Obituaries are a case in point. We read obituaries of people we have never heard of precisely because they invite us to think about what we ourselves have done with our lives, what we could still do with them, and so, ultimately, about what it is possible to make out of a human life, and how the world shapes that making.

In *The Second Sex* Beauvoir finds her voice by representing her world—which, as she just has made very clear, is a woman's world—as honestly as she can. It is by trying to understand her own situation as fully as she can that she will be able to inspire me, her reader, into examining my own condition. What I have been trying to show in this paper is that her writing in the beginning of *The Second Sex* is uniquely powerful as philosophy *because* it is fully marked by Beauvoir's own subjectivity. The difference between the Beauvoir who feels tempted to answer 'I say it because it is true' to the man in the abstract discussion, and the Beauvoir who writes *The Second Sex* is that whereas the former would have been obliged to eliminate her subjectivity, the latter has refused to do so. As Stanley Cavell puts it, this woman has eliminated her defensiveness.[123] Nor is the woman who writes *The Second Sex* a prisoner of her female subjectivity. In these pages Beauvoir's *voice* shows that she speaks as the woman and philosopher she is, neither more nor less. If we now understand what this means, we also understand why she does not need constantly to preface her claims with 'in my view', or 'speaking as a white French bourgeois woman'.

A somewhat different form of arrogance still remains to be discussed. That is Beauvoir's outrageous ambition to speak for all.

---

[123] Private communication in response to an advanced draft of this paper.

Cavell considers that ordinary language philosophy has much in common with aesthetic judgements, which according to Kant are judgements in which we aspire to speak with a 'universal voice'. Throughout this essay I have argued that Beauvoir's particular kind of philosophy is illuminated by comparisons with ordinary language philosophy such as Cavell understands it. So also in this case. Cavell takes Kant to mean that in making aesthetic judgements we are not simply making gratuitous remarks about our own personal tastes, but aiming to achieve universal agreement: ideally we would like everybody else to come to see what we see. The hope of agreement constitutes the aspiration towards the universal. It is in order to be as convincing as possible that critics of various kinds engage in rational argument, in building our 'patterns of support', as Cavell labels them ('Aesthetic Problems' 94). To say that they do this in the *hope* of agreement, however, is not to claim that such agreement will ever be reached. Even more important, perhaps, is the fact that, as Cavell puts it, 'even were agreement in fact to emerge, our judgments, so far as aesthetic, would remain essentially as subjective, in [Kant's] sense, as they ever were' ('Aesthetic Problems' 94).

In the text of *The Second Sex* the anecdote about the abstract discussion is intended as an illustration to Beauvoir's claim that whenever 'woman' is defined, it is as a limitation. But it also resonates with her own defiant 'I am a woman', and so reveals the enormous ambition that informs her project. Beauvoir's aim is nothing short of revolutionary: she wants to produce the dramatic changes necessary to *make* the statement 'I am a woman' appear as something else than a limitation, to place woman in a reciprocal relationship to man. And now it is possible to see why her 'arrogation of voice' is a necessary part of this project. For how can we ever achieve reciprocity between men and women if women are denied the right to speak for all, to speak with the ambition of the universal, to speak in the outrageous hope that we will all agree with them, a right that men have considered unproblematically theirs for so many centuries? For women to gain the right to speak for all is, as a matter of course, also to gain the right to be philosophers, the right to define themselves at once as women and as lovers of wisdom and seekers of truth. It is no coincidence that throughout *The Second Sex* Beauvoir insists that one of the worst effects of sexism is that it excludes women from the universal at every turn.[124]

If the ambition to reach the universal can be understood as speaking in the hope of encountering agreement, and if at the same time the fundamental strategy of the ordinary language philosopher or the literary critic may be characterized as an appeal to the subjectivity of the other, an appeal that occurs in the very act of staking one's own subjectivity in one's claims, then the arrogance of Beauvoir's 'I am a woman' consists precisely in the fact that she *arrogates to herself the right to speak as the woman she is with the ambition of the universal.* In so doing she exemplifies the kind of freedom *The Second Sex* is about.

Failure and Freedom

Beauvoir's ambition is to make the other see what she sees. The reception history of *The Second Sex* shows that she was remarkably successful in this enterprise. But in some cases the attempt at making the other see what we see fails. These are not only cases where we disagree, but cases where we don't even start to see what the other sees. What would happen if we imagine that Beauvoir is addressing the sentence 'I am a woman; this truth is the background from which all further claims will stand out' not to essentialists (as I basically did in my reading of the sentence) but to a nominalist who is also an epistemological sceptic? The problem Beauvoir would face then is not how to avoid essentialism, but how to convince the other that there are women and that she is one of them.

Beauvoir's syntax gives prominence to her truth claim. 'I am a woman' is the *truth* that forms the unavoidable background for

---

[124] By this she means that sexist thought deprives women of the chance to make their own experience exemplary, and blocks them from having the ambition or hope that their experience might one day come to speak for all. See e.g. Beauvoir's discussion of Hegel's notion of the universal in ethics and the prosecution, sometime in the 1890s, of two little girls who had been put to work in a brothel (*SS* 612–17; *DSb* 503–8). Naomi Schor's 'French Feminism is a Universalism' is a useful overview of different kinds of universalism in French feminist theory.

everything she will go on to say. In what way are we to take this? Is
Beauvoir inviting us to consider 'I am a woman' as an empirical
hypothesis to be verified by a checking of pre-existing facts? In so
far as she is trying to answer the question of what a woman is, this
seems rather to beg the question. Moreover, an existentialist
philosopher would hardly take the view that objective facts somehow speak for themselves. It is highly unlikely that Beauvoir's 'I
am a woman' represents a concession to objectivism or empiricism. On the other hand, the weight of the word 'truth' precludes
subjectivist interpretations: Beauvoir is not saying that although it
is her private opinion that she is a woman, you may be equally
justified in thinking that she is a man, a child, or a Martian.
Clearly, she would like us all to agree that the claim is true. But
how would she go about convincing the sceptic?

　　Just because you say you are a woman, the sceptic might say, it
doesn't follow that you are one. (In fact, this is a response one
doesn't have to be an epistemological sceptic to share.) You
might be psychotic (think of Freud's Schreber), or you might be
a pre-operative male-to-female transsexual. In Jenny Livingston's
documentary *Paris is Burning*, for example, both Octavia St
Laurent and Venus Xtravaganza refer to themselves as women.
Venus Xtravaganza may have died because someone took her too
literally.[125] Just as Descartes worried that the figures whose hats
and coats he saw in the street below him might turn out to be
automata and not human beings, I might worry that although
you are in every respect the physical incarnation of a highly
attractive woman, you may still be a monstrous alien from outer
space (this is the theme of innumerable films, including the relatively recent *Species* movies). Or perhaps I don't even suspect that
although you have a perfect female body, you are in fact an
outrageously sexist and selfish man who has just been forcibly
sex-changed by a gang of Mother-worshipping female terrorists
(this is the fate of Angela Carter's protagonist in *The Passion of
New Eve*). These are the familiar questions of philosophical scepticism, and as everyone knows who has ever been caught up in

---

[125] See Judith Butler, 'Gender Is Burning', esp. 128–37 for an interesting
discussion of Jenny Livingston's film.

them, there is no way to satisfy this kind of doubt by appeals to empirical facts.[126]

In the context of such doubt, the autobiographical form of Beauvoir's sentence ('I am a woman' as opposed to 'there are women') is not coincidental. It is as if Beauvoir wants to convey something she has learned from experience. Trying to make the epistemological sceptic understand that she is a woman, Beauvoir is in a position similar to that of Shylock in *The Merchant of Venice* trying to convince hostile Christians that a Jew is a human being just like them:

> Hath not a Jew eyes? Hath not a Jew hands, organs, dimensions, senses, affections, passions; fed with the same food, hurt with the same weapons, subject to the same diseases, healed by the same means, warmed and cooled by the same winter and summer as a Christian is? If you prick us do we not bleed? If you tickle us do we not laugh? If you poison us do we not die? And if you wrong us shall we not revenge? (III. i. 54–62).

There is helplessness, exasperation, and eloquence in Shylock's speech. The emphasis on the most material of human attributes, the body, is striking. Yet none of this moved his Christian opponents. For how can one *prove* by argument alone, even by arguments that place all the stress on the body, that one is a human being, or a woman for that matter?[127]

In a famous incident in 1858 Sojourner Truth's right to speak in the name of enslaved women was challenged by pro-slavery men, who claimed that she wasn't a woman because she had a male voice (the reference to Truth's voice is particularly symbolic here, I think). 'Denying the womanliness of women speaking in public was a familiar ploy', Nell Irvin Painter writes: 'Hostile audiences questioned the sexual identity of American women preachers like Harriet Livermore, of lecturers like the antislavery poet Frances Ellen Watkins Harper, and of actresses like Rachel, the great French tragedian' (139). In response to the challenge,

[126] I am inspired to say this by my reading of Cavell's 'Austin and Examples' in *The Claim of Reason* 49–64.

[127] Judith Butler's struggle to prove by rational argument alone that the body is material may be considered a parallel case (see my discussion of Butler's understanding of the body in Ch. 1, above).

Sojourner Truth bared her breasts and taunted the racist men by saying that many white babies had sucked these breasts and grown up to become far more manly than these hecklers, and then asked if they too wanted to suck (see Painter 139). Truth's chances of success were no better and no worse than Shylock's. The naked breasts or the body that bleeds when pricked will not overcome the fundamental doubt of the sceptic.[128] Even in the most convincing of cases there is always the possibility that Descartes so richly acknowledges, namely that my perception of your body is caused by some evil spirit, a malevolent devil intent on playing tricks on me.

Beauvoir's 'I am a woman' can be made to sound both as the fairly level-headed beginning of a conversation, and as the exasperated end point of the same conversation hours later. If we place Beauvoir in the company of Shylock and Sojourner Truth, then 'I am a woman' becomes a last ditch appeal to the other: 'Don't you *see* that I am a woman?' or 'What will it take for you to realize that I am a woman?', are possible glosses here. If we imagine that the sentence is the end of a long and futile conversation, a certain feeling of helplessness may be apparent in Beauvoir's voice. For how can she convince her interlocutors that she is a woman if they can find no way out of their fundamental scepticism?

At this point—where I imagine Beauvoir throwing up her

---

[128] Deborah McDowell discusses white feminists' use of the figure of Sojourner Truth to represent black women or black feminists in 'Transferences' (see esp. 158–63). I am using her famous statement here to exemplify a specific epistemological dilemma. In this case, Sojourner Truth represents all women asked to prove that they are women (not just black women, since the hecklers don't seem to have doubted that Soujourner Truth was black). I suppose one could say that I am choosing to foreground Truth's sex, and in so doing, I am placing her race in the background. The implication is not that race always has to be considered the background of sex. (In the case of Fanon (see above, 203) I foreground his race, not his sex.) McDowell writes that 'Truth's declarative question—"Ain't I a Woman"—might be read as "political" and "epistemological" simultaneously (159). This is obviously right. But what aspect (these two or others) of Truth's speech act to foreground is not given once and for all: the reason for turning to her experience will determine the interpretation given of her famous statement. Those reasons are themselves open to criticism. There are bad reasons as well as good reasons for using a given example.

hands in despair at ever being able to communicate her sense that she is a woman to her interlocutor—I am reminded of Stanley Cavell's discussion of the peculiar feelings of exasperation and helplessness that arise when discussions between a positivist analytic philosopher and a philosopher proceeding from ordinary language reach an impasse:

> The positivist grits his teeth when he hears an analysis given out as a logical one which is so painfully remote from formality, so obviously a question of how you happen to feel at the moment, so psychological; the philosopher who proceeds from everyday language stares back helplessly, asking, 'Don't you feel the difference? Listen: you *must* see it.' Surely, both know what the other knows, and each thinks the other is perverse, or irrelevant, or worse ('Aesthetic Problems' 90).

There is the same sense of impasse, of having reached bedrock, at the bottom of some aesthetic disagreements: 'It is essential to making an aesthetic judgment', Cavell writes, 'that at some point we be prepared to say in its support: don't you see, don't you hear, don't you dig? The best critic will know the best points. Because if you do not see *something*, without explanation, then there is nothing further to discuss' ('Aesthetic Problems' 93). Addressed to the sceptic, Beauvoir's 'I am a woman' takes on the same status as sentences such as: 'Can't you hear the desolation in this line?' or 'Don't you see that this painting treats light in a different way from that one?'

Efforts at agreement must end somewhere. The sceptic may never agree that Beauvoir is a woman, just as she may never agree that we know that there is a tomato on the table. Even after the best and most genuine effort we may still fail to see what the other sees. In the end, when all attempts to find agreement have failed, thinkers of Beauvoir's and Cavell's kind must stake their claims on their own experience. Cavell writes: 'At some point, the critic will have to say: This is what I see. Reasons—at definite points, for definite reasons, in different circumstances—come to an end' ('Aesthetic Problems' 93). Cavell is here alluding to Wittgenstein's famous comment 'If I have exhausted the justifications I have reached bedrock, and my spade is turned. Then I am inclined to say: "This is simply what I do" ' (*PI* §217).

Wittgenstein's image is arresting: when it is impossible to dig any further, when productive labour comes to an end, then there is nothing left but to say 'This is what I do'. It should be noted that he does not necessarily say this: he reports, rather, that he is *inclined* to say this. The parallel to Beauvoir's 'I knew that my only defence would be to say . . .' is quite striking. What Wittgenstein does not say or do is equally revealing: he does not, for example, lift up the spade and hit his interlocutor over the head with it. Nor does he continue to hack furiously away with the bent spade. Rather, he recognizes bedrock when he hits it. Whether or not he actually says 'This is what I do', the inclination to say so is an acknowledgement of the nature of bedrock, an acknowledgement that bedrock is the kind of thing that no amount of spadework will ever make a dent in. Wittgenstein's attitude here is quite gentle, without being in the least submissive. 'This is what I do' and the silence that follows are restful and utterly non-defensive. They indicate that Wittgenstein accepts that the other will never see what he sees, understand what he is doing. He is not prepared to go any further: he will neither use violence, nor keep battering away at the other. What he will do, however, is to take his stand on the value of his own view. He is *not* saying 'This is what I have been doing, but now that I realize that you are unable to see it in the way I do, I will stop doing it.' Had he said something like that, he would have let the other's inability (however well founded) to see what he sees determine his own perception; in Beauvoir's terms this would be tantamount to alienating his own subjectivity into an image projected by the other. In the abstract conversation, Beauvoir is, as it were, searching for a path towards this kind of non-defiant silence.[129] The whole of *The Second Sex* is an attempt to explain why it is so much harder for a woman than for a man to find this path.

Leaning on his bent spade, Wittgenstein demonstrates respect for the other's difference, for the other's right to continue to see what he sees. If the sceptic simply cannot see that there are women in the world and that Beauvoir is one of them ('It may

---

[129] I want to acknowledge that it was Stanley Cavell's extremely apt comments on a draft of this paper that helped me to bring out the value of the silence—the non-defensiveness—in these cases.

look like that, but how do I know these are not just appearances, induced by evil demons or regulatory discourses?'), then Beauvoir's spade will also be turned. She cannot continue to insist for ever. In this context, saying 'This is what I do' means acknowledging that the sceptic will not be able to share her perspective, without taking this as a reason to abandon her own project. Instead she will continue to show what the world looks like from the point of view of a person who takes herself to be a woman, in the hope that others will come to see what she sees. In the case of the abstract conversation, we might hope, then, that a woman could find a silence accompanied not by aggression but a sense of restful self-respect, a knowledge that the resistance and aggression of this other is no longer enough to eliminate her subjectivity.

The case Wittgenstein has in mind when he finds that he has to say 'This is what I do' is a philosophical conversation, in which both parties have made a serious good faith effort to understand the source of their divergence, but which nevertheless failed. This parallels Beauvoir's understanding of the ideal conditions of intellectual dialogue, namely that I should be free to speak and that you should be free to respond:

> First I must be allowed to appeal. I shall therefore fight against those who want to choke my voice, prevent me from expressing myself, prevent me from being. . . . Then I need to have before me human beings who are free *for me*, who can respond to my appeal (*PC* 113).[130]

To choke someone's voice is to deprive them of their fundamental freedom to speak, to participate in human decision making. A writer needs the response of the reader. If her response is to be worth anything, however, it must be freely given. (This is why Beauvoir considers both reading and writing to be acts of generosity.) For this reason I shall have to fight not only against those who attempt to choke my voice, but also against those who attempt to choke your voice. If, as I have tried to show, the beginning of *The*

---

[130] Eva Lundgren-Gothlin's 'Simone de Beauvoir, Jean-Paul Sartre' uses this quotation. The connection that Beauvoir makes here between *appeal* and *voice* brings out the parallels between her philosophy and that of Cavell.

Second Sex is an invitation to the other to consider her own experience in response to the text, it now becomes apparent that such an invitation presupposes Beauvoir's commitment to the other's freedom as well as to her own.

Intellectual exchanges nevertheless take place in all kinds of situations. The restful non-defiant and self-respecting silence arising after (or instead of) Wittgenstein's 'This is what I do' will not necessarily arise in other situations. Ruth Behar's story about the woman who ended a presentation by telling about the husband who beat her, also produced silence.[131] In that case, the silence was one of deep embarrassment, a sense that nothing can count as a valid academic response to such experiences. I may also remain silent in response to your appeal because I have resolved to fight it with all my might, and find that my best strategy involves a refusal to talk to you. Silence in the face of the other's appeal, Beauvoir writes, may also be a sign of indifference or icy contempt:

> If we fight against a project, we choose to appear as an obstacle in relation to it. There are projects which simply are of no concern to us; we envisage with indifference the judgments where they are expressed. . . . It happens that my disdain covers not a particular project but a whole human being. Then it is the global project of his being that we refuse and fight against. In that case disdain becomes contempt. I am indifferent to every opinion of those I despise. . . . True contempt is silence: contempt takes away even the wish to contradict and our sense of outrage [*scandale*] (*PC* 106–7).

To Beauvoir there is nothing intrinsically wrong with contempt: the meaning and value of my contempt will depend on the situation in which it occurs. In the same way, indifference in relation to the other's project is sometimes an appropriate and sometimes an inappropriate response. The value of this passage is that it encourages us to think of the many different ways of being silent. Whether my silence is caused by self-respect, exhaustion, opposition, indifference, or contempt it still represents a response to the other's appeal (as Beauvoir would put it), or, as Cavell would put

---

[131] See n. 14, above.

it, a form of acknowledgement of the other's presence.[132] For these thinkers, once an appeal has been expressed, whatever we do (including callous disregard or violent suppression) is a response to it, and that response is our responsibility. (Here we should remember that the man's 'You say that because you are a woman' is not an appeal in Beauvoir's sense of the word, since his intervention clearly shows that he doesn't imagine the woman to be as free as he is.)

To conclude: *The Second Sex* is an appeal to the reader's freedom. By arrogating voice to herself, by staking her own subjectivity in her claims, and by taking herself to be neither more nor less capable of philosophy than the reader whom she is addressing, Simone de Beauvoir shows us how to write personally and philosophically at the same time, without abandoning the outrageous ambition of speaking for all and without silencing the other.

III. SOME CONCLUDING THOUGHTS

In the introduction to this essay, I wrote that I wanted to see if I could find a way to write theory without neglecting or repressing the claims of the personal, but also without dismissing or diminishing the claims of the impersonal, the objective, and the universal. Have I succeeded? By reading *The Second Sex* I have discovered that to write theory in a way that does not neglect the personal entails, among other things, finding a voice of one's own and a way to write that acknowledges the presence of others. It also entails being able to stake one's own experience (subjectivity) in one's general claims, and to do so in a way that addresses the other's freedom.

---

[132] In his fabulous essay on *King Lear*, Cavell writes: 'Whether or not we are acknowledging others is not a matter of choice, any more than accepting the presence of the world is a matter of choosing to see or not to see it. Some persons sometimes are capable of certain blindnesses or deafnesses toward others; but, for example, avoidance of the presence of others is not blindness or deafness to their claim upon us; it is as conclusive an acknowledgment that they are present as murdering them would be' ('Avoidance' 332).

In this essay I place dialogue, exchange, conversation, engagement, and response at the heart of intellectual life.[133] It is not a coincidence, I think, that my engagement with Beauvoir takes the form of extremely attentive close reading. Beauvoir herself thinks of reading as a generous engagement of one's own freedom in the encounter with the other. In a different way, this essay is also a response to the work of Stanley Cavell. Although my main concern is with Beauvoir, I hope that the very fact of placing Beauvoir and Cavell in each other's company sheds new light on both of them. Finally, in the most obvious way the whole of this essay is my belated response to Jane Tompkins's 'Me and My Shadow'. Finding a way to address her concerns without abandoning my own took eleven years.

There is no all-purpose recipe for 'personal' writing of theory here. There are innumerable ways of fulfilling the criteria I arrive at in the last two sections. *The Second Sex* itself certainly does not lend itself to imitation. If I set out to write *like* Beauvoir, I would be denying the lessons I claim to have learned from her. In particular, I would have overlooked the vast differences between her situation and mine, between her audience and the one I can hope for, and of course, between our different experiences. Identifying with Beauvoir, imitating her style, I would only succeed in alienating myself, just as surely as if I identified with some other model for theoretical or personal writing. What Beauvoir teaches me, is that regardless of the mode or style of my writing (theory or autobiography) I have to find a voice of my own, even if the voice I find is a voice that in every way is unlike hers. What Cavell in particular helps me to see, is that the personal is not something given, it is a task (Beauvoir would surely say a 'project'); the personal is not a possession, but something to be learned and refined.[134]

How does Section II of this essay illuminate Section I? Working on Beauvoir's philosophical style I have found myself thinking about the ordinary, the concrete, and the everyday, about situations and

[133] The attitude I explore here has considerable implications for one's way of teaching, whether on the graduate or undergraduate level.

[134] This sentence is based on Cavell's expressions, in a personal communication.

examples, about staking one's subjectivity in one's claims, about dialogue and response, about the difficulty of finding a voice, about generosity, responsibility, and freedom, and a host of other things, too: what it means to be a woman, to have a female body, what it means for a woman to write philosophy; and how style and tone matter to philosophical and theoretical writing. Set against such concerns, contemporary debates about the personal and the theoretical have come to look conceptually impoverished to me. All too often current discussions turn out to be based either on the idea that we *must* choose between 'speaking for' or 'speaking as', between writing personally or writing theoretically, between the personal and the impersonal, and between subjectivity and objectivity; or on the equally lame idea that we don't have to choose at all since the two (meaning, the two parts of the same binary oppositions) always go together. The problem is not that the old binary grid is always wrong or mistaken. I have no objection to using words like 'personal' and 'impersonal' and so on. The problem is that it makes us believe that no alternatives are available (except the predictable and to my mind boring deconstruction of the very same binary grid). What I have tried to do is to show that there are alternatives to the binary straitjacket. Investigation of other examples will surely produce other alternatives. I am struck by the fact that theories that make such enormous claims for the virtues of location in practice rarely demonstrate anything like attentive interest in specific cases or situations. In contrast, I have tried to show by example that close attention to a particular case (in this case the beginning of *The Second Sex*) can produce serious theoretical insights.

Working on Beauvoir has also taught me that there is no one way of 'getting personal'. The effects of autobiographical material or emotionally painful revelations in scholarly writing will vary as much as the effects of the most impersonal and objective prose. General claims for the 'vulnerability' or 'openness' of this or that form of writing are hollow. The same rhetorical or thematic elements may have widely varying effects in different contexts, as any literary critic knows. In the same way there is no such thing as one monolithic form of 'theory-writing' which is bound always to have oppressive and silencing effects. Nor can one assume that 'writing personally' always has a set of predictable political effects that 'writing impersonally' somehow does not have. As Cora Diamond might have put it, such effects will depend.

Some theoretical writing is execrable, but so is some so-called 'personal' writing. Explicitly autobiographical and emotional writing can be genuinely open and revealing or just as 'silencing'—just as closed off to engagement from others—as the most arrogantly impersonal prose. A friend of mine who has written both theoretical and autobiographical material once told me that when she wrote theory she didn't think about the reader, but when she wrote more personal work she did. No wonder that she thought that her personal work was far more lively, better written, and more interesting. Beauvoir thinks that all kinds of writing, including theory and philosophy, are appeals to the reader, whether the writer knows it or not. My friend's experience indicates that the tone and style of the finished text will depend a great deal on the writer's own understanding of what she is doing.

Contemporary debates about the personal and the philosophical have been productive for scholars who wish to write in autobiographical ways. In the 1990s, autobiographical and other kinds of personal writing have definitely become more acceptable within the American academy, if not necessarily elsewhere.[135] On the other hand, the limited conceptual range and the fairly anti-intellectual tenor of some of the more common arguments have made the same debates quite unproductive for anyone who really wants to write theory and philosophy. As a result it has been all too easy for theorists and philosophers to turn their back on the important questions about the role of the theorist's or philosopher's subjectivity and about writing style raised by critics such as Jane

---

[135] I do not mean to give the impression that personal writing only takes place in the USA. In some other countries that I know of, explicitly feminist forms of personal writing have been developed. I am thinking of the 'memory work' pioneered by Frigga Haug in Germany which links work on individual memory with theories of oppression and exploitation (see esp. Haug's *Female Sexualization*). In 1994, the Swedish sociologist Karin Widerberg published a much discussed book in Norway entitled *Kunnskapens kjønn* ('The Sex of Knowledge') inspired by Frigga Haug's work. Haug and Widerberg both see 'memory work' as a way to develop and continue the insights of the feminist consciousness raising groups of the 1960s and early 1970s.

Tompkins. The result has been that theory-writing has proceeded with business as usual, and that 'confessionalism' or 'personal writing' has become an academic subgenre like any other without influence on that other subgenre known as 'theory'. To me, this is an indication that unless the personal critic is willing to engage in genuine dialogue with people who do take theory seriously, she will not be able to show why they should care about her point of view. Turning one's back on theory, as Jane Tompkins recommends, will only make one end up 'all alone and feeling blue'.

The anxiety of excluding others has been prominent in the turn away from theory and towards the personal, and in many arguments about location. The worry is that by speaking or writing theoretically, I will falsely subsume the point of view of others under my own. In the frequent expressions of this anxiety I hear a recurring fantasy: the fantasy of being able to speak in a way that would genuinely be all-inclusive. What this fantasy denies (or tries to forget) is that the very moment of speaking (or writing) is a moment of *arrogation of voice,* as Cavell puts it (see above, 233–4). Cavell speaks of an arrogation of voice because he recognizes that each one of us is different from others, and that each of us is separated from all other human beings. (In this he is very much like Lacan.) To deny the moment of arrogation—the moment of injustice, of unfoundedness—in the act of writing, is to wish for a kind of imaginary non-separation from the other. The fantasy is one of merger, in which one would not have the problem of separating one's own voice from that of others, so that, ultimately, it would not matter who was speaking. Denouncing every attempt to arrogate voice to oneself as a denial of voice to others, the critic of 'speaking for' may be attempting to cure her own guilt feelings about speaking and writing at all. (If I understand this fantasy, it is because I have come to realize that I have at some point shared it.)

I don't mean to say that every critique of 'exclusionism' is based on guilt feelings about the writer's own arrogation of voice. Some such critiques are entirely valuable and necessary. My point, rather, is that the usual catch-all critique of 'exclusionism' is far too simple and unspecific, and particularly, that it often confuses the question of arrogation of voice (to which there is no alternative) with questions of style, tone, contents, and address (here the potential choices and effects are endlessly varied and variable). Critics of 'exclusionism' need to establish more specific criteria, ask more specific questions, and—above all—read more carefully if they want to produce genuinely important critiques of *The Second Sex* or any other text.

Our speaking—even the most deep-felt critique of 'exclusionism'—is never justified by anything but our own wish to speak: 'Who beside myself could give me the authority to speak for us?' Cavell writes (*Pitch* 9). There is something arrogant and something unjust about writing anything at all. How can I write when my mother, who never got more than seven years of primary education, cannot? How can I justify my arrogation of voice? How can anyone? If we do decide to write, it is pointless to consume ourselves in guilt about the 'exclusionary' effects of writing per se. The question, therefore, is not how to justify writing anything at all, but rather what one aims to do with one's writing. I can spend my life feeling guilty about having more opportunities to express myself than my mother ever had, or I can try to write in a way that may inspire more women (and perhaps some men, too) to find a theoretical voice of their own. This is not a revolutionary act. It will not turn society upside down, at least not in the short term. It does not make up for the inexpressive life my highly intelligent mother has had to lead. Because I understand that nothing can make up for that, I have found the courage to write about things that matter to me in the hope that they will also matter to others.

Works Cited

For individual essays published in anthologies or collections, cross-references have been used, except for cases where it seemed unnecessarily fussy. For examples of cross-reference, see the entries under Altieri and Cavell. For examples where cross-references have not been used, see the entries under Baym and Stone.

Alcoff, Linda, 'The Problem of Speaking for Others', *Cultural Critique* 20 (Winter 1991–2), 5–32.

Altieri, Charles, 'What Is at Stake in Confessional Criticism', in Veeser 55–67.

Audry, Colette, *La statue* (Paris: Gallimard, 1983).

Austin, J. L., 'A Plea for Excuses', in *Philosophical Papers* (3rd edn. Oxford: Oxford University Press, 1979), 175–204.

Barthes, Roland, *Mythologies*, trans. Annette Lavers (New York: The Noonday Press, 1972).

—— 'The Writer on Holiday', in *Mythologies* 29–31.

Bauer, Nancy, *Simone de Beauvoir, Philosophy, and Feminism* (New York: Columbia, 2001).

Baym, Nina, 'The Madwoman and her Languages: Why I Don't Do Feminist Theory', in Shari Benstock (ed.), *Feminist Issues in Literary Scholarship.* (Bloomington, Ind.: Indiana University Press, 1987), 45–61.

Beauvoir, Simone de, *America Day by Day*, trans. Carol Cosman (Berkeley and Los Angeles: University of California Press, 1999); trans. of *L'Amérique au jour le jour* (Paris: Gallimard, 1948).

—— *The Ethics of Ambiguity*, trans. Bernard Frechtman (New York: Philosophical Library, 1948); trans. of *Pour une morale de l'ambiguïté* (Paris: Gallimard (Coll. Idées), 1947).

—— *L'existentialisme et la sagesse des nations* (Paris: Nagel, 1948).

—— *Force of Circumstance*, trans. Richard Howard (Harmondsworth: Penguin, 1987); trans. of *La force des choses*, 2 vols. (Paris: Gallimard (Coll. Folio), 1963).

—— *Memoirs of a Dutiful Daughter*, trans. James Kirkup (Harmondsworth: Penguin, 1987); trans. of *Mémoires d'une jeune fille rangée* (Paris: Gallimard (Coll. Folio), 1958).

—— '*La phénoménologie de la perception* de Maurice Merleau-Ponty', *Les temps modernes*, 1/2 (Nov. 1945), 363–7.

—— *The Prime of Life*, trans. Peter Green (Harmondsworth: Penguin,

1988); trans. of *La force de l'âge*, 2 vols. (Paris: Gallimard (Coll. Folio), 1960).

—— *Pyrrhus et Cinéas* (Paris: Gallimard, 1944).

—— *The Second Sex*, trans. H. M. Parshley (New York: Vintage Books, 1989); trans. of *Le deuxième sexe*, 2 vols. (Paris: Gallimard (Coll. Folio), 1949).

—— *She Came to Stay*, trans. Yvonne Moyse and Roger Senhouse (London: Fontana, 1984); trans. of *L'invitée* (Paris: Gallimard (Coll. Folio), 1943).

Behar, Ruth, *Translated Woman: Crossing the Border With Esperanza's Story* (Boston: Beacon Press, 1993).

—— *The Vulnerable Observer: Anthropology That Breaks Your Heart* (Boston: Beacon Press, 1996).

Bergoffen, Debra B., *The Philosophy of Simone de Beauvoir: Gendered Phenomenologies, Erotic Generosities* (Albany, NY: State University of New York Press, 1997).

Bleier, Ruth, *Science and Gender: A Critique of Biology and Its Theories on Women* (New York: Pergamon Press, 1984).

Bornstein, Kate, *Gender Outlaw: On Men, Women and the Rest of Us* (New York: Routledge, 1994).

Bowie, Malcolm, *Mallarmé and the Art of Being Difficult* (Cambridge: Cambridge University Press, 1978).

Brooks, W. K., *The Law of Heredity: A Study of the Cause of Variation, and the Origin of Living Organisms* (Baltimore: John Murphy, 1883).

Burton, Christine, 'Golden Threads', *Off Our Backs* 24/9 (Oct. 1994), 14–15.

Butler, Judith, *Bodies That Matter: On the Discursive Limits of 'Sex'* (New York: Routledge, 1993).

—— 'Critically Queer', *GLQ* 1/1 (1993), 17–32.

—— 'Gender as Performance', in Peter Osborne (ed.), *A Critical Sense: Interviews with Intellectuals* (London: Routledge, 1996), 109–25.

—— 'Gender Is Burning: Questions of Appropriation and Subversion', in *Bodies That Matter* 121–40.

—— *Gender Trouble: Feminism and the Subversion of Identity* (New York: Routledge, 1990).

—— 'Sex and Gender in Simone de Beauvoir's *Second Sex*', *Yale French Studies* 72 (1986), 35–49.

Bynum, Caroline, 'Why All the Fuss about the Body? A Medievalist's Perspective', *Critical Inquiry* 22/1 (Autumn 1995), 1–33.

Calhoun, Randall, *Dorothy Parker: A Bio-Bibliography* (Westport, Conn.: Greenwood Press, 1993).

Carter, Angela, *The Passion of New Eve* (1st pub. 1977; London: Virago, 1997).

Case, Mary Anne C., 'Disaggregating Gender from Sex and Sexual Orientation: The Effeminate Man in the Law and Feminist Jurisprudence', *Yale Law Journal*, 105/1 (1995), 1–105.

Caughie, Pamela L., 'Let It Pass: Changing the Subject, Once Again', *PMLA* 112/1 (Jan. 1997), 26–39.

Cavell, Stanley, 'Aesthetic Problems of Modern Philosophy', in *Must We* 73–96.

——— 'Austin at Criticism' in *Must We* 97–114.

——— 'The Avoidance of Love: A Reading of *King Lear*', in *Must We* 267–353.

——— *The Claim of Reason: Wittgenstein, Skepticism, Morality, and Tragedy* (Oxford: Oxford University Press, 1979).

——— 'Knowing and Acknowledging', in *Must We* 238–66.

——— *Must We Mean What We Say? A Book of Essays* (Cambridge: Cambridge University Press, 1969).

——— 'Must We Mean What We Say?', in *Must We* 1–43.

——— *A Pitch of Philosophy: Autobiographical Exercises* (Cambridge, Mass.: Harvard University Press, 1994).

——— 'The Politics of Interpretation (Politics as Opposed to What?)', in *Themes Out of School: Effects and Causes* (Chicago: University of Chicago Press, 1984), 27–59.

Chanter, Tina, *Ethics of Eros: Irigaray's Rewriting of the Philosophers* (New York: Routledge, 1995).

Christian, Barbara, 'The Race for Theory', in Linda Kauffman (ed.), *Gender and Theory: Dialogues on Feminist Criticism* (Oxford: Basil Blackwell 1989?), 225–37.

Copjec, Joan, 'Sex and the Euthanasia of Reason', in *Read My Desire: Lacan Against the Historicists* (Cambridge, Mass.: MIT Press, 1994), 201–36.

Danius, Sara, 'Själen är kroppens fängelse: om den vanskliga distinktionen mellan kön och genus', in Claudia Lindén and Ulrika Milles (eds.), *Feministisk bruksanvisning* (Stockholm: Norstedts, 1995), 143–66.

Darwin, Charles, *The Descent of Man and Selection in Relation to Sex* (rev. edn., New York: Merrill and Baker, 1874).

Delphy, Christine, 'Rapports de sexe, genre et universalisme', interview with Myriam Lévy and Patrick Silberstein, *Utopie critique: Revue internationale pour l'autogestion* 2 (1995), 9–23.

Derrida, Jacques, *Limited Inc.* (Evanston, IL: Northwestern University Press, 1988).

Diamond, Cora, 'Knowing Tornadoes and Other Things', *New Literary History* 22 (1991), 1001–15.

Eagleton, Terry, *The Illusions of Postmodernism* (Oxford: Blackwell, 1996).

Ebert, Teresa L., *Ludic Feminism and After: Postmodernism, Desire, and Labor in Late Capitalism* (Ann Arbor: University of Michigan Press, 1996).

Ellmann, Mary, *Thinking About Women* (New York: Harcourt, 1968).

Evans, Mary, *Simone de Beauvoir: A Feminist Mandarin* (London: Tavistock, 1985).

Fallaize, Elizabeth (ed.), *Simone de Beauvoir: A Critical Reader* (London: Routledge, 1998).

Fanon, Frantz, *Black Skin, White Masks*, trans. Charles Lam Markmann (New York: Grove Weidenfeld, 1967); trans. of *Peau noire, masques blancs* (Paris: Seuil, 1952).

Farnham, Marynia F., 'The Pen and the Distaff', *Saturday Review of Literature* (22 Feb. 1947), 7 and 29–30.

Fausto-Sterling, Anne, 'The Five Sexes', *Sciences* (Mar./Apr. 1993), 20–4.

Feinberg, Leslie, *Stone Butch Blues* (Ithaca, NY: Firebrand Books, 1993).

—— *Transgender Warrior: Making History from Joan of Arc to Dennis Rodman* (Boston: Beacon Press, 1996).

Fernald, Anne, 'A Room of One's Own: Personal Criticism and the Essay', *Twentieth Century Literature* 40/2 (Summer 1994): 165–89.

Fineman, Joel, 'The History of the Anecdote', in *The Subjectivity Effect in Western Literary Tradition: Essays Toward the Release of Shakespeare's Will* (Cambridge, Mass.: October Books, 1991), 59–87.

Fish, Stanley, 'How Ordinary is Ordinary Language?', in *Is There* 97–111.

—— 'How To Do Things with Austin and Searle: Speech-Act Theory and Literary Criticism', in *Is There* 197–245.

—— *Is There A Text In This Class? The Authority of Interpretive Communities* (Cambridge, Mass.: Harvard University Press, 1980).

'Forum', *PMLA* 111/5 (Oct. 1996), 1146–69.

Foucault, Michel, *The History of Sexuality: An Introduction*, trans. Robert Hurley (New York: Vintage Books, 1990).

Frank, Francine Wattman, and Treichler, Paula A., *Language, Gender, and Professional Writing: Theoretical Approaches and Guidelines for Nonsexist Usage* (New York: MLA, 1989).

Franke, Katherine M., 'The Central Mistake of Sex Discrimination Law: The Disaggregation of Sex from Gender', *University of Pennsylvania Law Review* 144/1 (Nov. 1995), 1–99.

Freud, Sigmund, *The Standard Edition of the Complete Psychological Works*, ed. and trans. James Strachey, 24 vols. (London: The Hogarth Press, 1953–74) (abbreviated to SE).

—— 'The Psychogenesis of a Case of Homosexuality in a Woman' (1920), *SE* 18: 147–72..

—— *Three Essays on the Theory of Sexuality* (1905), in *SE* 7: 125–243.

Fuss, Diana, *Essentially Speaking: Feminism, Nature and Difference* (New York: Routledge, 1989).

Gallop, Jane, *Feminist Accused of Sexual Harassment* (Durham, NC: Duke University Press, 1997).

—— *Thinking Through the Body* (New York: Columbia University Press, 1988).

Garber, Marjorie, *Vested Interests: Cross-Dressing & Cultural Anxiety* (New York: Harper Perennial, 1993).

Gardner, Martin, 'The New New Math', *New York Review of Books* (24 Sept. 1998), 9–12.

Gatens, Moira, 'A Critique of the Sex/Gender Distinction' (1983), in Sneja Gunew (ed.), *A Reader in Feminist Knowledge* (London: Routledge, 1991), 139–57; repr. in Moira Gatens, *Imaginary Bodies: Ethics, Power and Corporeality* (London: Routledge, 1996).

Geddes, Patrick, and Thomson, J. Arthur, *The Evolution of Sex* (London: Walter Scott, 1889).

Gilligan, Carol, *In a Different Voice* (Cambridge, MA: Harvard University Press, 1982).

Gothlin, Eva, 'Simone de Beauvoir's Notion of Appeal, Desire, and Ambiguity and Their Relationship to Jean-Paul Sartre's Notions of Appeal and Desire', *Hypatia*, 14/4 (Fall 1999), 83–95.

Gould, Timothy, 'The Unhappy Performative', in Andrew Parker and Eve Kosofsky Sedgwick (eds.), *Performativity and Performance: Essays from the English Institute* (New York: Routledge, 1995), 17–44.

Grosz, Elizabeth, *Sexual Subversions: Three French Feminists* (Sydney: Allen & Unwin, 1989).

—— *Volatile Bodies: Toward a Corporeal Feminism* (Bloomington, IN: Indiana University Press, 1994).

Gubar, Susan, 'What Ails Feminist Criticism?', *Critical Inquiry* 24/4 (Summer 1998), 878–902.

Haraway, Donna J., ' "Gender" for a Marxist Dictionary', in *Simians, Cyborgs, and Women: The Reinvention of Nature* (New York: Routledge, 1991), 127–48.

Harding, Sandra, *The Science Question in Feminism* (Ithaca, NY: Cornell University Press, 1986).

—— and O'Barr, Jean F. (eds.), *Sex and Scientific Inquiry* (Chicago: University of Chicago Press, 1987).

Haslanger, Sally, 'Disembodying Race and Gender', unpublished lecture (Mar. 1996).

—— 'Natural Kinds and Social Construction: Butler on Subjects of Sex/Gender/Desire', unpublished manuscript (Dec.1995).

Haug, Frigga, *Female Sexualization* (London: Verso, 1987).

Hausman, Bernice L., *Changing Sex: Transsexualism, Technology, and the Idea of Gender* (Durham, NC: Duke University Press, 1995.)

Heinämaa, Sara, 'What Is a Woman? Butler and Beauvoir on the Foundations of the Sexual Difference', *Hypatia* 12/1 (1997), 20–39.

Heinämaa, Sara, 'Woman—Nature, Product, Style? Rethinking the Foundations of Feminist Philosophy of Science', in Lynn Hankinson Nelson and Jack Nelson (eds.), *Feminism, Science and the Philosophy of Science* (The Hague: Kluwer, 1996), 289–308.

Howells, Christina, 'Conclusion: Sartre and the Deconstruction of the Subject', in Christina Howells (ed.), *The Cambridge Companion to Sartre* (Cambridge: Cambridge University Press, 1993), 318–52.

Hull, Carrie L., 'The Need in Thinking: Materiality in Theodor W. Adorno and Judith Butler', *Radical Philosophy*, 84 (July/Aug. 1997), 22–35.

Ibsen, Henrik, *Et dukkehjem* (1879), in *Samlede Verker,* ii (Oslo: Gyldendal, 1993).

Irigaray, Luce, *Speculum of the Other Woman,* trans. Gillian Gill (Ithaca, NY: Cornell University Press, 1985); trans. of *Spéculum de l'autre femme* (Paris: Minuit, 1974).

—— *This Sex Which Is Not One,* trans. Catherine Porter with Carolyn Burke (Ithaca, NY: Cornell, 1985); trans. of *Ce sexe qui n'en est pas un* (Paris: Minuit, 1977).

Jeanson, Francis, *Simone de Beauvoir ou l'entreprise de vivre* (Paris: Seuil, 1966).

Kaplan, Alice, *French Lessons: A Memoir* (Chicago: University of Chicago Press, 1993).

Keller, Evelyn Fox, *Reflections on Gender and Science* (New Haven: Yale University Press, 1985).

Kessler, Suzanne J., 'The Medical Construction of Gender: Case Management of Intersexed Infants', *Signs* 16/1 (Autumn 1990), 3–26.

Kruks, Sonia, 'Simone de Beauvoir: Between Sartre and Merleau-Ponty', *Simone de Beauvoir Studies,* 5 (1988), 74–80.

—— 'Simone de Beauvoir: Teaching Sartre About Freedom', in Ronald Aronson and Adrian van den Hoven (eds.), *Sartre Alive* (Detroit: Wayne State University Press, 1991), 285–300.

—— *Situation and Human Existence: Freedom, Subjectivity and Society* (London: Unwin Hyman, 1990).

Lambert, Helen H., 'Biology and Equality: A Perspective on Sex Differences' (1978), in Harding and O'Barr 125–45.

Lang, Candace, 'Autocritique', in Veeser 40–54.

Laqueur, Thomas, *Making Sex: Body and Gender from the Greeks to Freud* (Cambridge, MA: Harvard University Press, 1990).

Le Dœuff, Michèle, *Hipparchia's Choice: An Essay Concerning Women, Philosophy, etc.,* trans. Trista Selous (Oxford: Blackwell, 1991); trans. of *L'Étude et le rouet: des femmes, de la philosophie etc.,* (Paris: Seuil, 1989).

Lorde, Audre, 'The Master's Tools Will Never Dismantle the Master's House', in *Sister Outsider: Essays and Speeches* (Trumansburg, NY: The Crossing Press, 1984), 110–13.

Lundberg, Ferdinand, and Farnham, Marynia L. Foot, *Modern Woman: The Lost Sex* (New York: Harper and Brothers, 1947).

Lundgren-Gothlin, Eva, *Sex and Existence*, trans. Linda Schenck (Hanover: Wesleyan, 1996); trans. of *Kön och existens: studier i Simone de Beauvoirs Le Deuxième Sexe* (Gothenburg: Daidalos, 1991).

McCarthy, Mary, 'Tyranny of the Orgasm', Review of *Modern Woman: The Lost Sex* by Ferdinand Lundberg and Marynia Farnham, *New Leader* (5 Apr. 1947), 10; repr. in *On the Contrary* (New York: Farrar, Straus and Cudahy, 1961), 167–73.

McDowell, Deborah E., *Leaving Pipe Shop* (New York: Norton, 1996).

—— 'Transferences. Black Feminist Thinking: The "Practice" of "Theory"', in *'The Changing Same': Black Women's Literature, Criticism, and Theory* (Bloomington, IN: Indiana University Press, 1995), 156–75.

McDowell, John, *Mind and World* (Cambridge, Mass.: Harvard University Press, 1994).

McIntosh, Mary, 'Review of *Gender Trouble*', *Feminist Review* 38 (Summer 1991) 113–14.

Mackenzie, Catriona, 'Simone de Beauvoir: Philosophy and/or the Female Body', in Carol Pateman and Elizabeth Gross (eds.), *Feminist Challenges: Social and Political Theory* (Boston: Northeastern University Press, 1987), 144–56.

MacKinnon, Catharine A., 'Feminism, Marxism, Method, and the State: An Agenda for Theory', in Nannerl O. Keohane, Michelle Z. Rosaldo, and Barbara C. Gelpi (eds.), *Feminist Theory: A Critique of Ideology* (Chicago: Chicago University Press, 1982), 1–30.

Mead, Margaret, 'Dilemmas the Modern Woman Faces', Review of *Modern Woman: The Lost Sex* by Ferdinand Lundberg and Marynia Farnham, *New York Times* (26 Jan. 1947), 18.

Merleau-Ponty, Maurice, *Phenomenology of Perception*, trans. Colin Smith (London: Routledge, 1962); trans. of *Phénoménologie de la perception* (Paris: Gallimard (Coll. Tel), 1945).

Miller, Nancy, *Getting Personal: Feminist Occasions and Other Autobiographical Acts* (New York: Routledge, 1991).

Millot, Catherine, *Horsexe: Essay on Transsexuality*, trans. Kenneth Hylton (Brooklyn, NY: Autonomedia, 1990).

Milton, John, 'The Doctrine and Discipline of Divorce Restored to the Good of Both Sexes' (1643), in Stephen Orgel and Jonathan Goldberg (eds.), *John Milton* (Oxford: Oxford University Press, 1991), 182–226.

Moi, Toril, *Sexual/Textual Politics: Feminist Literary Theory* (London: Methuen, 1985).

—— *Simone de Beauvoir: The Making of an Intellectual Woman* (Oxford: Blackwell, 1994).

—— 'While We Wait: The English Translation of *The Second Sex*', *Signs*, 27/4 (Summer 2002), 1005–35, repr. in Emily R. Grosholz (ed.), *The Legacy of Simone de Beauvoir* (Oxford: Clarendon Press, 2004), 37–68.

Money, John, 'The Conceptual Neutering of Gender and the Criminalization of Sex', *Archives of Sexual Behavior*, 14/3 (1985), 279–90.

——Hampson, Joan G., and Hampson, John L., 'An Examination of Some Basic Sexual Concepts: The Evidence of Human Hermaphroditism', *Bulletin of the Johns Hopkins Hospital*, 97/1 (1955), 301–19.

Nicholson, Linda. 'Interpreting Gender', *Signs* 20/1 (Autumn 1994), 79–105.

Osborne, Peter (ed.), *A Critical Sense: Interviews with Intellectuals* (London: Routledge, 1996).

Painter, Nell Irvin, *Sojourner Truth: A Life, A Symbol* (New York: Norton, 1996).

Parker, Andrew, and Sedgwick, Eve Kosofsky, 'Introduction: Performativity and Performance', in Andrew Parker and Eve Kosofsky Sedgwick (eds.), *Performativity and Performance: Essays from the English Institute* (New York: Routledge, 1995), 1–18.

Prosser, Jay, 'No Place Like Home: The Transgendered Narrative of Leslie Feinberg's *Stone Butch Blues*', *Modern Fiction Studies*, 41/3–4 (Fall–Winter 1995), 483–514.

Raymond, Janice G., *The Transsexual Empire: The Making of the She-Male* (New York: Teachers College Press, 1994).

Remnick, David, 'Inside-Out Olympics', *New Yorker* (5 Aug. 1996), 26–8.

Rogers, Arthur, 'Legal Implications of Transsexualism', *The Lancet*, 341 (1993), 1085–6.

Rubin, Gayle, 'Thinking Sex: Notes for a Radical Theory of the Politics of Sexuality', in Carole S. Vance (ed.), *Pleasure and Danger: Exploring Female Sexuality* (Boston: Routledge & Kegan Paul, 1984), 267–319.

—— 'The Traffic in Women: Notes on the "Political Economy" of Sex'. in Rayna R. Reiter (ed), *Toward an Anthropology of Women* (New York: Monthly Review Press, 1975), 157–210.

Russett, Cynthia Eagle, *Sexual Science: The Victorian Construction of Womanhood* (Cambridge, Mass.: Harvard University Press, 1989).

Sartre, Jean-Paul, *Anti-Semite and Jew*, trans. George Becker (New York: Schocken Books, 1948), trans. of *Réflexions sur la question juive* (Paris: Gallimard (Coll. Folio), 1946).

—— *Being and Nothingness*, trans. Hazel E. Barnes (New York: Washington Square Press, 1992); trans. of *L'Être et le néant* (Paris: Gallimard (Coll. Tel), 1943).

—— 'What Is Literature?', And Other Essays*, introd. and ed. Steven Ungar (Cambridge, Mass.: Harvard University Press, 1988).

—— 'What Is Literature?', in *What Is* 21–238, trans. Bernard Frechtman; trans. of *Qu'est-ce que la littérature* (Paris: Gallimard (Coll. Idées), 1948).

Sayers, Janet, *Biological Politics: Feminist and Anti-Feminist Perspectives* (London: Tavistock, 1982).

Schor, Naomi, *Bad Objects: Essays Popular and Unpopular* (Durham, NC: Duke University Press, 1995).

—— 'French Feminism is a Universalism' in *Bad Objects* 3–27.

—— 'This Essentialism Which Is Not One: Coming to Grips with Irigaray', in *Bad Objects* 44–60.

Scott, Joan Wallach, 'Gender: A Useful Category of Historical Analysis', in *Gender and the Politics of History* (New York: Columbia, 1988), 28–50.

Sedgwick, Eve Kosofsky, *Epistemology of the Closet* (Berkeley and Los Angeles: University of California Press, 1990).

—— 'Gender Criticism', in Stephen Greenblatt and Giles Gunn (eds.), *Redrawing the Boundaries: The Transformation of English and American Literary Studies* (New York: MLA, 1992), 271–302.

—— 'Queer Performativity: Henry James's *The Art of the Novel*', *GLQ* 1/1 (1993), 1–16.

Shakespeare, William, *The Merchant of Venice*, in *The Complete Works*, ed. Stanley Wells and Gary Taylor (Oxford: Clarendon Press, 1994).

Shumway, David R., 'The Star System in Literary Studies', *PMLA* 112/1 (Jan. 1997), 85–100.

Simons, Margaret, 'The Silencing of Simone de Beauvoir: Guess What's Missing from *The Second Sex*', *Women's Studies International Forum* 6/5 (1983), 559–64.

Simpson, David, *The Academic Postmodern and the Rule of Literature: A Report on Half-Knowledge* (Chicago: University of Chicago Press, 1995).

Soper, Kate, *Troubled Pleasures: Writings on Politics, Gender and Hedonism* (London: Verso, 1990).

—— *What Is Nature? Culture, Politics and the Non-Human* (Oxford: Blackwell, 1995).

Spelman, Elizabeth V., *Inessential Woman: Problems of Exclusion in Feminist Thought* (Boston: Beacon Press, 1988.)

Spivak, Gayatri Chakravorty, *Outside in the Teaching Machine* (New York: Routledge, 1993).

Stanley, Liz, and Wise, Sue, *Breaking Out: Feminist Consciousness and Feminist Research* (London: Routledge & Kegan Paul, 1983).

Steedman, Carolyn, *Landscape for a Good Woman: A Story of Two Lives* (London: Virago, 1986).

Stoller, Robert J., 'A Contribution to the Study of Gender Identity', *International Journal of Psychoanalysis*, 45 (1964), 220–6.

—— *Sex and Gender: On the Development of Masculinity and Femininity* (New York: Science House, 1968).

Stone, Martin, 'Focusing the Law: What Legal Interpretation is Not', in Andrei Marmor (ed.), *Law and Interpretation: Essays in Legal Philosophy* (Oxford: Clarendon Press, 1995), 31–96.

—— 'Wittgenstein on Deconstruction', in Alice Crary and Rupert Read (eds.), *The New Wittgenstein* (London: Routledge, 2000), 83–117.

Stone, Sandy, 'The Empire Strikes Back: A Posttranssexual Manifesto', in Julia Epstein and Kristina Straub (eds.), *Body Guards: The Cultural Politics of Gender Ambiguity* (New York: Routledge, 1991), 280–304.

Strindberg, August, *The Father, in Strindberg: Five Plays*, trans. Harry Carlson (New York: Signet, 1984); trans. of *Fadren* (1887), ed. Gunnar Ollén, in *August Strindbergs Samlade Verk* 27 (Stockholm: Almqvist & Wiksell, 1984).

Thernstrom, Melanie, 'Sexuality 101', *Details* (Feb. 1998), 96–100.

Tompkins, Jane, *A Life in School: What the Teacher Learned* (Reading, Mass.: Addison-Wesley, 1996).

—— 'Me and My Shadow', in Linda Kauffman (ed.), *Gender and Theory: Dialogues on Feminist Criticism* (Oxford: Basil Blackwell, 1989), 121–39.

Trebilcot, Joyce, 'Dyke Methods: or Principles for the Discovery/Creation of Withstanding', *Hypatia* 3/2 (Summer 1988), 1–13.

Van Doren, Dorothy, 'To Save Us From Women', Review of *Modern Woman: The Lost Sex* by Ferdinand Lundberg and Marynia Farnham, *New York Herald Tribune Weekly Book Review* (9 Feb. 1947: 16).

Veeser, H. Aram (ed.), *Confessions of the Critics* (New York: Routledge, 1996).

Vintges, Karen, *Philosophy as Passion: The Thinking of Simone de Beauvoir,* trans. Anne Lavelle (Bloomington, Ind.: Indiana University Press, 1996).

Ward, Julie K, 'Beauvoir's Two Senses of "Body" in *The Second Sex*', in Margaret A. Simons (ed.), *Feminist Interpretations of Simone de Beauvoir* (University Park, PA: Pennsylvania State University Press, 1995), 223–42.

Wertham, Frederic, 'Ladies in the Dark', Review of *Modern Woman: The Lost Sex* by Ferdinand Lundberg and Marynia Farnham, *New Republic* (10 Feb. 1947), 38.

West, Candace, and Zimmerman, Don H., 'Doing Gender', *Gender & Society*, 1/2 (June 1987), 125–51.

Widerberg, Karin, *Kunnskapens kjønn: minner, refleksjoner, teori* (Oslo: Pax, 1994).

Wittgenstein, Ludwig, *Philosophical Investigations*, trans. G. E. M. Anscombe (3rd edn. New York: Macmillan, 1968).

Wittig, Monique, *The Straight Mind and Other Essays* (Boston: Beacon Press, 1992).

Woolf, Virginia, *A Room of One's Own* (1929; London: Granada, 1977).

Young, Iris Marion, *Throwing Like a Girl and Other Essays in Feminist Philosophy and Social Theory* (Bloomington, IN: Indiana University Press, 1990).

Index

Note: In order to avoid long strings of entries under frequently cited authors' names, entries have as far as possible been alphabetized under the relevant subject heading. With the exception of the principal entry for each term, 'Simone de Beauvoir' has been abbreviated to 'SdB', and *The Second Sex* to *SS*. References of the type '150–78 *passim*' indicate that the subject matter of the heading is to be found in scattered passages throughout those pages of the text.